LANGUAGE AND MEDIA

Routledge English Language Introductions cover core areas of language study and are one-stop resources for students.

Assuming no prior knowledge, the books in the series offer an accessible overview of the subject, with activities, study questions, sample analyses, commentaries and key readings – all in the same volume. The innovative and flexible 'two-dimensional' structure is built around four sections – introduction, development, exploration and extension – which offer self-contained stages for study. Each topic can also be read across these sections, enabling the reader to build gradually on the knowledge gained.

Language and Media:

- is a comprehensive introduction to how language interacts with media
- investigates the forms of language found in media discourse; how patterns in such language contribute to recognisable media genres and styles; and broader social themes and consequences that arise from media language
- uses a wide variety of real texts from the media that include newspapers covering events such as the Asian tsunami, speeches, blogs, emails, advertisements and interview transcripts from television talk shows including *Oprah*
- provides classic readings by the key names in the discipline including David Crystal, Norman Fairclough, David Graddol, Allan Bell and Theo van Leeuwen
- is accompanied by a supporting website with extra activities and weblinks.

Written by two experienced teachers and authors, this accessible textbook is an essential resource for all students of English language and linguistics.

Alan Durant is Professor of Communication at Middlesex University Business School, London, UK.

Marina Lambrou is Senior Lecturer in English Language and Communication at Kingston University, London, UK.

ROUTLEDGE ENGLISH LANGUAGE INTRODUCTIONS

SERIES EDITOR: PETER STOCKWELL

Peter Stockwell is Professor of Literary Linguistics in the School of English Studies at the University of Nottingham, UK, where his interests include sociolinguistics, stylistics and cognitive poetics. His recent publications include *Language in Theory*, Routledge 2005 (with Mark Robson), *Cognitive Poetics: An Introduction*, Routledge 2002, *The Poetics of Science Fiction*, *Investigating English Language* (with Howard Jackson), and *Contextualized Stylistics* (edited with Tony Bex and Michael Burke).

SERIES CONSULTANT: RONALD CARTER

Ronald Carter is Professor of Modern English Language in the School of English Studies at the University of Nottingham, UK. He is the co-series editor of the *Routledge Applied Linguistics* series, series editor of *Interface*, and was co-founder of the Routledge *Intertext* series.

OTHER TITLES IN THE SERIES:

World Englishes 2nd edition
Jennifer Jenkins

History of English
Dan McIntyre

Practical Phonetics and Phonology 2nd edition
Beverley Collins and Inger Mees

Pragmatics and Discourse 2nd edition
Joan Cutting

Sociolinguistics 2nd edition
Peter Stockwell

Child Language
Jean Stilwell Peccei

Language in Theory
Mark Robson and Peter Stockwell

Stylistics
Paul Simpson

Psycholinguistics
John Field

Grammar and Vocabulary
Howard Jackson

LANGUAGE AND MEDIA

A resource book for students

ALAN DURANT AND MARINA LAMBROU

Routledge
Taylor & Francis Group
LONDON AND NEW YORK

First published 2009
by Routledge
2 Park Square, Milton Park, Abingdon, Oxon OX14 4RN
Simultaneously published in the USA and Canada
by Routledge
711 Third Avenue, New York, NY 10017

Routledge is an imprint of the Taylor & Francis Group, an informa business

Typeset in Minion Pro by The Running Head Limited, Cambridge, www.therunninghead.com

British Library Cataloguing in Publication Data
A catalogue record for this book is available from the British Library

Library of Congress Cataloging-in-Publication Data
Durant, Alan.
Language and media: a resource book for students / Alan Durant and Marina Lambrou.
p. cm. — (Routledge English language introductions)
1. Mass media and language. 2. English language—Discourse analysis. 3. Discourse analysis.
II. Lambrou, Marina. II. Title.
P96.L34D87 2009
302.2301'4—dc22

2008053203

ISBN10: 0–415–47573–2 (hbk)
ISBN10: 0–415–47574–0 (pbk)
ISBN13: 978–0–415–47573–0 (hbk)
ISBN13: 978–0–415–47574–7 (pbk)

Printed and bound in Great Britain by
TJ International Ltd, Padstow, Cornwall

HOW TO USE THIS BOOK

The Routledge English Language Introductions are 'flexi-texts' that you can use to suit your own style of study. The books are divided into four sections:

A Introduction – sets out the key concepts for the area of study. The units of this section take you step-by-step through the foundational terms and ideas, carefully providing you with an initial toolkit for your own study. By the end of the section, you will have a good overview of the whole field.

B Development – adds to your knowledge and builds on the key ideas already introduced. The units in this section might also draw together several areas of interest. By the end of this section, you will already have a good and fairly detailed grasp of the field, and will be ready to undertake your own exploration and thinking.

C Exploration – provides examples of language data and guides you through your own investigation of the field. The units in this section will be more open-ended and exploratory, and you will be encouraged to try out your ideas and think for yourself, using your newly acquired knowledge.

D Extension – offers you the chance to compare your expertise with key readings in the area. These are taken from the work of important writers, and guidance and questions are provided for your further thought.

You can read this book like a traditional textbook, 'vertically' straight through from beginning to end. This will take you comprehensively through the broad field of study. However, the Routledge English Language Introductions have been carefully designed so that you can read them in another dimension, 'horizontally' across the numbered units. For example, units A1, A2, A3 and so on correspond with units B1, B2, B3, and with units C1, C2, C3 and D1, D2, D3, and so on. Reading A5, B5, C5 and D5 will take you rapidly from the key concepts of a specific area, to a level of expertise in that precise area, all with a very close focus. You can match your way of reading with the best way that you work.

The Index at the end of the book, together with the suggestions for further reading, will help to keep you orientated. Each textbook has a supporting website with extra commentary, suggestions, additional material and support for teachers and students.

LANGUAGE AND MEDIA

Language and Media has nine units, each following the above four-part structure. Section A units introduce the key topics in language and media, as well as how these two concepts relate to one another. Section B develops these issues with additional detail and discussion. Attention is also drawn in this section to work by key thinkers. Section C offers opportunities for further study and your own research, by following through examples and controversies in the field. Finally, the readings in Section D bring together the various threads developed through the book and are accompanied by suggestions for further study and discussion.

The nine horizontal threads begin with ideas of what media language is (in A1, B1, C1 and D1). Thread 2 explores different varieties of language used in media discourse; thread 3 considers what is specific to media texts, as regards the particular roles played by the speaker/writer and different constructions of audience; thread 4 investigates media genres. Units A5, B5, C5 and D5 all examine, from different perspectives, how information is presented in media discourse. These units also look at techniques used to persuade an audience towards some point of view being presented. Thread 6 explores media storytelling. Thread 7 focuses on how words are linked with still and moving images, focusing in particular on the form of captions and voice-over on media soundtracks. Units A8, B8, C8 and D8 examine the boundaries of what can be said in different kinds of media language. The final thread, thread 9, looks into the media future and evaluates alternative accounts of what that media future may mean as regards the structure and use of language. Further material and activities can be found on the website which accompanies the book: http://www.routledge.com/textbooks/reli.

CONTENTS

C EXPLORATION *Analysing media language*

FIGURES

TABLES

TRANSCRIPTIONS

ACKNOWLEDGEMENTS

Bell, A., *The Language of News Media*, Blackwell, 1991: 156–8. Reprinted with permission of Wiley-Blackwell.

Biber, D., 'Compressed noun-phrase structures in newspaper discourse: the competing demands of popularization vs. economy' in J. Aitchison and D. L. Lewis, *New Media Language*, Routledge, 2003: 169–71 and 179–80. Reprinted with permission of Taylor & Francis Books UK.

Big Words . . . Small Worlds, transcription reproduced with permission of Curtis Brown Group Ltd on behalf of David Lodge, copyright © David Lodge 1987.

'Character matters', 22 February 2008, www.onthemedia.org/transcripts/2008/02/22/05, reprinted with permission of On the Media.

Clayman, S. and Heritage, J., *The News Interview*, Cambridge University Press, 2002: 6–25. © Steven Clayman and John Heritage, 2002. Reproduced with permission of Cambridge University Press.

Crystal, D., *Language and the Internet*, Cambridge University Press, 2nd edition, 2006: 258–61 and 271–2, © David Crystal 2006. Reprinted with permission of Cambridge University Press.

Durant, A., *Meaning in the Media: Discourse, Controversy and Debate*, Cambridge University Press, 2009: 9–12 © Alan Durant, 2009. Reproduced with permission of Cambridge University Press.

Fairclough, N., *Media Discourse*, Hodder Arnold, 1995: 201–5. Reprinted with permission of Edward Arnold (Publishers) Ltd.

Finnegan, R., *Communicating: The Multiple Modes of Human Interconnection*, Routledge, 2002: 40–3. Reprinted by permission of Taylor & Francis Books UK.

Graddol, D., 'The visual accomplishment of factuality' in D. Graddol and O. Boyd-Barrett, *Media Texts: Authors and Readers*, Open University, 1994: 136–42. Reprinted with permission of David Graddol.

Kress, G. and van Leeuwen, T., *Multimodal Discourse: The Modes and Media of*

Contemporary Communication, Hodder Arnold, 2001: 1–9. Reprinted with permission of Edward Arnold (Publishers) Ltd.

Montgomery, M., *The Discourse of Broadcast News: A Linguistic Approach*, Routledge, 2007: 145–8. Reprinted with permission of Taylor & Francis Books UK.

Myers, G., *Words in Ads*, Hodder Arnold, 1994: 30–44. Reprinted with permission of Edward Arnold (Publishers) Ltd.

Ong, W. J., *Orality and Literacy: The Technologizing of the Word*, Routledge, 1982: 133–4. Reprinted with permission of Taylor & Francis Books UK.

The Police, *Every Breath You Take*, Sumner (100%). Reprinted by permission of EMI Music Publishing.

Thompson, J. B., *The Media and Modernity: A Social Theory of the Media*, Cambridge: Polity Press, 1995: 83–7.

Toolan, M., *Narrative: A Critical Linguistic Introduction*, Routledge, 2nd edition, 2001: 221–8. Reprinted with permission of Taylor & Francis Books UK.

Wales, K., 'Keywords revisited: media', *Critical Quarterly*, issue 49 (1) 2007: 6–13. Reprinted with permission of Wiley-Blackwell.

Williams, R., *Keywords: A Vocabulary of Culture and Society*, HarperCollins Publishers Limited (Fontana), 1983: 203–4. Reprinted with permission of HarperCollins Publishers Limited.

Every effort has been made to trace and contact copyright holders. The publishers would be pleased to hear from any copyright holders not acknowledged here so that this acknowledgements list may be amended at the earliest opportunity.

Section A
INTRODUCTION
KEY CONCEPTS IN LANGUAGE AND MEDIA

A1 MEDIA AS LANGUAGE USE

Is a book called *Language and Media* really two books: one book about 'language', the other about 'media'? Or is such a book a single, coherent enterprise? If a book dealing with 'language and media' *is* to be a coherent undertaking, then we need to ask what connects the two terms that make up its title: 'language' and 'media'.

This may seem an abstract question with which to begin a set of resources to be used in practical study of media language. At least a provisional answer is essential, however, if the topics that follow are to be seen as fitting together. Without a sense of why particular aspects of language and media are highlighted, what would remain is simply a cluster of miscellaneous topics. The question is made all the more important because there is no established discipline of 'language and media' in the way that there is a linguistic field of 'sociolinguistics', 'pragmatics' and 'stylistics'. Reading through the topics discussed in this book might still leave a sense that each domain, 'language' and 'media', isn't fully covered.

So in this opening unit, we

- outline some commonly accepted notions of 'language and media',
- show how 'media language' is a sub-set of uses of language in all the many different conversational and public settings in which you encounter language in use,
- describe use of the term 'media language' to indicate language transmitted by means of specific channels: spoken/written, combined with images, amplified, broadcast, recorded, streamed online, etc., and
- explain how the term 'media' is also used to indicate professional 'institutions' of communication, each of which can be traced in its historical development and current ways of working.

Contemporary conventions and styles of media language, which may seem fixed and even natural now, are likely to alter in future. This is something we need to allow for and to anticipate (we address this issue directly in thread 9). Together, the themes of this unit establish a framework for our coverage of the topics which follow, and should make it easier to see the structure of the book as a whole.

Different ways of looking at language and media

At first glance, 'language' in media is a matter of particular collected data. There are specific words, idioms, sentence structures, and styles of language use, written or spoken, to be appreciated, discussed and set in context. We can download discourse from the internet, print off incoming emails, or record people talking on TV programmes. Faced with such data, we can examine the verbal evidence in front of us.

Such activity, however, leads into a further, slightly more abstract perception: that language use in different media may show recurrent features and raise common questions across the different media channels. For instance, we may find regularities

in how persuasive effects are achieved in different media formats, or in how a sense is established of something being real or true, for example in news or documentaries. We might find similar problems in different kinds of potentially offensive material, or in how fraudulent online identities are created. Such patterns require us to *compare* stretches of media discourse across media.

Beyond such regularities, we may be tempted to view media language as a specialised kind of sign 'system': a structure of words, images, music and sound effects governed by rules or conventions. It is this sort of perception that leads people to speak of a 'language of television', a 'language of film', or to refer to 'music as a language'. Currently, there is considerable debate about whether there is a single, overall semiotic or language of multimodal discourse such as web pages and other online content.

These different understandings of 'media language' are of course connected. The particular data of language use in a given email, a TV programme or a website provide evidence when speculating about wider questions about media communication such as questions about realism, bias, newsworthiness or offensiveness. In turn, our view of whether the 'language of media' is some kind of general system involves inferences that we draw from evidence pieced together from language data in front of us. We need, therefore, to keep the different senses of 'language and media' in mind, simultaneously, and to develop a habit of switching between the level of precise description and the level of generalisation.

Media

Some initial clarification is needed of the term 'media' if we are to be clear about what the sub-set of uses of language that constitute 'media language' is.

Are communications media, we need to ask, something distinctively modern and electronic? Or have there always been media of one kind or another – e.g. papyrus, slate, megaphones, etc. – perhaps as long as there has been language (and possibly *before*, if we include human-made marks and artefacts used in pre-linguistic and non-verbal kinds of communication)?

We might want to say that communication always relies on some given infrastructure of technology or industry. In this sense, communication always involves a 'medium' or different 'media'. If we take this view, then further questions rush in.

- Do people use language differently in what we now call 'media discourse' than they do in everyday face-to-face interaction (i.e. in what is now typically thought of as 'non-media discourse')?
- Do they use language differently in different media?
- Is language change accelerated or distorted from its typical patterns by the massive (rapid and often global) influence of media language idioms, styles and formats?
- Is expression and the circulation of messages in media form always a good thing – or is there sometimes a need to restrict or even ban public communication, precisely because of the amplifying, and what is now called 'viral', power of media dissemination?

A book of this kind and length cannot offer a comprehensive treatment of each of these questions. Limits apply especially to the historical and social dimensions of the development of communications media. (We do, however, provide a timeline appendix giving key historical dates, such as the invention of writing, printing, telephone, typewriter, radio, television, mobile telephony, the internet, etc., in order to help you place modern media in a larger historical context.) We also present three extracts explaining different understandings of the term 'media', and the difficulties that the word can present in discussion, in unit D1.

Consider the evidence

Let's develop a little further our suggestion that looking closely at media language data leads into several different ways of understanding 'language and media'. We can be more specific about this, if we describe the various things we have in mind when we talk about media *discourse*.

Firstly, we may think of language *in* media, as viewed at a particular time. This, as we have suggested, is largely a matter of different varieties of language that we encounter. Think of the distinctive style of newspaper headlines, or email messages, or rapping, or contributions to live online chat. In each, choices are made about which words to use, how to combine them, how those words will be pronounced if they are spoken rather than written, and how to spell them if they are written. We can count and describe different sorts of words, idioms, length of sentences. We can compare patterns of this type between media texts of various kinds. Choices have been made in creating the given text, and those choices are distinctive because of their contrast with choices that would have been made in a different context. This is largely what enables us, for example, to imitate a news broadcast, a citizens' band radio conversation, a celebrity interviewer, or a football or horse-race commentator, for example as pastiche or as part of a joke. We investigate such media language varieties in more detail in thread 2.

In investigating varieties of discourse, we can see that consistent patterns of choices, developed over the course of some longer stretch of discourse, make the style of a discourse appear unified. The unified appearance of such choices, considered together, is often referred to as genre. Think now of the horror movie, internet shopping confirmation email, chat show, news interview, or radio quiz programme. These are conventional formats, or genres. Each involves extended *systems* of choices, which give a kind of identity to texts that, as a result, become easily identifiable as being of a particular kind. Such choices are not only a matter of choosing words, sentence structures, or style of intonation: they can also involve patterns of turn-taking, how themes are handled, and other larger discourse structures. We investigate the formal qualities and expectations surrounding recognised media genres in thread 4. Generalisations may follow here too. We might note, for example, that genres differ among different media; and they differ between historical periods. It may accordingly be possible to put forward general hypotheses based on observation. Such hypotheses might be fairly specific, for example about how news styles, magazine genres or sports commentary have changed in recent years. Or they may be broader, for example about how broadcast media discourse as a whole (and perhaps other kinds of public interaction) has

undergone a process of 'conversationalisation' over time: that is, whether the adopted styles have shifted away from the formal, public style of early mass media towards echoing patterns of apparently informal spoken conversation.

Understanding media language is about investigating such patterns and general claims, as well as describing what we see and hear in front of us. For example, we might trace, in the history of media language, constant interaction between spoken and written styles. In oral societies, communication took the form of speech (where it was 'verbal', rather than expressed by using objects and gestures as signs, such as those described by Ruth Finnegan in our first reading in unit D1). With the advent of writing, some discourse continued to be produced as speech. But other kinds were added, in written (at first manuscript) form. With the development of printing, some forms of discourse shifted from speech or manuscript into the form of books and other printed documents. Some of that discourse was especially influential, either because of its use for religious purposes, or as authoritative information (e.g. for legal purposes), or because it provided new kinds of entertainment. But a further reversal of influence and prestige associated with 'medium' was to follow. With the advent of radio, television and the telephone, media became more closely associated again with speech (though of course books and other written documents continued to be produced and read). Think of radio, the telephone, and film and television soundtracks. Some people, as we will see, have argued that this 'secondary orality' (or renewed dominance of speech, now amplified, broadcast and reproduced) represented a fundamental shift, likely to shape the future of media language forever. That was before the internet. The rapid rise and influence of the internet and associated communication technologies appears, however, to have shifted the balance away – at least temporarily – from speech technologies back in the direction of written discourse (see discussion in our David Crystal extract, in unit D9). The 'internet revolution' has also moved media language towards multimodal kinds of textual organisation. In multimodal discourse, images, written text, music and sound combine and function together (see the Kress and van Leeuwen reading in unit D7). But these changes are as yet incomplete. We don't yet know how they will develop or turn out. In later units, we describe large-scale social contexts of this kind for different varieties of media language use.

Why investigating media discourse is interesting

What makes 'language and media' interesting as a topic is largely that insights can follow from many different ways of looking at media discourse. We might say, for instance, that styles of language in media, at different times or at different stages of social development, reflect the capabilities and availability of media technologies, as well as necessary skills or aptitude associated with them. Such a belief may not be just a presumption or prejudice. It can follow from specific observations about discourse varieties. For example, we might notice distinct letter-writing styles in populations where few, many or virtually all people are able to read and write their own letters. Or we might develop an idea in connection with social, as much as linguistic, factors. For instance, phone conversation styles seem to vary with the relative cost of making calls; and telegrams seem to differ in style from fax communications partly because of how they were charged (by counting the number of characters used, rather than duration of the connection). What should we make, in this context, of condensed styles of SMS texting? Such styles may be driven by the frequency and circumstances of sending and receiving messages, including the speed with which they are composed. Or perhaps they reflect the changing quality of resolution of the screens on which they are composed and read? This is a genuine and worthwhile debate – partly because it affects how texting styles will evolve in future, as screen resolution, text prediction and voice recognition technologies all develop. We consider these questions in unit C8. In general, we may speculate that media technologies, including how they are financed, distributed and made available to different sections of a community, both facilitate and constrain kinds of communication, including the patterns of language use in which it is conducted.

We may also develop more sociological lines of enquiry into language and media. For example, we might explore the levels and kinds of literacy that are required for people to access and participate in production and reception of media communications of different kinds. As media discourse comes to play an increasingly important part in social and professional relationships, such access and participation are more and more important in how people's personal and professional relationships are defined.

Identifying different approaches to understanding language in its various connections with media allows us to focus on particular idioms, styles and genres, as well as neologisms (i.e. new, media-specific words, such as 'blog', or 'wiki'). We can link the buzz of such new words and practices to underlying issues of our media ecology. If we link together different kinds of perception and argument, then we should be able to place the excitement and occasional confusion of the contemporary 'industrialisation' or 'technologisation' of communication in a larger social and historical context. We should also be able to understand tensions in current media and to look into the media future. One thing that is certain about that media future is that it will bring many new, and highly socially influential, directions of change.

Activity 

- ❑ To follow up topics introduced in this unit, you will often need to use the words 'language' and 'media'. But it is important to be careful with these words. Look 'language' up in a dictionary and see how differently it is defined by different people or on different occasions (e.g. as a human capacity, as a nationally or regionally based code, etc.). Try this with several dictionaries and write down the main differences.
- ❑ When you have thought about 'language', consider 'media' in the same way.

In English, the most detailed dictionary in which we can look 'media' up – or 'vocabulary of culture and society', as it was called by its author – is Raymond Williams's *Keywords* (2nd edition, 1983). An abridged version of Williams's entry is given as one of our three extracts in D1. Williams doesn't offer an equivalent entry for 'language'. But he does have an entry for 'communication', which encompasses meanings ranging from channel of communication (such as post-carriages and canals), through letters or messages, to a human sense of mutual awareness, whether achieved by 'language' or simply by tacit, shared understanding.

Finally, it is interesting to consider whether – and if so how far – keywords for language, communication and media function differently in different languages. Compare words for 'language', 'communication' and 'media' that you may be familiar with in other languages. Do these equivalent words have the same range of senses as 'language', 'communication' and 'media' in English? Make up some phrases or sentences to highlight any relevant differences you find.

REGISTER AND STYLE

A2

This unit outlines the huge variety of kinds of language found in media discourse. It illustrates the concept of 'dialect' as language used by a given speaker (e.g. differences between speakers from different regions, classes or ethnic backgrounds) and also the concept of 'register' as language style appropriate to a given social setting. We describe such language variety in media to show how patterning of linguistic register contributes to media genres (discussed separately in unit 4). Media genre, in turn, is what makes different broadcasting formats almost instantly recognisable. We

- introduce the ideas of 'dialect' and 'register', drawn from linguistics, as ways of identifying style differences between language users and different kinds of use in different settings,
- look at accents and, in particular, at use of Received Pronunciation in broadcasting, noting the contribution a particular accent can make to overall style, and
- illustrate differences between speech and writing, as 'modes' of language use, and consider convergence and interaction between speech and writing in recent media technologies.

Language variety

The terms *register* and *style* are often used interchangeably. Each describes patterning in speech and writing, and shifts we make in order to ensure that the form of language we adopt for a particular context is appropriate. In other words, we match *how* something is communicated to *what* is being communicated and to *whom*. An obvious example is degree of formality: that is, consideration of whether our discourse needs to be formal or informal for its function or purpose in a given situation. Consider the two following openings to utterances:

1 Yo . . . Listen up, dudes!
2 Unaccustomed as I am to public speaking . . .

Just as we would not expect a lecturer in linguistics to begin a class with *Yo . . . Listen up, dudes!* (unless the utterance is meant to illustrate a point about register, style or social dialects) we would neither expect one of a group of teenagers to begin speaking

to the others by announcing, *Unaccustomed as I am to public speaking* . . . In both scenarios, choice of language jars with the context and the particular language users. The effect could be confusing, even comical. The incongruity reminds me of when, at the end of a seminar on Standard English and appropriate language use, I raised a laugh by asking students *Know wot I mean?* instead of the more fitting *Does everyone understand this point?* Fortunately, the students *did* get the point.

Register, as a language variety, may also be confused with the notion of *genre*. When we think of different types of media discourse, such as those found in tabloid newspapers, adverts, television soaps, or gossip magazines, we are thinking about different genres or text types. Each type is identifiable because of specific features commonly associated with both its form and function. In each of the above cases, language choice will differ at a lexical and/or grammatical level. For discourse in the written medium, there will also be typographical variation. With the spoken soundtracks of soaps and television adverts, choice will also reflect regional and social dialects phonologically (something discussed below in the section 'Accents in broadcasting'). No single word is an island: language in use differs, and its texture – that is, the qualities or characteristics of the language that make up the text type – reveals it to be of a given type because of its social use.

We have said that register and style are often considered as if they are the same. But there are differences between these two aspects of style. When we are faced with variation according to different situations and functions, the linguistic term is *register*. Register is a technical term used to describe a variety of language which is distinctive for a specific context. Register is created by a combination of choices a speaker makes in each area of language production: vocabulary, grammar, pronunciation, layout and other features of text design. Together, the result of such choices is a particular style, which is conventionally associated with some specific range of uses (formal, technical, legal, intimate, etc.). So register creates or contributes to style.

Consider an example. A personal blog is written in a different register from a legal contract. It uses different vocabulary, punctuation, layout on the page, etc. To see that this is the case, look at columns 1 and 2 in Table A2.1. Which column represents the typical register of a blog? And which is the typical register of a legal contract?

Table A2.1 Register in legal contracts and blogs

Level of variation	*1*	*2*
vocabulary	henceforth	you're
punctuation	:	!
layout	numbered pages	two words on a line
typeface	Times Roman	Comic sans
spelling style	Standard English	text messaging style

Clearly, column 1 relates to the legal contract. Use of exclamation marks (as in column 2) would undermine the seriousness of a legal contract's function. On the other hand,

two-word phrases as a whole line would appear inconsistent with the formal syntax and sentence length normally associated with legal contracts.

What makes style 'appropriate'?

We have established that register consists of 'style choices appropriate to a situation'. But what makes a style appropriate? In mass media discourse (such as magazines, television or radio), there is no immediate audience. So there is no given 'situation', other than the very general one of someone reading the magazine, watching TV or listening to the radio. What happens then, as regards the communicator's choice of appropriate style? Media create their own styles of address: specialised registers that may be public, formal and ceremonial; or they may be personal, as if talking with a friend. Or they may switch between the two, or mix the two. In later units (B3, C4) we look at how media discourse creates 'imaginary relationships' with addressees, and how such styles gradually become conventionalised as not just what you recognise but also as 'what you expect'.

Before we engage with such topics, however, we look at accent as an aspect of register in the media. We then go on to analyse stylistic differences between speech and writing, paying attention to overlap and convergence between the two mediums.

Accents in broadcasting

What is an accent and what is a dialect? The two terms describe differences or variation in the way different people speak. An accent describes variation at the phonological or sound level. So for example, in England, someone from the southern counties is likely to pronounce *bath* as /ba:θ/. The *a* is so long that northerners may protest that there is no *r* in bath! A northerner, on the other hand, would be likely to pronounce the word /bæθ/. By contrast with accent a dialect, on the other hand, describes variations not only at the phonological level, but also at the level of lexis (vocabulary) and syntax (grammar). Dialects are the broad range of social as well as regional varieties. With English as an increasingly global language, the term dialect is widely used to refer to the many different *Englishes* around the world.

Received Pronunciation (RP)

Received Pronunciation (or RP, as it is sometimes known) is the accent most identified with the BBC (sometimes it is also known as the Queen's English, or Public School English). In the 19th century 'standard pronunciation' of English was largely associated with the army, public schools, universities and civil service. But the term 'RP' itself seems to have been coined by the phonetician Daniel Jones as late as the 1920s. Jones described RP as 'most usually heard in everyday speech in the families of southern English persons whose menfolk have been educated at the great public boarding schools'. Unlike other accents, RP is not associated with a region or country. It is an accent of socio-economic status, most notably membership of a traditional upper class.

RP became much more influential as a style of speaking when Lord Reith (the first head of the BBC) adopted it in the early 1920s as his preferred broadcasting standard, hence the term BBC English. Reith was not directly concerned with class in his choice. He believed that Standard English, spoken with an RP accent, would be the most widely understood variety of English, both in the UK and overseas. He was also conscious that choice of a regional accent as a preferred model in broadcasting might alienate many listeners. Reith's policy of using RP, especially for news, prevailed at the BBC over approximately four decades, and probably reinforced the sometimes negative perception of regional varieties of English. The notion of standard pronunciation of US English, which has an otherwise very different history, is similarly related to broadcasting by the term 'network standard' (McCrum, Cran and MacNeil, 1986).

More recently, there has been a shift in Britain towards regional accents among television and radio presenters. With less than 2 per cent of the British population speaking with an RP accent, this 'standard' has been increasingly widely recognised as no longer reflecting – in fact it never did – the voice of the majority of the audience. The accent could even be thought potentially alienating, in the way that it had been feared regional accents would be. A push towards more regional and friendly accents, however, has also attracted criticism for eroding standards in the media, since certain accents are sometimes viewed as being less acceptable than others. (We discuss the issue of included and excluded accents in more detail in unit B8.)

Activity 

Reflect on your own preference as regards accent choice in broadcast media.

- ❑ Are there certain accents that you prefer to hear on television or the radio?
- ❑ Do you think that some accents sound more authoritative than others, particularly for news reporting?
- ❑ List the following (generalised) accents in each column, in order of preference: American, RP, Indian (English), Estuary, Liverpudlian, Irish. Your 'most strongly preferred' accent to hear in the given context should go in row 1. Put each accent in each list.
- ❑ Now compare your two lists. If there are differences between the two lists, why do you think that is? Do such differences, where they exist, help explain why you put the different accents in the order you chose?

	In general broadcasting	For news in particular
1		
2		
3		
4		
5		
6		

Stylistic differences between speech and writing

Speech and writing are contrasting channels of communication. But the differences between them are not always clear cut. Jenkins (2003) examines differences between speech and writing as part of her account of international variation in English. In her description, she draws on the work of Baron (2000: 21–2) who usefully summarises three different approaches to speech/writing differences: an Opposition View, a Continuum View, and a Cross-over View.

Each of these three views is now outlined.

Opposition View of speech and writing

In this approach to the differences between speech and writing, the two mediums are considered to have clear, contrasting characteristics (Table A2.2).

Table A2.2 Opposition View of speech and writing

	Writing is	*Speech is*
1	objective	interpersonal
2	a monologue	a dialogue
3	durable	ephemeral
4	scannable	only linearly accessible
5	planned	spontaneous
6	highly structured	loosely structured
7	syntactically complex	syntactically simple
8	concerned with past and future	concerned with the present
9	formal	informal
10	expository	narrative
11	argument-oriented	event-oriented
12	decontextualised	contextualised
13	abstract	concrete

Continuum View of speech and writing

The 'continuum' approach, as the name suggests, looks at speech and writing in variable contexts of use. It locates examples at points on a continuum (Table A2.3).

Table A2.3 Continuum View of speech and writing

Traditional writing			Face-to-face speech
◄			►
Word-processors	Telephones	Videophones	Teleconferencing
◄			►
Newspaper		Television news	Personal report on events
◄			►
Script of a play		Radio discussion	Phone conversation

Cross-over View of speech and writing

The 'cross-over' view takes into account the fact that, while a linguistic message may have been designed to be spoken or to be written, it may be experienced in a medium other than the one in which it originated. This is what happens with 'talking books', for example, in which a written version is read aloud on audio cassette. Almost the opposite happens with spoken lectures, which can be posted in written form on course websites. In both cases, the result is texts with a strikingly hybrid character. This inevitably complicates how we locate forms of communication around the middle of the continuum: play scripts, sermons, and other texts developed in an interaction between one medium and the other, or planned in one medium but delivered in the other.

Are differences between the three accounts of contrasts between speech and writing significant? The cross-over view of speech and writing works particularly well for the informal vernacular style found in emails. Jenkins (2003: 121–4) suggests that emails show a distinct kind of e-style that is neither simply writing nor speech. Following Baron again on this point, Jenkins concludes that such e-style is largely 'speech by other means'. She also emphasises that, as with speech and writing, there will always be differences of email style, depending on who is doing the emailing, to whom, and on the age, sex and first language of the emailer.

Blogging styles, such as the example we present in unit C2, also take on characteristics of speech despite their circulation in written form. Like speech (and contrary to what the *Opposition* View of speech and writing suggests) blogging can also be:

interpersonal,
a dialogue,
loosely structured,
concerned with the present,
informal,
narrative,
event-oriented,
contextualised, and
concrete.

Convergence between mediums

In media discourse, spoken and written styles are varied unexpectedly, and sometimes combined together. For this reason, media discourse plays an important part in social style change. Every day we can find new examples in newspaper headlines, advertising language and in our email inboxes.

These are some examples of media discourse in which writing reflects or simulates speech:

blogs, MSN and other instant messaging
contemporary screen-writing
email discourse

These are some examples of media discourse in which speech reflects or simulates writing:

- TV speeches read from scripts
- use of script cards, transparent lecterns and autocue as ways of assisting fluency on TV
- audio books (of novels and poetry, etc.)
- scripted phone interaction (call centres, etc.)

Semiotic register

As we shall see further in our discussion of typeface in unit B2, as well as throughout thread 7, register contrast is not only achieved linguistically. It can be created in other ways as well. In audio-visual and multimodal texts, design elements other than language play an increasingly important role in signalling such contrast. Design elements that contribute to register include font (e.g. Gothic vs. Courier); photo tinting (e.g. sepia to indicate a historical or retro effect); and overall layout (to indicate accessibility or expectation of relative technicality – compare tabloid and broadsheet newspaper layout). Design elements work together. They also work in conjunction with features of accompanying language to create an overall discourse style. Design elements are a sort of border zone between linguistic contrastivity, considered narrowly, and more general visual imagery. When stylistic effects of different kinds function together, they build up not only a sense of overall, general style but – if linked to a clear idea of purpose, anticipated effect or reader expectation – also of genre (see unit A4).

MEDIATED COMMUNICATION

A3

In this unit we move slightly away from the surface texture, or fabric, of language used in media discourse that we considered in unit A2. There, we were concerned with choices made between alternative words and grammatical forms that constitute register. Now we look at how whatever kind of language is chosen becomes a concrete media *utterance*. Such media 'utterances' are communicative acts, or events. They depend on some specific situational relationship between participants in a given setting. With media utterances, the relationship between participants is 'mediated' by media technology that extends or transforms the properties and expectations of verbal communication, especially those associated with conversation. We

- ❑ describe different kinds of 'communicative event',
- ❑ show how they relate, in different ways, to the 'canonical speech situation' traditionally described in linguistics, and
- ❑ explore what is sometimes called the departure from 'co-presence', or 'spatio-temporal distanciation', of media discourse: the fact that media language is often

> received at a distance from the situation in which it is produced and is often fixed or recorded and then consumed at a different time from the time of production.

By classifying media communication in terms of the properties of different kinds of 'communicative event', we can begin to see aspects of variation in language use that are specific to media styles.

Canonical situation of utterance

Some of the key features of media communication events are developments, in different ways, from a default structure of face-to-face interaction. Such face-to-face interaction is commonly described, in linguistics, as communication taking place in a 'canonical speech situation'.

In Ferdinand de Saussure's *Course in General Linguistics* (perhaps the key, founding text of how modern linguistics can analyse language as a system), linguistic interaction is famously depicted as a diagram of two (male) heads facing each other and exchanging messages (see Figure A3.1).

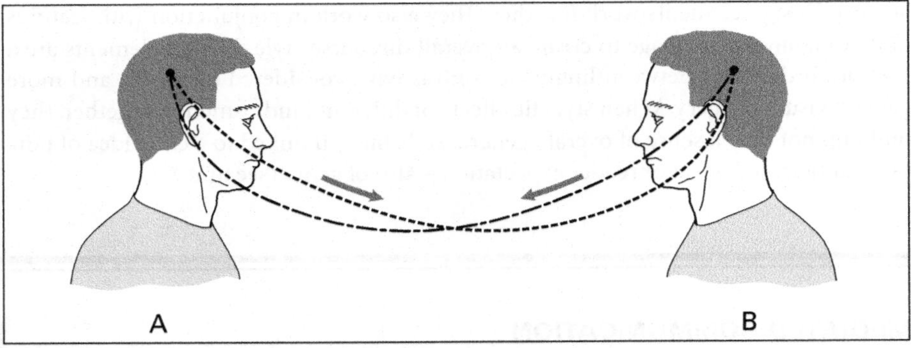

Figure A3.1 Ferdinand de Saussure's talking heads (1983: 11)

A's thoughts are converted into an utterance conveyed along a channel to B, the recipient. B decodes the message into thoughts that, as far as the meaning-bearing properties of the code allow, resemble A's original thought. Typically in spoken face-to-face interaction, the roles are then reversed: B thinks, expresses those thoughts by transmitting a coded message carried back along the same channel to A, etc.

John Lyons (1977: 637–8) has described the key features of this situation more exactly. He explains that the canonical speech situation involves

> one–one, or one–many, signalling in the phonic medium along the vocal–auditory channel, with all the participants present in the same actual situation able to see one another and to perceive the associated non-vocal paralinguistic features of their utterances, and each assuming the role of sender and receiver in turn. There is much in the structure of languages that can only be explained on the assumption

> that they have developed for communication in face-to-face interaction . . . Many utterances which would be readily interpretable in a canonical situation-of-utterance are subject to various kinds of ambiguity or indeterminacy if they are produced in a non-canonical situation: if they are written rather than spoken and dissociated from the prosodic and paralinguistic features which would punctuate and modulate them; . . . if the participants in the language-event, or the moment of transmission and the moment of reception, are widely separated in space and time; if the participants cannot see one another, or cannot each see what the other can see; and so on.
>
> (Lyons, 1977: 637–8)

The model of communication described here has been developed in many different directions. It has also been challenged as an adequate account even of face-to-face interaction, let alone of media communication. The model nevertheless in some form underpins most accounts of communication. It is sometimes described as the 'transmission' or 'conduit' model of communication, because of the central idea of messages being transmitted along a 'conduit' from A to B. Sometimes the model is called a 'dyadic model' of communication, because it is based on turn-taking between two people interacting with one another.

Among the main extensions of the model of communication described in Figure A3.2 is Roman Jakobson's (1987: 66) mapping of a principal function associated with each key aspect: what special power or effect that aspect is responsible for. In Jakobson's description, the 'context' dimension of a communication plays an important role in how information is conveyed. The 'conative', or persuasive, functioning of a communication results particularly from how the addressee is approached or appealed to. The 'code' aspect can have attention drawn to it if we comment on or discuss what words were used, or how words were used. And so on. Jakobson's functions are not mutually exclusive. In any given text, they function together. But they form a changing hierarchy in different texts, with different degrees of prominence. In one text, one function will be emphasised or more prominent; in another text, a different function.

	Context *Referential*	
Addresser *Emotive*	Message *Poetic*	Addressee *Conative*
	Contact *Phatic*	
	Code *Metalingual*	

Figure A3.2 Roman Jakobson's linguistic functions

Essentially the same communication model has been developed in different ways in other disciplines. Carried over into marketing and political science, for example, the same model forms the basis of the so-called Lasswell Formula (Figure A3.3) put forward by the American political scientist Harold D. Lasswell in 1948 (see McQuail and Windahl, 1993: 13).

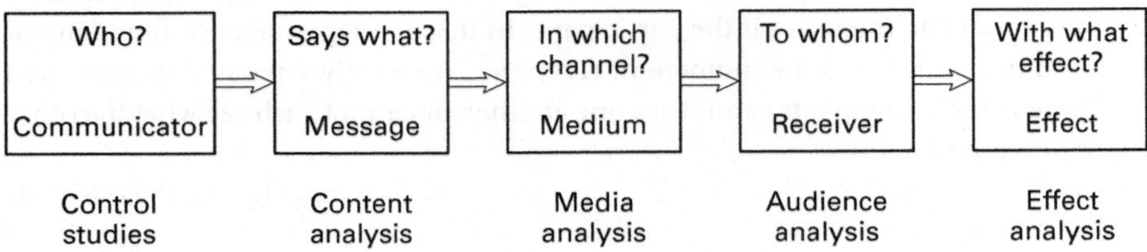

Figure A3.3 Harold D. Lasswell's Formula model (1948)

For Lasswell, a convenient way of describing an act of communication is to answer the following questions: Who? Says what? In which channel? To whom? With what *effect*? Where Lasswell feels answers will be found to each of these questions is indicated by the different approaches to analysing media texts he names beneath the boxes.

Media communicative events

Most media discourse takes place, almost by definition, in events that differ significantly from the model of the canonical speech situation. 'Mediated' communication involves specialised adaptations of the resources of face-to-face verbal interaction.

Communicative events in the media take many forms. At one end of a scale, they can still be 'dyadic communication' (two-way conversation between two interactants in a phone conversation). At the other end of the scale is what people traditionally think of as 'mass communication' (e.g. radio or television broadcasting). In his many books on the subject, the communication theorist Denis McQuail (1969) has distilled characteristics of mass communication into seven major features, which might be summarised as follows:

1 They normally require complex formal organisations.
2 They are directed towards large audiences.
3 They are public – content is open to all.
4 Audiences contain many different kinds of people.
5 Mass media can establish contact simultaneously with very large numbers of people at a distance from the source, and widely separated from one another.
6 Relationships between communicator and audience are managed by people who are known only in their public role, as communicators.
7 The audience for mass communications involves people coming together because of some common interest, even though the individuals involved do not know each other, have only a restricted amount of interaction, do not orient their actions to each other, and are either not at all or only loosely organised as a group.

This type of mass communication can be described in another way that we will develop in this unit: as 'non-reciprocal public address' (i.e. mass communication from some central point of production to large, dispersed audiences who have limited or no scope to reply). In between one-to-one dyadic (or dialogic) interaction and one-way mass communication can be found varying structures of 'mediated communicative event'. A phone call can reach someone's voicemail, rather than the person; it may be picked up later rather than allowing reciprocal turn-taking and interaction. Messaging can be synchronous (live) or it can be asynchronous (added to, as a thread). Films and TV can involve live transmission or exhibition, or they can be selected and watched from a list or archive, time-shifted. Classifying different 'communication event' structures allows us to see the capabilities of media technologies as what Marshall McLuhan (1964) called 'extensions of man' (sic). We consider this way of understanding media more closely in unit B1.

Present communications media vary on a range of dimensions:

- Role-reversibility (part of what is thought of as interactivity): this means whether it is possible to be alternately speaker and addressee, or whether you can only listen or watch.
- Co-presence/distance: most media technologies – from letters and telegraphy through to instant messaging and mobile phones – permit messages to be communicated at a distance (including globally), subject to network and cost considerations. By contrast, face-to-face speech doesn't.
- Co-temporality: this means whether there is a 'live' link, creating communication simultaneously in real-time, or whether communication is reproduced or time-shifted.
- Fixation/relative permanence: this means whether (now only in a minority of cases) media discourse exists only at the moment of its utterance – as was the case earlier for nearly all communication – or whether it has been fixed in permanent, or at least durable, textual form (e.g. in the form of writing, on tape, as a file).
- Spontaneity/rehearsed and scripted: this means whether the discourse is simultaneously planned, executed and monitored, or whether it is prepared and scripted (and so likely to be structured in more deliberate ways than if unplanned).

Other significant dimensions of media communicative events might also be proposed. Can you think of any not covered by this list?

What makes media discourse distinctive?

Two general properties stand out in the list of features of media discourse above. First, you may have noted what we will call a 'reification' of spoken communication. Second, there are different capabilities that create interactivity. We should explain each of these concepts further.

1 'Reification' means turning something that is a process or set of relationships into something fixed, a product or thing. Reification of spoken verbal discourse is sometimes called 'fixation' (e.g. by Thompson, 1995). It transforms spoken communication into an object or kind of commodity. Speech can be captured as writing, for example. Later in its history, writing could be turned into printed text. Both formats convert the evanescent character of speaking into something permanent and reproducible: a fixed text or artefact. Media 'speech' is also reproducible, in different circumstances from those in which it was created. It takes on many of the properties of writing, while continuing to have the apparent spontaneity of speech. Where spoken media discourse is planned, rather than spontaneous, it differs from conversational speech in another respect too: it is often produced by co-ordinated production teams rather than by individuals. Such speaking involves a complex division of labour between scriptwriter, director, sound recordist and others. Also, in broadcast form media speech tends to require a scale of investment from which financial return or benefit will be expected, in order to repay production costs and earn profit. This leads to a channelling of all the various kinds of speech that *might* be recorded and/or broadcast into a narrower range of media speech genres (of news, chat shows, corporate PR presentations, political soundbites, etc.). We consider some of these media speech genres in more detail in other units.

Activity 

- ❑ Some people say that the internet makes this 'mass media' view of spoken discourse and media speech largely redundant. How far do you agree?
- ❑ Make one list of points that suggest that the 'mass media' perspective is less relevant now than previously, and another list of points that suggest it still largely applies.

2 'Interactivity' is associated with most contemporary media technologies, which are typically to some degree 'interactive'. Being interactive is rather like 'reciprocity' in the canonical situation of utterance: it involves turn-taking – and so interaction – rather than only one-way transmission of a communicated message. But the degree of interactivity varies. It may involve recipients of a media text simply reacting, or making their own sense out of some piece of media content. This is the kind of 'active reception' or receiver interaction with media texts researched by David Morley and others in the field known as New Audience Studies (Morley, 1992). Such reception is active, but there is little feedback into or control over the content or direction of the message. Alternatively, interactivity may refer to a process of *using* media. The user interacts by choosing: targeting and selecting material, for example, using Google searches, message alerts, RS feeds, or following hypertext links. Such use is still passive, however, to the extent that it doesn't affect the content being presented. But the act of selection may be extended further, for example with so-called interactive television, until the user becomes in effect a mini-director of the content, pressing the red button on the remote control for alternative camera angles or extra information. Even our conventional expectations of linear narrative text can be modified, where interactivity includes choosing alternative story endings. In (currently experimental) cases of this kind, the media text user is to some extent co-creating the discourse that they are, in

another sense, a recipient of. 'Interactivity' of each of these kinds still of course only involves interaction with textual material presented by the machine, rather than interaction with other users. Other kinds of interactivity again involve interaction *between* users, creating two-way forms of communication (as with email, instant messaging, mobile telephony, or online electronic games and interaction in virtual worlds). In all cases of interactivity, however, what is involved is some combination of the following:

- the degree to which two or more parties to a communication event act on each other,
- how far their interaction affects the unfolding direction of the communication, and
- how far such mutual influence is synchronised.

Contemporary language and media environment

What is particularly striking about the current phase of media technologies is the way that different communicative capabilities combine together. We consider some of these ways in thread 7 and in thread 9. Some of the traditional distinctions of communication theory – for instance between 'live' and 'recorded' media, or between reciprocal (dyadic) communication and centre–periphery 'mass' communication – seem to be breaking down in the face of communications technologies that deliver combined capabilities and ease in switching between them.

Activity

Describe as precisely as you can the different 'communicative event' capabilities involved at each stage of the following chain: a friend thanks you, during a phone conversation, for an audio recording you forwarded to them as an email attachment of a phone-in radio programme you had enjoyed listening to on the internet.

Examples of mediated communications of the kind presented in the activity above involve combined forms of reification and interactivity. New mixed forms are changing our media discourse environment, which is presently one in which face-to-face interaction coexists with many other modalities of more or less mediated and more or less interactive discourse. Each different case has its own implications as regards styles adopted in contemporary media communication.

With the advent of radio, film and television, for example, millions of people were simultaneously able to 'overhear', in an unprecedented way, exact depictions of one person or actor whispering intimately to another. This innovation opened up new possibilities that could be exploited for creative purposes unforeseen at the time. Details of accent, intonation, tempo and precise gesture spread from the realm of what you could only know from personal experience and other people's descriptions into more public conventions of acting and presentation. Styles of stage acting and film acting have diverged ever since.

Private and public communications

The mediated character of verbal discourse being described here contributes, over time, to a fundamental redrawing of lines between personal and public, between self and community, and between close-up interaction and mass assembly and spectacle. You can read or listen to material and absorb ideas from other cultures and earlier periods. Personal communications to which previously you could not have had access become something you can read or listen to again and again. You can contribute to public display of the personal yourself, too, by blogging, online social networking, or contributing to an online discussion thread. Public figures you would never have come into contact with are subject to your close-up scrutiny of their words and how they deliver them (Thompson, 2000). Acknowledging such profound extensions of our productive and receptive linguistic experience is crucial in appreciating the massive capability of modern communication media.

Media-performed language also allows people or characters merely to *seem* intimate or informal in media presentation. They can use first-name terms or second-person direct address to an unseen (and largely unknown) audience; they can draw freely on conventionally personal topics and use an informal register, even in situations that do not allow for reply or dialogue that we typically associate with informal or personal interaction (Hoggart, 1957). Such appearance of informality and contrived intimacy can spill over, too, into more calculated kinds of dissembling and fraud: emails that purport to come from online identities very different from the actual writer or speaker projecting them; contributions to customer websites posted by employees or agents of the company whose product is being discussed but which present themselves as enthusiastic consumer endorsement; and media public relations announcements directly at odds with a situation as understood by the people who make them. Elsewhere in thread 3 we discuss examples of a number of these kinds of discourse, and some theoretical approaches to them.

A4 MEDIA DISCOURSE GENRES

In this unit, we introduce the idea of specialised media discourse genres. In doing so, we bring together considerations introduced in the previous three units. We look at the general question of how far genres can be categorised, and then consider some specific examples. We consider

- how the idea of 'genre' is used in communication and media studies
- what happens when genres become blurred, or where conventions associated with a genre are disrupted in what are felt to be inappropriate ways.

Genre as text type

In its most general sense, 'genre' simply means a sort, or type, of text: thriller, horror movie, musical, autobiography, tragedy, etc.

There is an obvious convenience in being able to label texts. We can fit any given text into a class or category that is then a convenient shorthand by means of which to describe what it is like: it resembles other texts that people already know. The notion is useful not only when applied to literary works and non-literary discourse, but also to the wide range of media texts. We can distinguish typical features of, say, a chat show from a political interview, a scripted soap from reality TV, and an email from a text message. 'Genre', in this sense, is generalisation or abstraction from specific textual properties.

For all its convenience, however, the notion of genre presents difficulties. It raises such questions as:

- ❑ Is there a fixed number of sorts of text?
- ❑ If so, when and how was this range defined, and on what basis?
- ❑ Who will decide 'genre' for still evolving types, such as emergent styles in popular music, texting or multimedia?

A more theoretical question also arises. Is genre a prescriptive category – grouping features that *should* be incorporated into writing or production of a given type? Or is it a descriptive category, generalising only after the event on the basis of agreement among text users? In the second view, any particular genre is whatever people say it is.

- ❑ One way to think about questions of genre is to consider a film you have seen recently (at the cinema, on DVD, or on TV). Decide what genre you would say it's in, and – more importantly – consider how you think you formed that view. Be as precise as you can about what makes the film belong to the genre you think it's in (e.g. particular features of style, development of plot, likely audience reaction, etc.).
- ❑ Here are two accounts (A and B) from our own recent experiences of talking about genre, with some questions added for you to think about:

A I saw a film on TV late last night – I missed the beginning and don't even remember its name. It seemed to me to be something I would call a 'revenge movie'.

- ❑ What would you expect that film to have contained?
- ❑ Can we identify a general 'formula' for such a film? If we can, how stable would such a formula be, for different kinds of cinema (such as Bollywood, or Chinese cinema)?
- ❑ Would the expected formula have been the same twenty years ago, or forty years ago?

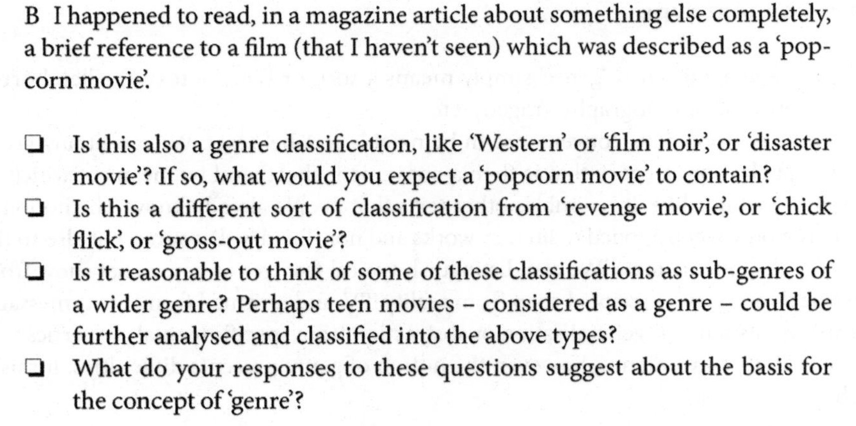

B I happened to read, in a magazine article about something else completely, a brief reference to a film (that I haven't seen) which was described as a 'popcorn movie'.

- ❑ Is this also a genre classification, like 'Western' or 'film noir', or 'disaster movie'? If so, what would you expect a 'popcorn movie' to contain?
- ❑ Is this a different sort of classification from 'revenge movie', or 'chick flick', or 'gross-out movie'?
- ❑ Is it reasonable to think of some of these classifications as sub-genres of a wider genre? Perhaps teen movies – considered as a genre – could be further analysed and classified into the above types?
- ❑ What do your responses to these questions suggest about the basis for the concept of 'genre'?

Attitudes vary towards creating texts which are recognisable within established genres. In some periods and places, it is considered a valuable achievement to produce a good 'generic text': a good detective thriller, an advertising campaign, a news report, or a stylised but not especially original pop ballad. In other circumstances, an ambition to do this is dismissed as being merely imitative and formulaic, lacking in creativity. (On the subject of pop ballads and 'imitative and formulaic' text creation, we illustrate a claimed method for producing the 'perfect' pop song below. Techniques used in creating song lyrics are also discussed in unit C3.) The wider point is that 'genre' production is often held to lack individual imagination by comparison with 'original' work.

However you view creativity in genre production, it is worth noting that genre always contributes to higher-level, social patterns of media production and circulation in a given society. Genre is part of a social system of what gets produced and why; what people like and why; what gets preserved, re-released, etc., and why. Historical and cultural differences as regards 'genre' suggest that this contribution is not fixed. It is something we need to think about and monitor, especially in a rapidly changing, globalised media environment.

Tell me about genres

How did genres develop? Our understanding or knowledge of genres is based on expectations we form about specific text types, whether these are literary works or media discourses. For example, we expect something classified as a pop song to have lyrics organised into verses and a chorus and set to a melody. We expect a political interview to consist of a sequence of turn-taking moves in a question–answer format, with field-specific vocabulary that is formal and serious in tone. Features of any exemplar of a genre are judged in terms of how well suited to the genre they are.

Classifying genres

Montgomery, Durant, Fabb, Furniss and Mills (2006) suggest a number of ways in which genres can be classified on the basis of properties that distinguish different text types:

1 Classification on the basis of formal arrangement: structure is the main property that distinguishes one genre from another, e.g. sonnets are composed of fourteen lines; poetry follows a certain rhythm and conventions of sound patterning, etc.
2 Classification on the basis of theme or topic: a biography (film or book) is about a person's life whereas a drama involves a plot that develops and is (usually) resolved. (Think about how books are arranged by theme or subject matter in a bookshop.)
3 Classification on the basis of mode of address: genre is identified by how the text addresses its audience (e.g. directly talking to the audience, in news reporting and sport commentary) or how it is presented as though the audience is overhearing named participants (e.g. chat shows, a lot of drama, phone-ins, and celebrity interviews).
4 Classification on the basis of attitude or anticipated response: this is perhaps the most complex of the categories. It involves how the audience's response is elicited in a variety of ways. An example cited by Montgomery et al. is that of war poetry, which can be either jingoistic or anti-war in its exploration of patriotism, moral values, loyalty, heroism, wasted life and political cynicism. We can extend such examples. Newspaper stories traditionally set out to inform but they may also encode political and ideological positions, which readers may then either agree or disagree with. In Britain, think about labels such as 'Guardian reader' and 'Sun reader' and the associations such categories give rise to. (We consider the relationship between informing and other kinds of persuasive discourse in thread 5.)

Film genres: expectation and verisimilitude

In film studies, the notion of genre is more than just a classification of bodies of work into categories such as those presented above. Genres are importantly about expectations that people bring with them when they go to see a particular type of film. Genre helps audiences to make sense of character and plot, for example. It is what Neale (1990) describes as offering 'a way of working out the significance of what is happening on the screen'; in order to understand genre expectations, individuals must have some knowledge of regimes of verisimilitude, or 'various systems of plausibility, motivation, justification and belief' (p. 46). In other words, what is probable in, and appropriate to, a specific genre must be intelligible and believable. (Neale's description of genre here can be likened to the notion of 'schemas' and schema 'reinforcement' and 'disruption' discussed in unit B4.)

Todorov (1981) identifies two types of verisimilitude, which he calls 'generic' and 'social or cultural' verisimilitude. Whereas generic verisimilitude embodies rules,

norms and laws that make the genre intelligible, cultural verisimilitude requires 'conventional notions of realism' to create an appearance of truth. Consider an example. In films about a war, realism can be achieved by a combination of drawing on facts from history, media sources and first-hand accounts. These sources create together a level of authenticity that is likely to be judged as acceptable or not by an anticipated audience. The types of verisimilitude work together in satisfying audience expectations. Often, generic knowledge merges with cultural knowledge to form what Todorov describes as overall 'public opinion'. If either form of knowledge is transgressed (or misunderstood), then audience and critics alike will make their (unfavourable) opinion known.

Sometimes, the genre of a piece of work may not be all that clear. A text can challenge or 'disrupt' expectations, though not necessarily in a damaging or negative way. One film that comes to mind as not fitting into any one obvious genre had critics very confused: *From Dusk Till Dawn*. The film was directed by Robert Rodriguez (1996), with a screenplay by Quentin Tarantino. *From Dusk Till Dawn* has been described as belonging to a number of genres, including action/horror/survival-horror/vampire and suspense genre. None of these categories on its own, however, captures what the film is about. As one online blog of critics' reviews states:

> **Consensus:** *From Dusk Till Dawn* starts out as one movie, but, about halfway through, it becomes an entirely different beast. While the odd mix is not entirely successful, the over-the-top action scenes and gore will please fans of the genre.
> (http://uk.rottentomatoes.com/movie-1069340/, 30 August 2008)

As for which genre the fans referred to are fans of, things remain not entirely clear.

Leading a song and dance

Earlier in our discussion of genre, we suggested that genres are often seen as 'imitative and formulaic'. Consider in this context what makes a perfect pop song (example 1) and how expectations are disrupted when a politician cracks a joke (example 2).

1 A perfect pop song

What is the perfect pop song? First, you need to define what you mean by 'pop' to establish the characteristics you associate with that *type* of song. Once you have done that, you need to say what you mean by 'perfect', because any definition you produce may not have universal appeal. Such questions are interesting because a psychologist at London University, Tomas Chamorro-Premuzic, has proposed a specific formula for the perfect feel-good pop song:

P + Pos + T + BPM + I S

(P = Pitch, Pos = the % of positive lyrics, T = tonality, BPM = beats per minute, I = images/memories associated with the music, S = serotonin level)

Chamorro-Premuzic's calculations suggest that the song *Wake Up Boo!* by the Boo Radleys tops his Top 10 list, which consists of the following songs:

1. Boo Radleys: *Wake Up Boo!*,
2. Beach Boys: *Good Vibrations*,
3. Jackson 5: *I Want You Back*,
4. Beatles: *Here Comes the Sun*,
5. Madonna: *Holiday*,
6. Van Morrison: *Brown Eyed Girl*,
7. The Foundations: *Build Me Up Buttercup*,
8. Michael Jackson: *Wanna Be Startin' Somethin'*,
9. John Paul Young: *Love Is in the Air*,
10. The Darkness: *I Believe in a Thing Called Love*.

Activity

- ❑ What do you think of this list? Do you see major differences between the songs listed here, either within the terms of Chamorro-Premuzic's formula, or beyond those terms?
- ❑ Are pop songs, and media genres in general, a matter of formula as this kind of song calculus suggests?

We look at conventional techniques used in pop songs further in unit C3.

2 A president's public gaffe

What sort of comments do you expect to hear in a broadcast made by a US president? Think about level of formality, the form and content of what is said, and use of field-specific language such as political jargon. Now consider how, in 1984, President Ronald Reagan, not realising that his microphone was on during a sound check, joked about bombing Russia with the now notorious gaffe, 'My fellow Americans, I am pleased to tell you today that I've signed legislation that will outlaw Russia forever. We begin bombing in five minutes'. Not surprisingly, this comment attracted international coverage and criticism.

Given this description of President Reagan's remarks, consider the following questions:

- ❑ What features of President Reagan's utterance, as quoted here, mark it out as unusual?
- ❑ How inappropriate was the comment in the context of the political climate of the day?
- ❑ How are discourse conventions you would usually associate with the genre of a political broadcast breached in President Reagan's comment?

A detailed discussion that examines the genre of a speech event using a model for analysis is presented in unit C4. We also consider this particular example, which has been discussed from a different point of view by the novelist and critic Umberto Eco, in unit B3.

A5 MEDIA RHETORICS

Two kinds of significance stand out in media language: whether it conveys information (and, if so, how reliably); and how far it seeks to persuade us towards some particular viewpoint, belief, or course of action. These two main functions of media language, and the interaction between them, create the huge influence that media discourse exerts. In this unit, we show how

- some media discourse makes truth-claims: it reports facts or gives information, and invites you to believe what is said or shown, and how
- other kinds of media discourse invite you to see them as persuasion or opinion, rather than as an account of how things are.

We contrast these functions with media discourse styles that function primarily as diversion and entertainment: they involve audiences in social interaction, often in the form of games and quizzes. To assess the relative 'authority' of media discourse, we shift emphasis to some extent away from local word-choice and style towards larger discourse functions. The persuasive techniques used in discourse may be usefully grouped together and called 'rhetoric'.

'Information' and 'persuasion'

The present period is commonly described using phrases such as 'media age' or 'the age of information'. These phrases are sometimes treated as if they are interchangeable, but there are important differences.

'Information' is a kind of content or raw material for perception or interpretation. It is a matter of how the world is. Ask people for examples and they say names and dates, numbers, prices and statistics. 'Media', on the other hand, are forms or channels for *presenting* such content. Information is intertwined with the means by which it is presented (e.g. whether information is presented in visual or verbal form, or in a humorous way). Sometimes we recognise media as being interwoven with kinds of content they present (see units A1 and D1, for how the word 'media' is understood in different ways). The basic contrast nevertheless remains. We should therefore ask if (and, if so, how) information is affected by the particular media forms that express it.

Asking this question raises another issue. Can information ever be represented neutrally, impartially or objectively? Or is there always some element of point of view, bias, even distortion in its presentation? Some thinkers – in a tradition of linguistics

that derives from the work of Sapir and Whorf (for the clearest statement of this view, normally associated with both editors, see Whorf, 1956) – have argued that concepts, and so information, are not just shaped by the terms of their expression; they do not exist separately from such expression. Changing your word for something, in this view, changes that something.

Even if you do not accept the contested viewpoint associated with Sapir and Whorf, it is clear that ideas and information can be packaged in different ways. Some sorts of discourse that 'present' information purport to be factual and objective. They include scientific discourse and public information. Other kinds of discourse are overtly forms of persuasion and advocacy, and are clearly based on a given point of view. They include statements of opinion, blogs, magazine features, personal reports, and adverts. Other kinds of discourse again are part of the category of fiction. 'Truthfulness' for texts in this category lies in how they capture deeper truths indirectly, by using a made-up story or imagined situation and events as a vehicle for revealing how things actually are.

How do we know which sort of discourse is serving which function? Sometimes, mode of presentation is a clear guide. The text may consist of explicit statements of what (you assume) the writer or speaker believes to be the case. Information provided by such discourse may still be either correct or incorrect. But whether it is true or false, the discourse is a matter of statements of information. This stands in contrast with obvious statements of opinion. Such statements tend to be marked by a subjective stance towards the material. That stance may be conveyed by words such as 'may', 'might', 'probably', 'in my opinion', 'seems' or 'all things considered'. Words of this kind contribute to what is called the modality of the discourse: the degree of conviction or authority with which it is presented. In this case, what is at stake is epistemic modality, which is concerned with how certain or uncertain the speaker wants to suggest they are about what they are saying (see Simpson, 1993). To give an example, Simpson (1993: 48–9) shows how these modal auxiliaries can be used in their epistemic sense to 'convey varying degrees of epistemic commitment to the basic proposition "You are right"':

You could be right
You may be right
You must be right
You might have been right
You should have been right

With some discourse, an addressee must work out whether what is being presented is 'information' or whether the discourse is trying to be persuasive. Working this out calls for understanding of the genre or idiom of the discourse, which can also act as a signal of what purpose it serves (see unit A4). It may also be necessary to extract general points or significance carried by specific case studies or stories that are being presented, for instance in documentaries, as accessible forms of illustration (see unit A6 on narrative). In broadcast media, as well as with direct mailing and on the internet, a great deal of discourse combines one form or style with the function of another. An apparent birthday card or blog entry may gradually reveal itself to be actually an

advert. A mini-drama about a car accident may turn out to be a public information warning about the danger of drinking and driving or not wearing a seatbelt. You are led into the text's actual purpose from an initial appearance that it is something else.

Because of these different ways that media language communicates, we need to understand the construction, or rhetoric, of media discourse. We need to appreciate selectiveness of material, as well as the point of view created by emphasis, sequence and chosen style. If you are looking for information on the internet, it matters whether the information you find is accurate and fair (e.g. when you are checking availability of products and services; when you are researching details of a medical condition; or when you read up about something in a Wikipedia entry). Attention to accuracy and fairness is particularly important with the genre of news, since we base much of our understanding of the world we are living in on news sources. Some media organisations or outlets (e.g. – in Britain – the BBC, *The Times*) enjoy or have enjoyed particular reputations for accuracy and authority. Others may present themselves differently, and have different reputations. Some news sources offer alternative views that the authoritative sources are unable or unwilling to provide. Similar awareness must be shown when engaging with advertising. Interpreting what is said in this case may result in making good or bad purchases. Or you may enter unwisely into some other kind of legally binding contract. It is an increasingly important part of modern media literacy to distinguish fact from opinion, and well-founded views and advocacy from scams, manipulation and deception.

Familiarity with the styles and rhetorical techniques of media language is also important for a further reason. Information is not a passive resource, waiting to be searched for and accessed. It is always in competition for people's attention with other information. For that reason, it is often designed in ways that seek to make it appear especially relevant, urgent, or sensational. Information and ideas may be selected, simplified and enhanced in various ways. Text producers may use dramatic language, selective presentation and exaggeration, and sensational detail in order to attract attention. The resulting styles of rhetoric may try to arouse emotion, or make what is said or written especially memorable; or they may try to excite and entertain in other ways. In such a media environment, information is not a neutral reflection of how things are. Rather it is a matter of representations that are, to different extents, calculated to achieve persuasive or rhetorical effects.

Rhetoric

The term 'rhetoric' is traditionally used to describe analysis of and training in how to persuade. Rhetoric is not just persuasive speech, but persuasive *public* speech. Public persuasion can take place in many different contexts: in assemblies of people in a common place, in courtrooms, at political meetings, in street markets, or on television and online. The term 'rhetoric' itself comes from Greek *rhêtorikê*, meaning 'art of speech'. Cockcroft and Cockcroft (2005) widen this sense of rhetoric to 'the art of persuasive discourse'. They point out that the term can refer to both written and spoken communication, including broadcast and recorded forms.

Two influential themes run through the history of rhetoric. Each originates in

classical Greek times. In Aristotle (and in followers of Aristotle), rhetoric is viewed as an important and necessary aspect of all human communication, not only important in government. In Plato, by contrast, rhetoric is viewed as manipulative language, wherever it occurs. It is not a good way of getting at truth. The two views amount, essentially, to approval and disapproval of using communication strategically, rather than supposing that it can *reflect* how things are or should be. These two views run through the subsequent history of rhetoric as a struggle between the relative merits of logic and science, on the one hand, and persuasion, on the other.

According to Aristotle, there are three ways that an audience can be persuaded:

1 ethos: audiences are persuaded because they believe the speaker to be fair and honest,
2 pathos: audiences are persuaded on the basis of emotion aroused by what is said, and
3 logos: audiences are persuaded by the reasoning contained in an argument conveyed by the speech.

Note incidentally a parallel here with models of communicative functions presented in unit A3, especially Jakobson's.

Nowadays, the term 'rhetoric' is mostly associated with public speeches, where speaking persuasively is important in influencing the public. Sometimes such persuasion occurs when rhetoric is used by a political candidate during an election campaign; sometimes by a politician in their justification for war or exhortation to members of the public to resist or stand firm in difficult times. As we have stressed, rhetoric also forms part of public relations discourse, propaganda and advertising, and also runs through more personal uses of language.

Devices in persuasive discourse

Rhetorical techniques are found at a number of different levels of discourse. Traditionally, skilled orators drew on a 'rhetorical toolkit' in persuading their audience. The devices they used can be categorised into three main areas:

- Lexical choices: choice of words is governed by such factors as who the speaker is and by the context and goal of the utterance. Word choice is part of what we now mostly call register (see unit A2).
- Tropes or figurative language: this aspect includes use of tropes such as metaphor and metonymy, among others. Tropes alter and often enrich the meaning explicitly communicated. In doing so, they can create new and striking perceptions.
- Sound patterning: this consists of repeated patterns of sound such as alliteration, assonance and rhyme. Such patterns bond ideas together and create memorable effects.

Slightly confusingly, the last of these three categories contains some effects that are commonly taught as 'figures of speech', even though they are not concerned, as tropes

traditionally have been, with transfer of meaning. Examples of many of these devices, as used in advertising, are discussed in the extract from Myers (1994) in unit D5.

Consider the following example of political rhetoric. On 20 March 2003, Tony Blair made a controversial address to the nation justifying imminent war in Iraq. In his speech, he deployed a number of rhetorical devices in developing his case, some more obvious than others. For instance, he said

> So our choice is clear: back down and leave Saddam hugely strengthened; or proceed to disarm him by force. Retreat might give us a moment of respite but years of repentance at our weakness would, I believe, follow.

1 We can illustrate persuasive discourse based on *ethos* here. Blair appeals for agreement on the basis of his status as speaker. He was prime minister, the nation's political leader.

2 *Logos* or reasoning is evident in Blair's construction of an argument against Saddam remaining in power (even though his use of modals *might*, *would* and the qualification *believe* all hedge his line of argument).

- ❑ Contrasting choices (an instance of antithesis) are presented by use of adversative conjunctions *or* and *but*, which contrast the consequences if action is taken and if it is not.
- ❑ Responsibility for the action being proposed is presented subtly through use of inclusive first-person pronouns, *our* and *us*. These pronouns personalise Blair's intentions by positioning him as 'one of us'. This inclusive function of the pronouns also suggests that 'we', the public, are involved in decision-making and will therefore share responsibility for the decision to invade.

Finding rhetorical devices and design in a speech justifying war emphasises that persuasion is not just a matter of ornamentation and pleasure. It can play an important part even in situations of political crisis and life-and-death.

Activity 

> The Blair speech considered here was made in 2003. Find an important political speech that has been made more recently and look for similar examples. (You may find it useful before doing this to look at our account of the speech by President Obama in unit C5.)

Beard (2000) presents a useful list of well-known strategies employed in political discourse that fall within the conventional category of verbal patterning:

1 Antithesis, or contrastive pairs: two parts to a clause are in opposition to each other, as in Nelson Mandela's 'I stand before you not as a prophet but as a humble

servant of you'. Contrasts of this kind are an illustration of the wider phenomenon in discourse of parallelism (see Montgomery et al., 2006).

2 Repetition, as a means of creating emphasis: a famous example is Winston Churchill's repetition of emphatic 'so' in praising Battle of Britain fighter pilots in 1940: 'Never in the field of human conflict has so much been owed by so many to so few'.

3 The 'list of three' (or three-part list): the three elements complement or reinforce one another, creating a sense of unity for the phrase as a whole. Consider Nelson Mandela's statement on his release from prison in Cape Town in 1990: 'Friends, comrades and fellow South Africans. I greet you all in the name of peace, democracy and freedom for all'.

This last example allows us to make some further points about rhetorical organisation.

Rhetorical design takes place, we have said, at several different levels of discourse simultaneously. We showed this in the Tony Blair example above. We can now note a further effect in Nelson Mandela's expression 'Friends, comrades and fellow South Africans': this phrase echoes the widely recognised phrase 'Friends, Romans, countrymen' used in Shakespeare's play *Julius Caesar*. It even includes a sound parallel between 'comrades' and 'Romans'. Memorable expressions can be chosen to echo specific other utterances.

Expectations about patterns such as the three-part list can be built on, to create extra effects. In Tony Blair's celebrated mantra, 'Education, Education, Education', the three terms in the three-term list are made one and the same. The rhetorical emphasis is accordingly that 'education' is not just one of three priorities, but stands alone as the single, topmost priority.

Finally, we can note that rhetorical styles vary between different traditions and different social roles. Some rhetorical styles draw on Classical learning. Others draw more on Biblical or other religious traditions. Some contemporary rhetorics draw on people's familiarity with established styles (such as the presidential address, the courtroom speech and conventional sales patter). Others allude to particularly well-known speeches that already exist (e.g. very commonly to Martin Luther King's 'I have a dream' speech).

We consider aspects of political rhetoric further in unit C5.

Metaphor

The trope metaphor requires further discussion. Many different definitions of this figure of speech have been put forward. There are also many different approaches to analysing how it works. Many traditions of poetic analysis of metaphor, for example, view this figure as a creative device that stands out against the background of discourse in which it occurs. Conceptual investigations of metaphor, by contrast, show how metaphor can involve ordinary words or phrases that routinely present one (usually more abstract) field in terms associated with another (usually more concrete) field.

Consider the following description from Lakoff and Johnson: 'The essence of metaphor is understanding and experiencing one kind of thing in terms of another' (1980:

5). Someone having a *heated argument*, it is significant in this view, may be told to *chill out*. Sensory metaphors of hot and cold, both of which are from the same semantic field, are used to represent intensity of an argument (heated) and a way of easing off, by reducing that intensity or 'cooling down' (chill out). Such examples suggest that metaphor isn't always a one-off creative insight against a more ordinary background. It can involve more extended, socially established patterns in how we see things.

The study of metaphor is accordingly of special interest to cognitive linguists, who are interested in metaphorical mappings of ideas that occur in everyday, non-literary discourse. According to Lakoff and Johnson again,

> metaphor is pervasive in everyday life, not just in language but in thought and action . . . Our ordinary conceptual system, in terms of which we both think and act, is fundamentally metaphorical in nature . . . Our concepts structure what we perceive, how we get around in the world, and how we relate to other people. Our conceptual system thus plays a central role in defining our everyday realities.
>
> (Lakoff and Johnson, 1980: 3)

Many everyday expressions share common conceptual structures of this kind, which are embedded in the mental life of large groups of people. A much-cited example from Lakoff and Johnson (1980) is the metaphorical proposition *argument is war*. This metaphorical proposition can be illustrated by such expressions as

- ❏ Your claims are indefensible.
- ❏ He attacked every weak point in my argument.
- ❏ His criticisms were right on target.
- ❏ I demolished his argument.
- ❏ He shot down all of my arguments.

The 'argument is war' metaphor has nothing to do with any argument *for* war (as Tony Blair's rhetoric above did). Rather, it concerns the typical way we perceive a person we are arguing with as an *opponent*. We *win* or *lose* an argument, in what is seen as a *battle*, where *attacks* are made. Spread across many individual words and idioms, this metaphor involves a network of conceptual connections rather than a single imaginative inspiration.

Framing

Metaphors form extended structures (as in the 'argument is war' metaphor). They play a role in social life by calling into play larger frames of perception and belief that they bring to life. In this way, metaphors reflect, and also contribute to shaping, general representations that guide how we view experience and events. They therefore also play a part in how we choose to act. They 'frame' ideas. Cognitive linguists have for this reason paid particular attention to the role of metaphor in persuasion, including how it is drawn on extensively in political speeches, advertising, public relations discourse and spin.

Here is George Lakoff (the same Lakoff as in Lakoff and Johnson above), at the beginning of his Preface to his book about political discourse, *Don't Think of an Elephant! Know Your Values and Frame the Debate* (2004):

> Frames are mental structures that shape the way we see the world. As a result, they shape the goals we seek, the plans we make, the way we act, and what counts as a good or bad outcome of our actions. In politics our frames shape our social policies and the institutions we form to carry out policies. To change our frames is to change all of this. Reframing *is* social change. [. . .] Reframing is changing the way the public sees the world. It is changing what counts as commonsense. Because language activates frames, new language is required for new frames. Thinking differently requires speaking differently.
>
> (Lakoff, 2004: xv)

Throughout *Don't Think of an Elephant!*, Lakoff links language to different points of view from which we perceive things. His first major example in the book is that of the commonly used political expression 'tax relief'. Lakoff suggests that

> when the word 'tax' is added to 'relief', the result is a metaphor: Taxation is an affliction. And the person who takes it away is a hero, and anyone who tries to stop him is a bad guy. This is a frame. It is made up of ideas, like 'affliction' and 'hero'.
>
> (Lakoff, 2004: 4)

Lakoff then builds on this example (which closely echoes 'argument is war'). He points out that 'for there to be relief there must be an affliction, an afflicted party, and the reliever who removes the affliction and is therefore a hero' (Lakoff, 2004: 4). Positive perception of the tax-relieving hero presented by the frame is then counter-balanced by negative perception: 'And if people try to stop the hero, those people are villains for trying to prevent relief' (Lakoff, 2004: 4).

Lakoff's work on framing in political discourse, along with that of other linguists and cognitive scientists working on similar lines, is outlined at the Rockridge Institute website (www.rockridgeinstitute.com). His research and proposals are partly linguistic and partly political. Lakoff describes such work as part of US progressive politics. Interestingly, however, he acknowledges that conservative politicians consistently match, and often surpass, the ability of progressive politicians to understand and act on findings about frames. Frames are not a partisan political tool. They are how media language works. For cognitive linguists they are how *all* language works.

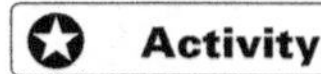

> Find a key term or phrase in a recent political speech. Give a name to the frame that it is part of. Your frame will take the form 'X is Y' (as in the 'argument is war' proposition, above. Look at some other examples as well.). List some other instances of the same frame. Now the hard part: look for reasons *why* that frame has been chosen in the context you found it in. What does use of this particular frame contribute to the political speech you found it in?

A6 MEDIA STORYTELLING

The significance or authority of a stretch of media language is often affected by a key dimension of its form: the tendency for storytelling to be adopted as the style of presentation. In this unit we

- analyse storytelling as a form, or cluster of genres,
- explain the difference between narrative and plot,
- illustrate features that distinguish narrative as a particular way of presenting news and information, and
- show how story structure fits into the sorts of media genre exemplified in earlier units.

Some claims about stories

Storytelling is usually held to be a universal activity. The psychologist Jerome Bruner suggests that there is an 'innate' human propensity to organise events into memorable stories (see Cobley, 2001). It is not surprising, therefore, that stories pervade our day-to-day lives in the form of anecdote, literary and non-literary narratives, and media representations. As long as there is an audience, there will be stories. Perhaps the most recognised way of presenting stories is through use of narrative structure: a form of presentation we see in TV drama and cinematic fiction, which is also common as a rhetorical vehicle for news, documentary and advertising.

It is worth noting a series of varying claims about stories to begin with that we will need to sort out.

- Stories seem suited to function as 'reports on reality poured into recognisable models'.
- Narrative seems to be either one genre or a cluster of genres. There are established formulae or templates for relaying complicated events and their significance.
- When you enjoy a story, you are experiencing an echo, or particular realisation, of other stories you already know (and which give rise to expectations about the one you are experiencing at the time).
- There are only a hundred great (or archetypal) stories in the world. They are told and retold many times, in many different forms (e.g. *Romeo and Juliet*, or Homer's *Odyssey*).
- Stories provide a way of making abstract information graspable, if it is made sufficiently concrete and personalised, hence the centrality of characters and events.
- Stories are useful as illustrations, or ways of propagating points in favour of an organisation. In its branding and public relations, an organisation may feel that on a certain theme it 'has a good story to tell'.
- Stories sometimes function as vehicles for stereotypes and are used for that purpose in propaganda and other ways of manipulating public opinion.

What makes a good story: narrative and plot

Various descriptions have been offered of what it is that produces expectation when you encounter a story for the first time.

Fundamental to almost any story appears to be a good plot. But what is a plot? We might begin by saying (with Scholes and Kellogg, 1966: 207) that plot involves 'the dynamic, sequential element in narrative literature . . . the only indispensable skeleton', the 'most essential' but 'least variable' element of narrative. Plot consists of three conditions that combine to form a minimum plot structure:

- Temporality: a time-ordered sequence of events, with a minimal narrative requiring three states – the beginning, middle and final state – linked together by conjunctions of time e.g. *firstly, then, finally.*
- Causation: the middle state causes the final state of the story. Events in different parts of the story are connected by causal links.
- Human interest: without this, there is no narrative. Human interest, however, is subjective and culturally specific – what appeals to one audience may not appeal to or have relevance for another.

A king and queen story

Contemporary media stories adapt established desires and expectations associated with stories in earlier forms, including oral narration and personal narratives as well as novels, drama and other media. Consider the following adaptation of E. M. Forster's (1927) famous exemplification of how the three conditions of *temporality, causation* and *human interest* interact with each other.

a The King died. The Queen died

The two sentences here provide factual information about two separate events. The lack of any conjunction of time allows that the two events may be unrelated.

b The King died and then the Queen died
(i) (ii)

Two kinds of conjunction have been added, which now connect the two events: (i) co-ordinating *and*; (ii) temporal *then*. The two events have been linked in a temporal sequence, so readers understand that the King died before the Queen. This is a minimal narrative, which the sociolinguist William Labov (1972) described as 'a sequence of two clauses which are temporally ordered'. The linking device *then* also functions here as an implicit causal conjunction: readers infer that the King's death may have caused the Queen to die. Perhaps the Queen died of a broken heart.

c The King died and then the Queen died of grief

By adding the prepositional phrase *of grief* to the second sentence, the cause of the Queen's death is made explicit: the first event resulted in the second. According to Forster, there is now a 'plot', whereas **b** is a narrative. Not only is temporality present but also causation. The important condition of human interest is also met by the events being about public figures. We could imagine that if example **c** appeared as a news headline, it would definitely sell newspapers.

A further distinction frequently made between narrative and plot is that a narrative tells you 'what happened' whereas a plot also tells you 'why'.

Using these observations, which apply across most or all forms of storytelling, we can now turn to examples of recent media headlines. It is instantly interesting to see how the word *plot* is often used in a different sense: to describe secretive, illegal and underhand activities that pursue the purpose of damage or devastation on a national or international scale. The examples of headlines given below show that 'plot' tends to collocate with (that is, commonly appear next to) 'bombs' and events involving acts of terrorism.

Details emerge on alleged plot to bomb airliners
The bomb plot that didn't make the news headlines
India's Jaipur bombing called 'terror plot'
Accused in alleged Toronto bomb plot tapped to behead PM, court hears
German Police Arrest 3 in Terrorist Plot

Activity 

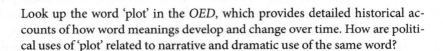

Look up the word 'plot' in the *OED*, which provides detailed historical accounts of how word meanings develop and change over time. How are political uses of 'plot' related to narrative and dramatic use of the same word?

Narrative and its relatives

Narratives offer one way of organising events into a story format. There are also reports, diaries, essays (and other forms that express general points and illustrations; arguments and implications, etc.). Each of these forms can overlap to varying degrees with narrative.

Consider some possible differences between a narrative and a police report of 'what occurred'. The researcher Polanyi suggests that a narrative illustrates 'some sort of general truth with implications for the world in which the story is told as well as for the impact of events in the story itself' (1981: 326). Police reports, on the other hand, 'give a picture of what went on during a particular period' but convey only the facts and not an evaluation of the events. Furthermore, recipients 'bear the burden of building the "story" out of the report', if that report was produced as an answer to a request for information (Polanyi, 1982: 515). In her study of personal narratives, Lambrou (2007) introduces a further distinction, between narrative and another mode of storytelling: a 'recount'. She suggests that 'If narratives are descriptions of "actions" then it can be argued that recounts are descriptions of "states"' depending on

the story topic, i.e. what the story is about. Drawing on extensive data, she goes on to provide evidence that 'story topic does go some way towards determining story form' (2007: 205). A further distinction between the two storytelling modes is the presence of evaluative strategies, which is discussed separately, in unit B6

Media storytelling, including stories found in news, presents many examples both of first-person accounts of events and more distanced and impersonal styles of reporting. Stories are 'representations' of news events, nevertheless, and may be influenced by factors such as culture and political beliefs, where ideology may differ significantly. Moreover, news stories are produced with a particular audience in mind, rather than being neutral accounts of events they depict (see unit B5). Even personalised reports, or first-person witness accounts in written form, are commonly subject to editing and may therefore contain interpretation at one or more removes of time and reflection from what actually occurred. Examples of first-person accounts can be found in unit C6.

Stories in adverts

Figure A6.1 is an excerpt from an advertisement that appeared in a Saturday broadsheet newspaper in 2007. The advert was published on behalf of the Bhopal Medical Appeal campaign, and appeals for donations to help victims of the chemical poisoning in Bhopal, India, in 1984, resulting from the gas leakage from a nearby chemical plant. At least 8,000 people died in what is still thought to be the world's worst industrial disaster. Ongoing contamination is estimated to have affected up to 100,000 people, who have injuries including genetic birth defects.

AMIR WHO'S EIGHT sadly holds up his hands. His fingers are joined together as if he's had an accident with a tube of superglue.

'Who called you such a thing?'

'A lady in Hamidia Road. She looked at me and said, "Ugh, too many monsters".'

'Why do you listen? Don't cry!' says his mother. Herself near tears, she asks furiously, 'What was she thinking, that woman? That he wouldn't hear? He wouldn't follow? His hands are that way so he must not have a brain?'

When she has calmed down she says that she no longer goes to family weddings: many people, even relatives, feel uncomfortable about having a malformed child at the festivities. 'In case it attracts ...'

She breaks off. 'That woman, you know what, I think she was scared. She knows the next one could be hers.'

'This is the way the world ends'

Amir is one of hundreds born damaged in a certain cluster of neighbourhoods in Bhopal. What all have in common is that they are near Union Carbide's haunted, derelict factory.

On a cold night 22 years ago, the factory sent a cloud 500 times deadlier than cyanide rolling out over the sleeping city of Bhopal.

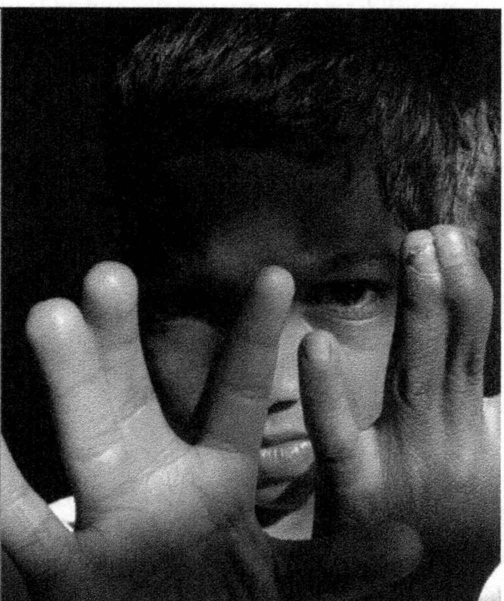

Figure A6.1 Bhopal Medical Appeal (*The Guardian*, May 2007)

The opening paragraphs of this advert resemble a fictional novel rather than a charity advert. Facts and figures surrounding the events and consequences of the poisoning are given later in the advert and provide the important contextual information to readers for the purpose of asking for their donation. But it is the personalised, subjective account of one family's experience that draws readers' attention. Such personalisation is achieved through use of literary techniques associated with fictional writing. The advert is first presented as a story; that story recounts the daily suffering of victims of the incident. We are told of Amir's experiences in particular, but we infer that his suffering is representative of many thousands of others who are victims of the same chemical poisoning.

Note some of the literary techniques used in the opening sequence of the Bhopal Medical Appeal advert:

1 Introduction of characters into the 'story':

   Amir, Amir's mother, the lady from Hamidia Road

2 Use of third-person narration:

   Amir who's eight sadly holds up his hands. His fingers are joined together . . .

3 Use of direct speech and inverted commas to move the story on while providing emotive details of what the child Amir has to endure:

   'Who called you such a thing?' 'A lady in Hamidia Road. She looked at me . . .'

Juxtaposition of the story with the photo of a child (which the author of this donation appeal confirms is Amir) holding up his hands to the reader, to show his genetic defects, validates the story visually, and adds to the shock value of the advert in general. (In thread 7, we consider how words and images create meaning together.)

Now look at the headline for this advert in Figure A6.2. The child-like presentation of the writing (combining upper and lower case characters in one word, having words and individual letters in words misaligned, and using different font styles) conveys obliquely the handwriting that children with genetic defects affecting their hands might produce.

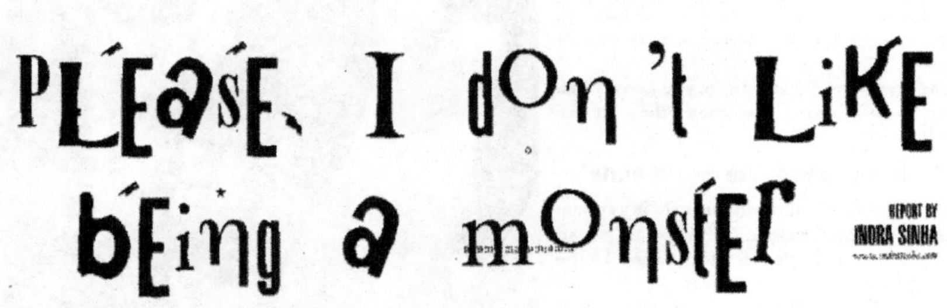

Figure A6.2 Headline, Bhopal Medical Appeal (*The Guardian*, May 2007)

In email correspondence (January 2009) with the author of this appeal, Indra Sinha explained that the appeals are not seen as adverts: that is, they were not conceived or written as conventional charity advertisements. From the earliest appeals, in 1994, the techniques of literary narrative were purposely used 'to tell stories and bring the suffering to life'. The result has been a successful campaign that has produced impressive donations, which now fund a clinic with almost 50 permanent staff and have given free care to more than 30,000 people. The appeal, according to Indra, works

> by engaging the imagination – and proceeds on certain assumptions, a certain philosophy, whose tenets are:
>
> 1 People are basically good
> 2 Our appeals are conversations in which the reader plays an equal part. This has to be allowed for in the writing
> 3 The work takes place inside the reader's imagination, into which we are temporarily invited
> 4 Storytelling can convey truths which facts are incapable of expressing.

Other Bhopal Appeals can be viewed online at: http://www.indrasinha.com/bhopal appeals.html

(Interestingly, many of the ideas for the Bhopal Medical Appeal found their way into Indra's novel, *Animal's People*, shortlisted for the 2007 Man Booker Prize.) The impact of narrative in advertising is considerable and, as has been shown in the Bhopal Medical Appeal example, can turn the 'experience of thousands of people into stories that can touch and move other people'.

- ❏ How successful is the storytelling format adopted in the Bhopal Medical Appeal in engaging readers?
- ❏ What general strategies are used in trying to persuade readers to donate?
- ❏ How far do you think the picture and the headline add to the shock value of the advert? Would removal of either make the advert less moving?
- ❏ Discuss Indra Sinha's four tenets above. How far do you agree with them?
- ❏ Find other examples of adverts where storytelling is used as the main rhetorical device. Evaluate their success by following the same procedure of description and analysis as we use for examples presented in this unit.
- ❏ Take a well-known product and write an advertisement, using some of the literary techniques described above.

A7 WORDS AND IMAGES

In this unit we address a question that is commonly raised about the interest or importance of studying *verbal* discourse in the media. Media, many people say, are not about 'language'. Rather, they suggest, media texts are primarily pictures and combinations of image, sound and music. This view has led many thinkers in semiotics to try to identify a distinct 'media language', rather than viewing verbal language as one element in a compound, multimodal media form.

- We outline the interaction that takes place between language (conceived as words, phrases and sentences) and 'media language' (thought of as a compound form in which words, images and sounds combine).

Why words with pictures matter

Why does the *visual* dimension of contemporary media present a challenge in investigating language and media? One answer is that it is because the visual element in contemporary media discourse has been so pervasive. Many contemporary media appear *primarily* visual. Historically, too, there have been a range of forms of combination between pictures and words:

- illustrated books, with captions of varying length and detail under diagrams and drawings,
- titles and captions added to paintings and other publicly displayed images (including sometimes the thought-provoking title 'Untitled'),
- photographic news images used to illustrate printed stories or articles,
- headlines and taglines used in advertising posters and magazine adverts that have one or more central images,
- the sound and image, audio-visual discourse of television and film, from the advent of talkies in the late 1920s onwards, and
- text and image combinations in multimedia presentations, including widespread use of PowerPoint slides.

Each of these media forms – as well as others – emphasises some kind of combination of image and verbal language.

Even with texts that have *no* pictures, we might say that features of design (including font, layout, colour, etc.) are significant in our perception of printed text. Such design properties foreground a communicative dimension of writing that goes beyond its representation of speech. (Again, there are historical precedents for this in the history of printing, such as elaborately decorative pages, especially frontispieces, and illuminated manuscripts.)

Faced with evidence of accentuated visual signification alongside speech and writing in modern media, we must ask whether there is some kind of interaction

between the two channels in shaping interpretation and response. How do pictures and writing, or pictures and sound, connect with each other? What effect do they have on each other? And *how* does their interaction shape interpretation and response?

This question is important in how we process all texts in our contemporary multimedia environment. It is also important in trying to grasp future directions that media technologies and genres are likely to follow (see thread 9).

Unsurprisingly, the question of how words and images work together has implications in relation to problems of bias, especially in news, discussed in thread 5. Commenting on bias in television news, for example, Gunter (1997) suggests that one reason why television news is considered so believable, by comparison with other news sources, is because of the 'simultaneous observation of action and verbal description of events' that it allows. In this view, it is as if seeing *confirms* what you hear or read. Seeing is believing. At the same time, though, the hearing or reading directs you ('talks you through') what you're seeing. It leads you towards a particular interpretation of it.

Analysing pictures and captions

Is Gunter's (and many other people's) idea of some kind of mutually reinforcing interaction between simultaneous channels well founded?

A lot of recent discussion of images presented with accompanying textual material in linguistics and semiotics (rather than in other fields, such as psychology) is based on a small number of essays by the French semiotician Roland Barthes (1977b), who took the press photograph (usually in news and advertising) as his case study. In unit B7 we explore two key concepts that Barthes proposed should guide analysis: 'relay' and 'anchorage'. Here, we explore Barthes's suggestion that we need different but complementary approaches to analysing mixed media or multimodal discourse. Barthes's approach may be usefully compared with more integrated, or synthetic 'multimodal' semiotic approaches, including the approach developed by Kress and van Leeuwen outlined in an extract in unit D7.

Barthes's point of departure in analysing how words work with images is the tradition of approaches to visual composition and iconography (i.e. the conventional associations that go with visual representations of objects, places, animals, people, etc.). But in the essay 'The Photographic Message', Barthes develops an alternative approach. His account seeks to show how photographs communicate in ways that are much closer to models of linguistic communication:

> The press photograph is a message. Considered overall this message is formed by a source of emission, a channel of transmission and a point of reception. The source of emission is the staff of the newspaper, the group of technicians certain of whom take the photo, some of whom choose, compose and treat it, while others, finally, give it a title, a caption and a commentary. The point of reception is the public which reads the paper. As for the channel of transmission, this is the newspaper itself, or, more precisely, a complex of concurrent messages with the photograph as centre and surrounds constituted by the text, the title, the caption, the lay-out

> and, in a more abstract but no less 'informative' way, by the very name of the paper (this name represents a knowledge that can heavily orientate the reading of the message strictly speaking).
>
> (Barthes, 1977b: 15)

Notice how Barthes begins here with the 'conduit model of communication' that is described in variant forms in unit A3. His model consists of

- ❑ a source of emission, or communicator,
- ❑ a text transmitted through a channel, and
- ❑ various points of reception, or an audience.

The photographic image itself, Barthes insists, involves 'a complex of concurrent messages'. These are the various things we can see in the image, and different meanings that what we see can evoke.

As regards how to analyse verbal aspects of media discourse, it is Barthes's next observation that may be most important. Barthes suggests that a press photograph is helped in its communication by a number of 'surrounds', or supporting devices: 'the text, the title, the caption, the lay-out and, in a more abstract but no less "informative" way, by the very name of the paper'. These 'surrounds' (what in a different vocabulary would be called aspects of 'paratext', Genette, 1997) are where interaction between verbal discourse and visual imagery takes place.

As the larger framework within which he develops his concepts of 'relay' and 'anchorage' (see unit B7), Barthes draws attention to questions of method in analysing the interaction between words and images:

> These observations are not without their importance for it can readily be seen that in the case of the press photograph the three traditional parts of the message do not call for the same method of investigation. The emission and the reception of the message both lie within the field of sociology: it is a matter of studying human groups, of defining motives and attitudes, and of trying to link the behaviour of these groups to the social totality of which they are a part. For the message itself, however, the method is inevitably different: whatever the origin and the destination of the message, the photograph is not simply a product or a channel but also an object endowed with a structural autonomy. Without in any way intending to divorce this object from its use, it is necessary to provide for a specific method prior to sociological analysis and which can only be the immanent analysis of the unique structure that a photograph constitutes.
>
> (Barthes, 1977b: 15–16)

The 'importance' Barthes attaches to his observations here is that analysing how an image signifies *fits with*, rather than being separate from or the same thing as, investigation of its social contexts of production and reception. Barthes's 'semiology' of images (or analysis of how images function as a sign system) is intended to account for the meaning-making processes of which images are capable. But that semiology, he insists, should then be brought into dialogue with sociological and

other approaches to understanding how communication functions as part of social behaviour.

Among the specific meaning-making processes associated with images, Barthes acknowledges that there will be pictorial qualities including composition, camera angle and conventional associations of particular themes or subjects. With audio-visual discourse such as television and film, those processes will include all of the above, plus others including editing tempo, music, choice of locations, and effects of lighting. Especially important among the signifying capabilities, however, will be the 'framing' role played by language that accompanies images.

- With still images, 'framing' language will consist largely of titles and captions.
- With television and film discourse, 'framing' language will consist either of spoken discourse that we can see being uttered in the image (diegetic speech), or alternatively it will consist of spoken discourse that is uttered by a voice not visible in the image (voice-over).

Consider each of these two types of speech in sound-and-image discourse. Utterances visible in the image (people talking to each other, or talking to the camera and so directly addressing the viewer) are standardly recognised as being important. For instance, it is common to analyse film scripts in ways that echo how we might analyse a play script. Or we might discuss studio interaction between chat-show guests or TV documentary interviewees in ways that build on how we analyse conversation (O'Keeffe, 2006; Montgomery, 2007). The functioning and significance of voice-over is less commonly acknowledged. But it is just as important. In a way that is similar to the functioning of titles and captions, voice-over tells us *how* we should see, and how we should make sense of, whatever we see in the image. In this respect 'language', in the traditional sense of verbal discourse, plays an important part in '*media* language', understood as a compound, multimodal form of discourse. This is the case even where the verbal discourse is least likely to be noticed. In units B7 and C7 we explore how.

BOUNDARIES OF MEDIA DISCOURSE

A8

In this unit, we consider kinds of media language that (under specific conditions that vary from medium to medium and between countries and periods) are subject to *restriction* or *exclusion*. Such 'taboo' media language includes kinds of swearing, insults and racial epithets, defamatory statements, verbal utterances that might incite crime or hatred, use of restricted trademark and copyright material, and – increasingly significantly – internet hate speech. We

- introduce the idea of regulated verbal content in media communication, and
- consider some of the grounds on which topics and forms of expression are judged to be unacceptable.

Kinds of trouble

Mostly media discourse is rightly seen as socially beneficial. It informs, offers variety in sources of opinion, entertains or inspires. Sometimes, however, media discourse gets into trouble. Recognising that there are variable boundaries in what is accepted in verbal discourse in the media is important in understanding both the power of and the risks involved in media communication.

Almost all societies have a notion of tolerance. Sometimes tolerance is freely extended towards different people, beliefs, religions and opinions. Sometimes it isn't. And sometimes it is, but only to a limited degree. Views vary on how restrictions should be imposed. They also vary as regards what the implications of such restrictions, if implemented, are likely to be. However these issues are viewed, some *framework* for deciding whether to tolerate or not tolerate is always in place. That framework is usually not a singular body or canon of law. It tends instead to be a mixture of legal and moral rules, compliance with social norms, and self-imposed restrictions on behaviour.

Activity 

The diagram in Figure A8.1 shows an area of legitimate or accepted types of media communication (e.g. on radio, TV, publicly accessible websites, etc.). Inside this conceptual area, you would expect to find most verbal discourse (e.g. about politics, sport, personal stories, fiction, celebrity gossip, etc.). At first, you might imagine that there is no limit at all to this field of discourse. This will be especially likely if you judge the internet to be 'public media' rather than a virtual space through which each person navigates towards their own actively chosen, and therefore partly private, discourse domains. Beyond the inner space in the diagram lie kinds of excluded, restricted or impermissible material. But what are they? Fill in this outer circle with different *kinds* or *characteristics* of discourse that you think are not permissible in a given situation. That 'situation' should for these purposes be a country you know fairly well. What is in question is not your own view. Explore instead what you believe will not be tolerated or accepted by whatever social forces govern public media for the particular situation. The main 'kinds' of excluded or restricted discourse are likely to take the form of

- topics that can't be publicly talked or written about, or shown in audio-visual form, and
- scandalous or outrageous styles of presenting content that could probably be depicted in a different (often more dispassionate or analytic) style.

There is no correct or complete answer. The aim here is to brainstorm as a way of identifying variables and issues. Each type of discourse you think of will raise questions in relation to at least the following considerations: the general media landscape you are talking about (where and when); who you take to be monitoring media output and doing the excluding, etc.

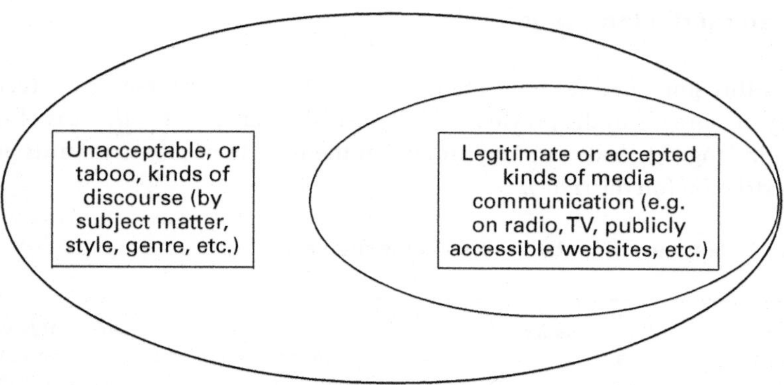

Figure A8.1 Boundaries of media communication

Here is some feedback to help guide this open-ended brainstorming activity. A number of major kinds of subject matter have typically given rise to controversy over whether an article, book or broadcast should be made public and allowed to circulate or not.

- Political information: what is going on, possibly secretly, at state or government level. How much information can be disclosed or reproduced in newspapers and media? This area raises questions about how much information needs to be protected by some arrangement for confidentiality or privacy. At what point do such arrangements create too much secrecy?
- Political opinion: the range of views allowable about how society should be organised or managed. What kinds of statement of political opinion should not be tolerated?
- Religious views: the boundaries, if any, that should exist on religious interpretation. What range of forms (documentary, fiction, drama, satire, etc.) should be tolerated as vehicles for religious comment or to express an individual's religious or secular sentiments or experience?
- Decency: boundaries drawn as regards legitimate expression of aspects of human life such as sexuality. How is a distinction to be drawn between artistic (e.g. creatively erotic) or scientific (e.g. sexological) expression in such areas and exploitative, pornographic representation?

Your allocation of material to the 'legitimate' and 'impermissible' fields in the diagram – whatever the outcome – involves modelling 'normative' or prescriptive judgements about language. Such judgements define what people should and shouldn't do on the basis of some established legal measure, social norm, or benchmark of behaviour. When you have made some decisions in relation to a society you know well, compare your diagram with how you would have filled it in for at least one other, very different society.

Limits to media language

Consider this simplified diagram (Table A8.1), which now reverses the direction of thinking encouraged in the previous activity. The diagram *starts with* areas of specific concern in language and communication (on the left), then moves towards areas of social restriction (on the right).

Table A8.1 Overview of verbal trouble in the media

	Area of concern in how language communicates	*Typical media areas for problem*	*Issues*	*Sources of discourse evidence*	*Areas of law and regulation (varying between different countries or jurisdictions)*
1	Truthfulness	News, advertising, propaganda aspects of public information campaigns, political spin, PR material	Statements of many different kinds that may not reflect the genuinely held view of the communicator News bias or distortion Misleading or deceptive claims made about a product or service being advertised Presentation of stereotypes as being true	Directly false statements Statements made selectively or out of context Understatement or overstatement so extreme that what is said is no longer credible Unduly vague statements and ironic evasion	Broadcasting law; laws governing misrepresentation; advertising standards regulation Distinction between opinion statements and statements of fact in journalism (encouraged and maintained in journalism training and professional codes of practice)
2	Defamatory statement	News, documentary, web pages, online discussion forums, faction films and features, gossip coverage	Falsity of statement affects perception of reputation	As above	Libel laws (slander, or face-to-face spoken defamation, becomes libel – the more permanent and serious harm – if communicated in media forms such as TV or film); malicious falsehood in advertising

	Area of concern in how language communicates	Typical media areas for problem	Issues	Sources of discourse evidence	Areas of law and regulation (varying between different countries or jurisdictions)
3	Offensiveness	Reality shows, web pages, adverts	Offensiveness (name-calling, inappropriate material in relation to sex and religion); calls made to phone-in shows that are not screened out before being broadcast; individually upsetting or abusive comments or messages	Swearing Epithets and other terms of abuse Inappropriate treatment of sensitive topics (sex, religion, etc.)	Legal measures where offence amounts to incitement or causes public disorder Programme codes promulgating standards of taste and decency in broadcasting Speech codes (e.g. campus rules or hospital radio broadcasting guidelines)
4	Originality	Everywhere where copy and paste is possible (TV, web content, adverts, radio material)	Plagiarism; copyright infringement; infringement of commercial and reputation rights in intellectual property generally	Substantial similarity between work copied or passed off as own and an original produced by someone else Derivation of copy from a non-permitted source	Copyright law Arrangements governing plagiarism (e.g. in professional standards codes)
5	Privacy and confidentiality	News and features in all media, especially celebrity coverage	Dissemination of information acquired through job or official position Intrusion into aspects of life conventionally thought personal and beyond legitimate public interest (e.g. health, private sex life)	Unauthorised publication of material dealing with conventional private sphere that goes beyond legitimate public interest Publication of material acquired in a private or protected relationship (e.g. during employment)	Privacy laws Breach of confidence actions Whistle-blowing (and public-interest disclosure) arrangements

Table A8.1 presents an overview of many different kinds of verbal trouble in the media. In practice, most controversies about media discourse cut across the simplified categories presented. Consider the points listed below:

- A magazine article, TV programme, or website can involve a complicated combination of acceptability issues. For instance, its language may appear to be misleading, offensive and intrusive into someone's privacy, all at the same time.
- Sometimes the sense of an audience being offended is clear enough, but the basis of that offensiveness is perceived differently by different people within the audience. One person's perception of an unacceptably blasphemous utterance, for example, may be based on the idea that the utterance is untrue. For another person, the same utterance may also be considered unacceptable, but on the grounds that it offends someone else's religious beliefs (which the person making the judgement may nevertheless consider incapable of being either true or untrue).

In units B8 and C8, we explore some particular areas of verbal offensiveness further. We also consider how difficult it is to draw boundaries, to make judgements and to arbitrate in disputes in a multimedia environment used by multicultural populations with different language standards and attitudes.

A9 THE FUTURE OF MEDIA LANGUAGE

One of the most frequent comments made about media is how rapidly they change. Even in a single lifetime – and allowing for variation by region or country – most people can expect to see massive change in the communication technologies available to them or around them. This unit considers the significance of technological change as it affects media language. We

- draw attention to recent technological developments in language production, distribution and reception, as well as in search techniques used to find and analyse individual words, idioms, or longer stretches of language, and
- assess how far thinking about past and present media language use can be helpful in making predictions about the future.

Language futurology

There is always a temptation to make predictions about the future. As well as specific predictions we make about what will happen tomorrow or next week, people also engage in extended, imaginative speculation in novels and films about what future societies will be like (e.g. in the genre of science fiction). Some forecasts highlight changes in how people will communicate. Think of the different communication styles and technologies represented in *Star Trek*, for instance, or *Star Wars*. Or think

of George Orwell's *1984* and Ray Bradbury's *Fahrenheit 451* (both discussed in unit B9), which stand out as presenting a more sustained language theme.

Often, predictions turn out to be wrong. Sometimes they are too fanciful. Sometimes they can be too conservative. It is interesting to look back fifty or a hundred years at predictions about communication technologies and behaviour of the future, and evaluate how reliable they were. You can explore the main lines of development in communication by looking at histories of media (e.g. Briggs and Burke, 2005; Scannell, 1991; Winston, 1998). Such histories tell you what happened. As far as possible, they also tell you why. But you must look to fictional representations, and philosophical and political arguments, for how people imagine things could have or might still turn out. The question of what people anticipated in relation to communication technologies at different times is interestingly explored by Crystal (2006), from which our final extract in D9 is taken.

In most discussion of 'language and media' futures, several different levels of prediction are involved.

1 Changes are anticipated at the level of invention of new technologies. Those technologies may be developed for one purpose but then applied to other purposes by creative users. Some of the initial research and development (R & D) is often military. But applications and spin-offs are often then adapted for civilian use. Interesting case studies in the social history of media inventions include the telegraph, telephone, talking film, radio, and television. More recently, you might investigate the development of the mobile phone or language-related software such as voice analysis and recognition software.

2 Other changes relate to policy directions that surround media inventions:

   Broadcasting has always had potential to develop either as a state-controlled or as a public-service network of institutions (in Britain, consider the BBC or find out about the founding vision and history of Channel 4 television as a provider of alternative content and editorial values). Or broadcasting could have developed, as increasingly it has done in most countries, as primarily a field of commercial enterprise and competition (e.g. carrying advertising and/or sponsorship; adapting editorial policy to the needs of advertisers; chasing ratings, etc.)

   There has always also been a question about broadcasting whether (and if so how far) minority languages should be protected against dominant neighbours. The mass media footprint of one language can cut directly into another language. The role of English-language media in Wales is a UK example.

   Literacy education is often directed towards comprehension and consumption of discourse produced by others (e.g. reading religious texts, evaluating bias in TV news, etc.). In other circumstances, however, it might be directed as much towards production of the user's own discourse (e.g. blogging, citizen journalism, uploading video or other kinds of online content).

3 Other changes again involve cultural shifts that reflect a combination of technical capabilities with changing policy frameworks, institutions and prevailing public opinion:

   How far should a society accept increased surveillance of personal communication, rather than maintaining personal privacy, when it acquires new technological

capabilities (e.g. intercepting and monitoring emails, recording telephone conversations 'for training purposes')? Surveillance of communication needs machines to make it possible. It also needs a legal or policy framework that legitimises surveillance. It also needs public perception that surveillance is an appropriate use for emerging communication technologies.

Policy questions also surround how far language use in media needs to be censored or regulated in order to maintain some recognised standard of interaction in a national or international public sphere. Control of media may nevertheless conflict with an aim of encouraging media to be a platform for all voices in a society to be heard. Words can be bleeped out on television using audio technology. Websites can be blocked technologically. But regulatory authorities of some kind also need to be in place to authorise or endorse editorial intervention. Public attitudes towards media discourse are needed to support such a direction for media policy.

Examples of each kind of media change can be found throughout the historical record. Making sense of them cuts across the fields of linguistics, media studies, sociology, law and politics (the work of Raymond Williams is exemplary in this respect). In unit B9, we look at influential approaches to the language issues raised by such changes.

Media technologies and language capabilities

Successive new media technologies – from writing on papyrus to instant messaging – have extended and reshaped how much, and in what circumstances, people communicate with each other. Because language change reflects patterns of language use, we might therefore expect that the rate, direction and extent of language change (including towards language standardisation) will all vary in relation to media available at any given time. This is where consideration of language and media intersects with sociolinguistics, historical linguistics and language planning.

One key historical period for exploring interaction between media and language change is the period following the introduction of printing in the 15th century (Eisenstein, 1979):

- ❑ Did printing affect perception of social class or communication between social classes?
- ❑ Did printing affect how people conducted business, or understood the law?
- ❑ Did printing open up new forms of entertainment, and if so of what kind and for whom?

The spread, influence, and growth or decline of any particular language is also affected by how accessible it is and the range of functions for which it is used. The question therefore arises whether broadcast media and online content may accelerate language death of some languages (Crystal, 2000), by spreading the impact of one dominant language in a given situation at the expense of other, more vulnerable minority languages.

- ❑ Does the organisation of broadcast media at a national level have an effect on convergence or divergence between regional accents?

Large-scale language changes of this kind cannot be understood by applying to them some simple general principle. They need to be traced through interlocking, concrete media developments. With differing amounts of evidence, this can be done for different historical periods. In Table A9.1 we list, in no particular time order, some recent (and ongoing) developments that are worth thinking further about.

Table A9.1 Some recent (and ongoing) developments in media and language technologies

1	Use of electronic cut, copy and paste techniques in word-processing, by comparison with bringing to mind and then writing down an extended stream of thoughts
2	Use of spell-checking and grammar-checking text-editing tools
3	Recording and editing of digital audio
4	Voice message storage and dictation capabilities on mobile phones
5	Text production and playback using voice recognition and speech synthesis software
6	Uploaded and web-streamed audio and audio-visual content, as a form of publication in parallel with traditional publishing and broadcasting
7	'Written' forms that combine speech styles, graphics and icons, such as email and instant messaging
8	Accumulating threads of written discourse, including blogging and interaction in discussion forums and chatrooms
9	Predictive text composition (e.g. on mobile phones) and auto-completion of manually entered text (e.g. of names and addresses)
10	Updatable 'live' online information (e.g. timetables, share prices)
11	Automatic translation of web content between languages
12	Use of the internet, including videophone, connections for conversations alongside telephones
13	Video recording and editing as ways of representing gesture and physical positioning of speakers in relation to one another
14	Desktop video recording and editing, as a parallel form of publishing alongside public broadcasting
15	Videoconferencing, as an alternative to physically travelling to meetings
16	Electronic search and concordancing techniques, applied either to constructed language corpora or to general web content (e.g. by use of search engines and web crawling software)

Activity 

Add some further items to the list in Table A9.1. Then decide whether you think the various developments can be sorted into more general categories. If so, what criterion makes classification work best – function?, medium?, historical sequence of invention?, etc. For each item in your list, consider how much relevant context you can provide at each of the three levels indicated above: technological, policy and cultural.

It is sometimes difficult to think about language and media at this level of abstraction. So here are a few generalisations about communicative capability to get you started with the activity above.

1 New forms of interaction and combination are emerging between speech, as a non-reproducible mode of interaction, and writing, as a permanent record (for background, see thread 1). It is increasingly possible to record speech. We can edit both speech and writing in non-destructive ways (i.e. keeping earlier versions, as with the 'track changes' function in word-processing software). We can store most kinds of discourse permanently. For instance, we can build up an archive of speech from earlier generations of speakers, as well as earlier utterances of present speakers. Our archive need not consist only of famous broadcast speeches. It might include call-centre conversations such as contested phone insurance claims, and/or old university lectures, toddlers' first words, air traffic control conversations, and personal voicemails. This capability radically affects the range of data available to future researchers of language (including language change).

2 The functions of searching and memory in relation to language input are changing. New capabilities for storage and replay allow us to access vast amounts of material almost instantly. We can search that material for relevant content whenever we wish or need to. Rather than keeping a personal note of what was said or written (e.g. by means of memorisation, rote learning, or use of a personal notebook), we can consult a book, an email, or a website once more. Or we can use a search tool to find a particular phrase or passage we wish to recall, or scan through voicemails or DVD scenes.

3 From some perspectives, the anchoring of interaction in particular places is less important than in earlier periods. Who you talk to, when, and how often is less and less dictated by where you are. As a result, beginnings and endings of conversations – along with the social messages such openings and closings convey – are less defined by co-presence. People sometimes defer the remainder of a continuing interaction to a subsequent email exchange, even when they are talking face-to-face about the same topic ('I'll email you . . .'; or 'email me'). The technological capability provided by computer-mediated communication (CMC) is preferred over the canonical speech situation.

4 Difficulties faced by speakers of different languages in their efforts to communicate with each other are mitigated by the availability of portable electronic dictionaries and translation devices. Communicating across languages is also

facilitated by automatic web page translation and by the availability, in many professional circumstances, of simultaneous translation audio equipment and translators.

Each of these four general trends emerges from a combination of language and media. We may start by thinking about technical devices or inventions. But we soon have to shift attention to human language capabilities. Each of the four topics above is concerned at one level with hardware and software innovation. In order to understand future directions of language and media, however, we need something else. Users need constantly to update their familiarity with communication technologies and strengthen their skills in using them. Understanding the social shifts involved in this aspect of language and media requires looking again at the functions of language, at values in communication, and at education related to how communication skills are taught.

In an influential work about the development and future of mass media, Marshall McLuhan (1964) calls media 'the extensions of man [sic]'. He sees media as tools for communication in the same way that manual tools extend reach, force or speed. If his analogy is a fair one, then thinking about media futures is partly a matter of weighing up human needs and capabilities, and seeing how they can be extended in different directions by new media. We consider McLuhan's perspective in more detail, as well as others critical of it, in unit B1. We consider media futures and forecasts more generally throughout the rest of thread 9.

Section B

Development STUDIES IN MEDIA LANGUAGE

B1 SPEECH, WRITING AND MEDIA

In unit A1, we introduced connections between 'language' and 'media' by considering how different understandings of 'media language' are affected by the meanings people give to the term 'media'. In this unit, we describe different senses that people give to another aspect of 'language and media': that the phrase is simply another way of saying 'language plus technology'. We

- ❑ review how different media technologies extend human language capabilities,
- ❑ consider the influential idea that writing functions as a 'technology of the intellect': a tool or instrument that helps us to think in new ways, and
- ❑ use writing to illustrate a contrasting interpretation of how media interact with language: that media help to create what sorts of people we are and how we think and function.

Extending human language capabilities

The writer Marshall McLuhan, as we noted in unit A9, gave his influential book *Understanding Media* (1964) the subtitle *The Extensions of Man*. This phrase evokes an idea of media as ways of extending our human capabilities in relation to language. In other words, human communication is given greater leverage or power.

A group of thinkers about communication now often associated with McLuhan, including Harold Innes, Elizabeth Eisenstein, Milman Parry and Albert Lord, took a similar stance. They investigated the impact on social life of our ability to convey verbal messages. What happens if we can remember, transmit and record communications in different ways? Their approach combined investigation of how language works with anthropological and sociological analyses, and with questions of historical development and future social directions. We explore the 'future forecasting' dimension of such an approach in thread 9.

Consider first the idea that even with face-to-face speaking there is an 'anatomical' technology involved in using language. In speaking, we draw on specialised vocal organs as well as organs which have speech production as an extra function (lungs, glottis, larynx, uvula, alveolar ridge, tongue, teeth and lips, etc.). These parts of the body all play a role in the articulatory mechanisms required for speaking. Reception and processing of the sounds of speech require an equivalent body technology: the biology of the human ear. We take this technological dimension of speech and listening for granted. Its necessity, however, becomes clear when relevant organs do not function, or function only incompletely, or need to be removed surgically.

In thinking about media rather than face-to-face interaction, it is common to call to mind raw materials (wood pulp for paper, silicon for computer chips), or to foreground the means by which communication technologies are powered (steam printing, electronic media). But we can also describe media as 'extensions' of capabilities conferred by our human, biological technology. We might then emphasise

- amplification as a kind of throwing of the voice (giving it further reach over distance), made possible by megaphones, microphones and amplifiers,
- writing as fixation of utterances, or transposition of the sounds of speaking into written signs (though there are also other systems of writing; for discussion see Gelb, 1952; Harris, 1995, etc.),
- printing as mechanical reproduction of signs into many copies that can be distributed over large distances and over time,
- audio recording technology as capability to capture and reproduce the speaking voice from one situation to another, including after the speaker's life has come to an end, and
- broadcasting as transmission of the voice (and images) over distances not physically possible in person, and as a result to audiences far greater than can be reached in face-to-face interaction.

We consider how different human language capabilities are extended selectively by different communication technologies in unit A3.

Writing as a 'technology of the intellect'

Media may be described as technologies that extend human communication capabilities. What implications follow from such extensions, as regards how we conduct our lives? Put like this, the question is rather like asking how our lives would be affected if we had massively stronger, bionic arms or legs, or if we had infinitely larger memories. But there is a difference. In the case of media, the technologies are outside the body, as tools: expandable, add-on memory; easily amplified volume and projection of the voice; and an ability at the flick of a switch or click of a mouse to send a verbal message somewhere without anyone having to go there.

Historians of writing have examined questions of the long-term impact of communication technology on human behaviour, learning, and social structure. Such impact is what connects the field of literacy studies (Levine, 1986; Maybin, 2007; Street, 1984, 1995) with questions of language and media. We can see the particular relevance of writing as a case study if we consider the idea of writing as a 'technology of the intellect', an idea formulated in a joint paper by the anthropologist Jack Goody and the literary historian Ian Watt (Goody and Watt, 1963).

A society organised around speaking – with no system of writing available to it – is an 'oral society' (Ong, 1982; Finnegan, 2002). Speaking and listening are the only channels through which communication in language takes place. Even today, the majority of languages in the history of the world, and most languages in use, are used primarily 'orally' in this sense. A society organised around communication not only through speech but also by its use of writing, on the other hand, is a literate society. Reading and writing give it an extra channel through which verbal communication can take place, alongside speaking and listening.

Notice that the terms orality and literacy do not form a straightforward opposition. Orality can exist without literacy. Wherever there is individual or collective literacy, however, there is also orality. Literate societies involve a mix of the written and

read with the spoken and heard. Notice, too, that when the term 'literacy' is used of individuals, it describes a set of skills in reading and writing. In this sense, it contrasts not with 'orality' but with 'illiteracy'.

To investigate how literate individuals function in their literate societies, the concept of 'functional penetration of literacy' has been widely adopted. Analysis is made of the range of roles or tasks generally performed by means of reading and writing (e.g. receipts, diaries, laws, etc., see Barton, 1994; Levine, 1986). By examining the various functions for which writing is used, it is possible to see changing social patterns in choices people make between the two mediums. We discuss such choices of technological medium for particular discourse functions in unit C1.

Major consequences for individuals and for social groups have been claimed to follow from a society's shift from orality to literacy. Stylistically, as we show in thread 2, there are marked contrasts between communications in speech and in writing. In spoken discourse, there is likely to be, for example,

- less syntactic embedding,
- less use of explicit connectives,
- greater dependence on non-verbal contextual clues, and
- more use of fillers and repetition than in written texts.

Goody and Watt (1963) (and Goody, 1977, 1987) have also argued that literacy creates a new relationship for any individual to language. Literacy in a society, they suggest, prompts new modes of thought and social organisation. Written language (unlike spoken language) can be kept stable for scrutiny on the page, and can be scanned forwards and backwards. Historically, such stability of language fixed on the page (they contend) facilitated argument and discussion, including complex logical derivations such as sequences of syllogisms. There has therefore often been thought to be special historical significance in the rapid development of logic in classical Greece, roughly coincidentally with first use of a phonetic-alphabetic script (a writing system that defines vowel values as well as consonants).

A cultural shift from orality to literacy has also been associated with changing social attitudes towards language. It is claimed, for example, that literacy in a society challenges magical or ritualistic beliefs about language characteristic of oral societies. It makes new levels of abstraction and objectivity possible. Greater accuracy in a society's historical record is also thought likely as a result of writing, by comparison with oral histories and genealogies that place less emphasis on historical fact than on present relevance. Literacy has been suggested to encourage 'scepticism', too: doubt about, and more frequent disagreement with, the established wisdom of a community or culture.

In each of these respects, literacy appears to be an agent of social progress. From the perspective of literate societies, as a result, written forms (as well as literate people) are often taken as being of higher cultural status than their oral equivalents. This is reflected as a question of social value and authority not only in terms of the importance of the written word in education, law and religion, but also in complicated arguments about the relative importance of speech and writing as objects of linguistic enquiry.

Media and the sorts of people we are

Describing writing as a 'technology of the intellect' emphasises use of this extra linguistic medium as a tool to extend what is possible. The 'language and media' tool brings about social change, and with a record of change come further possibilities for social *progress*.

A contrasting view of the relationship between humans and language technologies has also been argued. This position (Street, 1984, 1995) views media technologies less as tools that we simply choose than as instruments of more powerful forces that determine how we apply such tools. The view of orality and literacy discussed above, as a result, is sometimes called an 'autonomous' view of literacy. It contrasts with this other, 'ideological' view of literacy, in which teaching and applications of literacy are considered inevitably part of an overarching framework of social goals and ideologies and a hierarchical distribution of roles and tasks. 'Literacy', in this second, ideological framework, is not a tool you pick up and use. As you engage with writing, you are drawn into and made the bearer of social values regarding how to think and what to believe. Literacy, in Paolo Freire's phrase, is simultaneously a way of 'reading the word and the world' (Freire and Macedo, 1987).

These two contrasting ways of assessing the impact of media on how we live are usefully compared in Street (1984) and Levine (1986). Each view has major implications. For instance, how should we teach reading and writing in schools? What approach to literacy education should be adopted in international development and aid programmes?

If we now extend discussion from the particular case of writing to take account of challenges presented by modern media, further issues arise. In his examination of 20th-century media, for example, Ong (1982, and elsewhere) described the impact of broadcasting and other electronic communications media on social structure and expectations. He proposed the term 'secondary orality' – by contrast with 'primary orality', as outlined above – to describe language skills, preferred styles, and attitudes towards language evolved in the new media environment that he and others faced. That environment combined established literate modes in new ways with re-engineered 'oral' abilities and perceptions associated with telecommunications, audio recording, radio, and television and film soundtracks. We include Ong's 1982 definition of 'secondary orality' as an extract in unit D9.

If we now extend discussion further, to include contemporary media technologies including the internet, as well as the likely influence of further, as yet unseen media and communication technologies of the future, questions of the relationship between language and technology continue to arise. Avoiding simplification of communication and media discourse to a simple sum of 'language plus technology', Raymond Williams expressed a preference for a wider term, 'cultural form', in his discussion of the relationship between technology, language and social function that came together in the development of television (Williams, 1974). That term 'cultural form' provides a useful reference in investigating future developments.

Activity

Consider the following questions as a way of thinking yourself into issues of the relationship between media and patterns of thought and social action.

- Does the option of googling, rather than having to know something or to remember it, lead you to think differently? How can you get beyond your own intuitions in assessing this?
- Does the option of meeting up with people by co-ordinating where you are using mobile phones affect your relationship to place and navigation? Is this the same effect as, or something different from, getting to wherever you're going by listening to satnav instructions as you drive?
- What both the above questions highlight is a reduced need for individuals to remember, and therefore recall, information because it can be stored or is available elsewhere. Is this a recent development? And is it a feature of literate societies only?

B2 DIFFERENT STYLES OF MEDIA LANGUAGE

This unit extends our discussion of work on register by exploring a well-known model for analysing communicative events. We

- outline how register can be analysed on three levels: field, mode and tenor,
- look at an example of a low-level transcript of an interview to illustrate convergence between the mediums of speech and writing, and
- consider the contribution made by one feature of text design, typeface, to signalling tenor.

Register in communicative events

Register, as the variety of language used for given types of situation, can be analysed into its linguistic and textual features using Michael Halliday's (1978) model. We can say that there are three different aspects of communication associated with any context or situation: field, mode and tenor. Each affects a text's register in ways we now describe (summarised from Montgomery et al., 2006):

Field

The purpose, or role, for which the language is being used, which typically derives from the field in which it is being used (its subject matter). Language can be used for a variety of different purposes: to convey information, to express feelings, to cajole, to pray, to produce aesthetic effects, to intimidate, etc. Each purpose leaves its mark on what is said and how it is said. In addition, however, many human activities have developed

their own characteristic registers by drawing on 'field-specific' vocabularies. Fields in this sense include the legal profession, the scientific community, cooking, religious rituals and practices, academic disciplines, advertising, and football commentary. The list could be extended indefinitely. All of these fields use some terms that are distinctive, in being particular to that field. Using the terms evokes particular situations.

Mode

The medium of communication. The medium of a text is the substance from which that text is made, or through which it is transmitted, or in which it is stored. For register, the most prominent difference of medium is that between speech and writing. Spoken forms in media include announcements; news-reading and video link-up with a reporter at a selected location; documentary voices, including voice-over; interviews; and chat show and studio discussion. Most of such talk is spontaneously planned and produced. Writing, on the other hand, may involve long periods of composition and revision. The resulting text may be read and re-read at leisure in circumstances quite remote – both in time and place – from those in which it was written. Written texts, in consequence, tend to be more formal than spoken texts, which, by contrast, tend to be looser and more provisional in their structure and feel less formal (see unit A2 for discussion). In public settings, spoken texts may be carefully prepared in advance and may take on many formal characteristics of the written mode.

Tenor

The social roles prescribed for, or adopted by, participants in the communication situation, which determines tone. There are typically markers in a text of whether the relationships between participants are informal or formal, familiar or polite, personal or impersonal. The tone of a text can in this way indicate the attitude or position adopted by the writer or speaker towards the reader or listener. Tenor can also be thought of in terms of the wider, interpersonal function of language, because of the importance of the relationship between participants to what and how they communicate. In 2006, a great deal of media coverage was devoted to President Bush's act of addressing the British prime minister of the time, Tony Blair, by calling out *Yo Blair!* in an unguarded moment. This form of address contrasts strikingly with the more formal address of *Prime Minister* typically used in public speeches.

We can now bring the three aspects of, for example, political register together, by illustrating how a text that we consider in more detail elsewhere (Barack Obama's presidential acceptance speech in unit C5) would be described in terms of Halliday's model. We would classify its register as follows:

Field	political
Mode	spoken (though prepared in advance in written mode and displaying many of the characteristics of writing)
Tenor	Formal, authoritative (but with some markers of informality and inclusiveness)

For each aspect, we should then be able to provide evidence of specific linguistic markers.

RBTL

In unit A2 we discuss differences between speech and writing and media-led convergence between these two mediums of communication. Recent developments in this type of convergence can be seen in text messaging, where much of the informality and spontaneity of speech is mimicked in written form. Use of shorthand codes to produce compact messages via mobile phones also provides much more rapid exchanges in communication. (For more detailed discussion of text messaging, see unit C9.)

Activity 

Translate the following examples of text speak back into their more conventional forms:

wu, omg, lol, u2, l8r
lmao, plmk, brb, y, gr8t
ova, nvm, wteva, idk, da

what's up?, Oh my God!, laugh out loud or laughing out loud or lots of love, you too, later
laughing my arse off, please let me know, be right back, why?, great
over, never mind, whatever, I don't know, the

The subheading by the way – RBTL – means *read between the lines.*

One of the first companies to exploit this new style in its corporate communication was the mobile phone company Phones 4 U. The company not only advertises itself through its company name, which incorporates text speak, but also promotes one of the main uses of the phones they sell by simulating some of the key strokes that might be used on them. The company's decision may have been aimed at attracting a younger market. But with texting being rapidly adopted as a mode of communication among all mobile phone users, its shortcuts and codes have become likely to be recognised by nearly everyone.

According to a recent poll of 1,000 adults on a single day:

- a third said they thought they spoke to people less because they email and text them,
- almost half said they liked texting because they did not have to bother with things like hello or how are you?
- the survey reported that the average person spends:
  88 minutes on an ordinary phone
  62 minutes on a mobile phone
  53 minutes emailing
  22 minutes texting.

Activity

Consider how your communication patterns compare with the figures presented in the list above.

- What else would you need to know about the survey from which these numbers are drawn in order to decide how reliable or authoritative you think this information is?
- How do your communication patterns compare, broadly, with the figures presented in this list?
- Do you think differences in communication patterns correlate with social factors such as an individual's age, gender, culture, level of education, etc.?
- How would you set about investigating such patterns?
- Design a questionnaire to investigate the communication patterns listed in the above survey as found among your classmates. Compare your findings with the survey results given above for similarities or differences.

Font, text design and register

In the final section of this unit, we consider how far one aspect of text design – choice of font in printing – contributes to register (alongside more recognised features such as lexical choice, accent, and grammatical constructions). We do this in two ways. First, we present an extract from an interview directly discussing the stylistic significance of font choice in political campaigns. Second, we present a short stretch of text in three different fonts and invite you to compare the resulting effects.

The transcript of the interview given below was chosen for this section because of its subject matter: the interview discusses the importance of typeface for political campaign logos. It explores whether choice of typeface as part of political branding creates register because of what it can connote.

We should also note, however, that transcripts of speech themselves provide a further example of convergence between speech and writing. After all, they are written forms of speech. There is no single form of transcription that can be used to represent speech definitively, however. A transcript will reflect the main features of speech that it is trying to show, and will pay less attention to other features. A transcript of a political interview or chat show interview is accordingly likely to be what is called a *low level representation* of talk, because it is primarily interested in communicating the ideas expressed: the content. Transcripts of such interviews are edited to remove many features normally found in natural speech, such as pauses, hesitations, overlaps, nonfluency errors, etc., in order to give emphasis to who says what. More formal, linguistic transcription conventions are kept to a minimum, as the priority is to ensure that the resulting text is clear and intelligible. (Other transcripts of political and chatshow interviews containing more features of speech can be found in unit C4.)

The interview discussion of whether the fonts used in campaign logos communicate in the same way that other aspects of register do is presented in Figure B2.1.

Figure B2.1 'Font, text design and register' interview

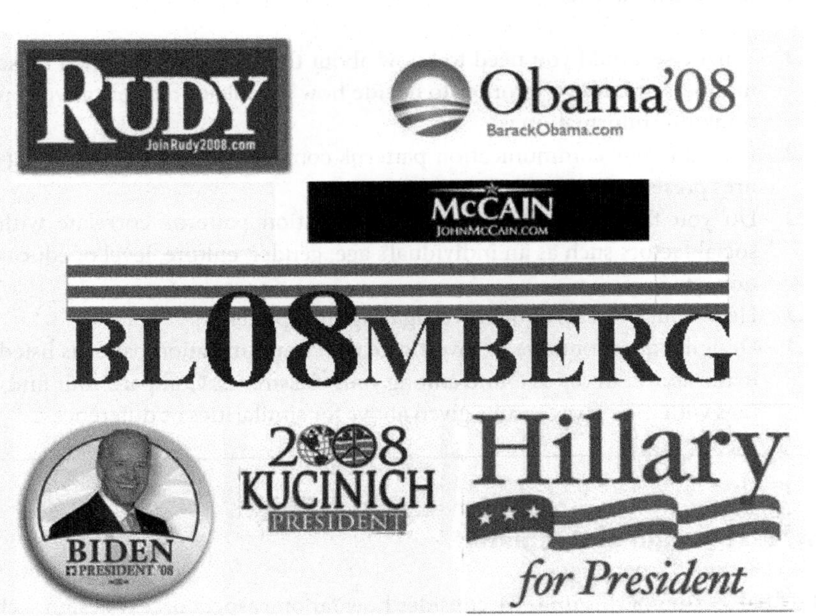

'Character matters' (http://www.onthemedia.org/transcripts/2008/02/22/05), 22 February 2008

The fonts that presidential candidates select for their campaign logos reflect an important act of political branding. Sam Berlow of The Font Bureau Inc. says the logos all speak volumes about the candidates they represent.

Brooke Gladstone: The typeface chosen for a logo can define a brand, just like a Coca-Cola or Fed-Ex or Google. But what about the brands known as Clinton, Obama and McCain? How much attention do their campaigns give to the marketing muscle of the humble font? And with the rise of the Web as a campaign tool, should they be giving more?

Sam Berlow, general manager of Boston-based design firm The Font Bureau, which has developed typefaces for companies including Apple Computer and The New York Times, *analyzed the candidates' logos for* The Boston Globe. *Welcome to the show, Sam.*

Sam Berlow: Hello, Brooke.

Brooke Gladstone: When we talk about logos, we often talk about serif and sans serif fonts. What are those?

Sam Berlow: A serif font has little feet at the end of the vertical characters whereas a sans serif is something you'd see like in the Best Buy logo, big,

strong, bold. There's less contrast between the thick and the thin strokes of the letters.

Brooke Gladstone: Do you think that typefaces really say anything about the candidates?

Sam Berlow: I think they say quite a bit. If you look at Bush/Quayle, Quayle is the very, very thin, spindly serif typeface and the Bush is a very strong sans serif and it's set really big. I think that said a lot about that campaign.

The Bush/Cheney was great. It just had that incredible NASCAR feel with the slanted sans serif saying, 'We're going really fast. Hang on.' [Brooke laughs] If you look at Hillary's campaign, it's really a throwback to Reagan and Bush. It has that feeling of old typography from the '70s and '80s. It's serif. It's sort of highwaisted, as if the lower case, the pants had been pulled up too high. It feels sort of like a bad Talbots suit. [*Brooke laughs*] Doesn't quite fit right.

Brooke Gladstone: What is the typeface that Hillary uses?

Sam Berlow: Oh, geez! The typophiles will talk about this for months on the blogs. I believe that it's a Baskerville, but it looks like the lower-case R has sort of been punched in the nose and the lower case has been jacked up a little bit to make it feel a little bit bigger and stronger.

Brooke Gladstone: If you liken Hillary's typeface to a Talbots suit, what sort of suit do you think it ought to be wearing and which font will get you there?

Sam Berlow: Well, I think something more like *The Wall Street Journal* fonts. That typeface is called Escrow. It was done especially for *The Wall Street Journal*. It's very classy and very clean. It has much more contrast between the thick and the thin strokes.

Brooke Gladstone: What kind of a suit?

Sam Berlow: More of a Brooks Brothers suit.

Brooke Gladstone: [*laughs*] Now, let's talk about Obama's. You think his is pretty hip and cool, right?

Sam Berlow: I do. They made big, beautiful posters that would say, South Carolina loves Obama, headlines set in a very classy sans serif font called Gotham. It's very clean. It doesn't have any lumps or big balls at the end of the characters. It sort of ends very crisply, like a manicured set of nails – very metrosexual.

Brooke Gladstone: If it were a suit, what would it be?

Sam Berlow: Armani.

Brooke Gladstone: [*laughs*] Now, you say that Huckabee's design is cluttered and confusing. Can you tell us about that?

Sam Berlow: Well, there are several oddities about the Huckabee design. The six stars that sort of floating down like snowflakes are a bit odd, and the swash

that reminds me of Coca-Cola. And then there's this yellow element in the type. [laughs] The only yellow that I could find in the past was Nixon/Lodge and Goldwater, which puts him in interesting company.

And then the type itself is squished together very tightly and artificially bolded as if they had so much they had to get on the page, like family and faith and freedom, as if the other candidates don't believe in those three things.

Brooke Gladstone: So what do you think would work better?

Sam Berlow: Well, if it didn't look like a Daytona 500 car [Brooke laughs] that would be a good start.

Brooke Gladstone: So what's your favorite logo of the candidates still in the race?

Sam Berlow: I think the McCain is fantastic. The star with the yellow bars clearly says he's a general, he's in charge.

Brooke Gladstone: So is this a serif or a sans serif font?

Sam Berlow: Well, it's interesting. It's in between, Brooke. It's –

Brooke Gladstone: [*laughs*] It's a moderate serif? [*laughs*]

Sam Berlow: It's a down-the-middle-of-the-aisle serif. It has elements of a sans serif but the ends of the strokes flare out a little bit.

Brooke Gladstone: So it's a nod to the serif crowd without a complete capitulation.

Sam Berlow: It's a typeface that can talk to Feingold and can talk to Bob Dole at the same time.

Brooke Gladstone: Sam, thank you so much.

Sam Berlow: Thank you, Brooke.

Activity 

- ❑ What are the main points about the semiotic potential of fonts made by Sam Berlow in this extract?
- ❑ Is it possible to talk about the register effect of fonts with the same degree of precision as it is possible to talk about the register properties of lexical items such as particular nouns, adjectives or verbs?
- ❑ Now think about register in this passage at another level. Interview transcripts reproduce a sense of the interaction that takes place between participants. Use the Halliday categories introduced above (and in particular the brief classification we offer of the register of Barack Obama's speech in Figure C5.1) to describe the register adopted by each of the participants in this interview. Find examples to support each of the three decisions you have to make in relation to each interactant (i.e. in relation to field, mode and tenor).

How important is typeface as an aspect of tenor? Compare the following National Audit Office press notices, which have been written using three different typefaces or fonts. Say whether one is more suitable than the others, and why. (Extract taken from *Crown Prosecution Service: Effective Use of Magistrates' Court Hearings*, 15 February 2006.)

a Georgia

Head of the National Audit Office Sir John Bourn said today: 'The Crown Prosecution Service is making efforts to improve its performance in magistrates' courts but needs to do more to modernise the way in which it prepares and brings cases to court. My recommendations will reduce the waste and delay caused by ineffective hearings and trials'.

b Comic Sans MS

Head of the National Audit Office Sir John Bourn said today: 'The Crown Prosecution Service is making efforts to improve its performance in magistrates' courts but needs to do more to modernise the way in which it prepares and brings cases to court. My recommendations will reduce the waste and delay caused by ineffective hearings and trials'.

c Franklin Gothic Demi

Head of the National Audit Office Sir John Bourn said today: 'The Crown Prosecution Service is making efforts to improve its performance in magistrates' courts but needs to do more to modernise the way in which it prepares and brings cases to court. My recommendations will reduce the waste and delay caused by ineffective hearings and trials'.

Now refer back to your reading of the Sam Berlow interview excerpt above. What aspects of Sam Berlow's opinions about presidential candidate logos, if any, apply to your comparison between the three fonts used here?

B3 MEDIATED PARTICIPATION

In unit A3 we describe how media communication events differ from face-to-face spoken interaction. How has this idea been developed by researchers? And what implications follow? We now look at how a number of scholars in related disciplines have investigated this aspect of language and media. We

- add precision to the notion that media language events differ from conversation,
- outline aspects of the work of Erving Goffman, who developed a pioneering 'participation framework' model of media utterances (Goffman, 1981),
- illustrate two directions in application of Goffman's approach: Allan Bell's (1991) analysis of print and broadcast news and Anne O'Keeffe's (2006) combination of Goffman's participation framework with investigative techniques from conversation analysis and corpus linguistics, and
- show how linguistic analysis can be relevant to wider cultural debate, by drawing attention to 'pseudo-intimate' media styles that construct (and may exploit) contrived interpersonal familiarity shown by media producers towards unknown audience members.

Media discourse is different from conversation

Unit A3 shows why it is necessary in considering media discourse to go beyond the two most influential models of communication:

- two people talking to each other in a 'dyadic' situation, and
- 'centre-to-periphery', one-directional public address, or 'mass communication'.

O'Keeffe (2006) usefully describes the main difference between mass media 'talk' and the underlying idea of two-person conversation from which our understanding of it is generally derived. She suggests that

> Media interactions are essentially conversations that are heard by others [. . .]. Many of our everyday conversations in public places such as in cafés or on public transport are regularly overheard. However, this 'overhearing' model is too narrow for media discourse. When a presenter and an interviewee or guest interact on television or radio, they do so with the knowledge not only that they are being overheard, but also that they are having a conversation in front of an audience. In this way, they are having a different kind of conversation than two people talking on a train beside others who cannot avoid hearing their conversation. The former requires inclusion and involvement of the audience, the latter very often requires exclusion (e.g. through guarded or coded references) and detachment (e.g. lack of eye contact and lack of inclusive reference).
>
> (O'Keeffe, 2006: 3)

Commenting on possible implications of the contrast, O'Keeffe continues:

> While the communication context and conditions of casual conversations and media interactions differ considerably, the internal features have much common ground, that is, in terms of spoken language itself. While many of the same features exist in casual conversation and media interaction, their form, function and distribution may differ and this is what proves very revealing when comparing the two types of interactions.
>
> (O'Keeffe, 2006: 5)

O'Keeffe's insight here consists of two interconnected claims:

1 that the relations structuring the communicative events of conversation and media talk are importantly different from each other; but
2 that those relations can seem to be the same, giving media talk an appearance of being 'natural' and 'ordinary': a kind of spontaneous, personal communication.

Goffman's participation framework

Most contemporary work on media talk draws on Erving Goffman's (1981) account of how communication events are structured. Goffman never presented his insights as a coherent, systematic model, but some general points can be drawn from his discussion and examples.

In his discussion of radio in particular, Goffman showed how analysis of media talk can go beyond a model of two people talking to one another about what each thinks. Instead, Goffman develops a model of communication based on multi-party social gatherings in which numerous people participate in different ways. He explores how speakers switch roles periodically in such talk. In doing so, they relate differently not only to the other people around them but also to what they themselves are saying. The other participants in the discourse situation in turn occupy varying roles in relation to the messages they communicate. Each participant is sometimes addressed directly, but at other times positioned as overhearing messages addressed to other people. Goffman calls his findings in this area a 'participation framework' for communication. He describes what he calls the 'participation status' of different roles in communication, both in relation to what in a conventional model would be simply the 'speaker' role and the conventional role of 'hearer'.

From 'hearer' to audience participation

Goffman shows how utterances aren't interpreted simply from the point of view of an undifferentiated receiver or 'hearer'. People exposed to a spoken communication stand in different relations to that communication. Some may be directly addressed, either implicitly or by name. Others may be unaddressed but nevertheless overhear a communication between a speaker and some other addressee in a way that is fully

anticipated and planned for (like an audience attending to the dialogue of a play or people listening to a trial from the public gallery of a courtroom). In Goffman's terms such listeners are 'overhearers'. Their participation status is 'ratified', in that their attention is planned for in the design of the utterance. Other people again may be 'eavesdropping'. They listen in, but they are not addressees nor ratified overhearing participants.

As with conversation, broadcast *media* talk can create each of these relations. Continuity announcements, weather forecasts and some other formats adopt a style of direct address to the audience. Interviews, studio discussion and other formats embed staged dialogue between designated performers (in the studio, linked by satellite, etc.) within the broadcast to the audience. That audience is accordingly cast in the role of overhearers of exchanges represented in the broadcast. Members of the audience are still ratified participants in the broadcast, nevertheless. Their presence and involvement are in fact its main purpose.

Whether members of a media audience are 'addressees' is more complicated. Production and reception of media discourse relate to one another across 'split contexts'. One place and time (or period) is involved in production but many different places (and possibly different times) are possible as the moment of reception. No particular audience member is known to or identified by broadcasters as they communicate. Nor do they know what mix of people will be watching or listening, even if they have access to generalised audience demographics (e.g. the proportion of people of different ages, or gender or class groups, likely to be listening or watching). In such circumstances, producers rely on their estimate of who the likely audience will be, how members of that audience may wish to be talked to, and how they will respond to various cues. Mode of address in media talk is based on a sense (sometimes a stereotypical sense) of what type of people might be listening or viewing and what those people want. To the extent that members of an audience recognise some aspect of themselves in the approach adopted, they allow themselves to be 'addressed' by the overall broadcast discourse. This is the case even if what they are listening to is embedded interaction that they 'overhear' between other, staged voices.

How speakers say what they say

For Goffman, and for researchers in several fields whose work he has influenced, the conventional 'speaker' role must also be sub-divided and made more precise. O'Keeffe (2006: 63) describes a general context for this. She summarises how any speaker simultaneously occupies three different *kinds* of role:

- a societal role (e.g. mother, father, daughter, American),
- a discourse role (e.g. doctor, patient, lawyer), and
- a genre role (e.g. 'architect' of an essay, MC of a public event).

Further layers of role-playing are superimposed when speech is recorded and/or broadcast. Goffman calls these extra layers the 'production format' of a media discourse (1981: 146).

Some roles in a production format may be occupied by different people but still function together (e.g. there are different professional roles in the industrialised division of labour that produces television programmes: producer, director, scriptwriter, autocue operator, actor/presenter, sound recordist, etc.). In some cases, a single role or function is performed by more than one person. An example of this is when two news anchors jointly present a TV news broadcast. Another example is when a DJ posse collectively presents a radio show.

The most interesting aspects of 'production format' arise when we consider the 'speaker' role not as something to be broken down into constituents but as a composite of different aspects functioning together. Goffman's contribution to understanding this aspect of language and media was his use of sociolinguistic insights into code-switching (i.e. shifting between alternative linguistic varieties) in accounting for speakers' strategies as they try to manage the reception of their utterances. In developing his account, Goffman draws attention initially to the sociolinguist John Gumperz's list of typical code-switching cues:

1 direct or reported speech,
2 selection of recipient,
3 interjections,
4 repetitions,
5 personal directness or involvement,
6 new and old information,
7 emphasis,
8 separation of topic and subject, and
9 discourse type, e.g., lecture and discussion.

Goffman points out that such switching cues are not just stylistic variation. They signal significant shifts of stance or alignment between 'the speaker' and her or his topic, as well as between different ways of addressing an audience. Goffman goes on to distinguish three overlapping but in principle distinguishable speaking roles: those of *principal*, *author* and *animator*. Together, these roles make up our commonsense notion of 'the speaker':

- The principal is the person (or organisation) 'whose position is established by the words that are spoken, someone whose beliefs have been told, someone who is committed to what the words say'.
- The author is the person who (or team which) 'has selected the sentiments that are being expressed and the words in which they are encoded'.
- The animator is the person who (or team of people which) performs the words (in Goffman's terms, the 'sounding box' or 'talking machine').

(adapted from Goffman, 1981: 144)

Activity 

Suppose you see an article on politics in a magazine with the byline 'Gordon Brown' (the British prime minister at the time of writing – leave aside the possibility of another Gordon Brown, despite Gordon Brown being a not uncommon British name). Which of the Goffman participation roles is it fair to assume that the prime minister played in its production: principal?/author?/animator?

Now consider this: in the course of a recent mini-controversy, the prime minister's office was asked about an article published in an American political magazine with the byline 'Gordon Brown'. The article, attributed to the British prime minister, discussed how the US presidential candidates stood on economic policy and appeared to favour one over the other. The prime minister's office confirmed the article's authenticity, but it said that Gordon Brown himself had neither written nor read it.

- ❑ What issues about communication (rather than about international politics) are raised by the suggestion that the prime minister didn't write or even read an article carrying his personal byline?
- ❑ Are those issues different from questions raised by a ghosted autobiography (i.e. a first-person narrative that purports to tell the author's life story but is in fact mostly written by someone else) or by the traditional letter of congratulation 'signed by the Queen' that is sent to British citizens who reach their one-hundredth birthday?

Footing and stance

In the course of a conversation or stretch of discourse, a speaker may shift their stance. A common shift is that from (informal) small talk into (more formal) discussion of a substantive topic. Or, on the main topic itself, the same speaker may present a viewpoint by directly attributing information or opinion to someone else. To do this, the speaker uses reported speech or thought: 'the company's view is that this should go ahead'. Alternatively, the speaker might put forward the same view as her or his own ('this should go ahead'). In overtly attributing an idea to someone else, the speaker in Goffman's terms occupies a position of 'animator' but not 'author' or 'principal' of what is being said.

Even when putting forward an idea as her or his own, a speaker may still be acting as a mouthpiece or spokesperson. The speaker may be speaking in an official capacity, rather than expressing a genuinely held personal opinion. In this case, the speaker is still 'animator' (and may or may not be also 'author', depending on whether the utterance was scripted by someone else). But the speaker is not necessarily the utterance's 'principal'. In all cases except speaking your own words straight from your own thoughts, what is said will not necessarily be the speaker's own content. What is said is framed by reference to another voice and/or interest.

Shifting between different speaker roles during the course of an utterance calls for

varied acts of projecting the self. This is an acting or theatrical approach to communicating that is amply reflected in much of Goffman's own imagery. In poetry, projection of a voice that is different from the speaker's 'own voice' is usually called adoption of a 'persona'. But strategic realignment of utterances with their content and their addressees doesn't only occur in poetry. It takes place all the time, both in conversation and in media discourse. Goffman calls the processes involved in maintaining and shifting between different stances 'footing'.

Activity

1. Select a piece of text which seems to you to involve a division between Goffman's different roles of 'principal', 'author' and 'animator'. Start with an obvious case, such as a radio or TV advert (where the copywriter role is a different job from that of the actors who perform and from the marketing managers in the company whose product is being promoted). Describe the roles as precisely as you can, and how each occupies a different stance in relation to the resulting 'message'.
2. Now select another piece of text, such as a public relations statement: a press or media release, or public statement made by a spokesperson for an organisation. Is it possible to identify equivalent distinctions within the speaker role?
3. In public relations, the source credibility of the animator (as someone likely to be believed or trusted) is usually thought essential in achieving a positive effect. Does it matter in such cases how far removed the animator role is from that of the author and principal (e.g. if a celebrity basketball player tells you on-screen that it's good to recycle plastic bottles; or if a soap actor endorses a political party's economic policies)?
4. Now look for a piece of media talk where you think the different roles coincide. Are there typical slots or functions for such stretches of discourse within the overall flow of a media text in which they occur (e.g. a radio or TV talk show, or a documentary)?
5. Finally, consider how each clip of talk is embedded as an item into an overall programme package. That package typically consists of an edited sequence of different voices (often joined by a presenter's links or voice-over). Can you distinguish the same kinds of role at the level of the overall programme speech event, rather than at the level of the various individual contributions to it?

Applying Goffman in specific analyses

Allan Bell has analysed in detail both the processes involved in producing print and broadcast news discourse and the resulting styles of news discourse itself (Bell, 1991). Bell (1991: 37–44) draws extensively on Goffman's classification. He lists the various professional and technical roles that make up news production (journalist, chief reporter, sub-editor, editor, etc.) and maps them onto Goffman's functional categories of principal, author and animator.

Bell also adds a category to Goffman's: that of editor, between author and animator. This extra category reflects a shift in processes of text production across most media over the last 30 years, towards iterative text editing and away from any single, decisive act of composition. Bell also shows how the principal role proposed by Goffman involves two sub-roles in print news media: a commercial proprietor role (the ultimate source of direction and strategy, even where there is no interference in day-to-day editorial policy) and a news professional role, focused on the editor and team of senior journalists.

As regards media audiences, Bell also extends Goffman's model of multiple participation roles. As we illustrate in Figure B3.1, he views roles 'as concentric rings, like the skins of an onion' (Bell, 1991: 91). Bell's categories are partly matched to a specific mode of address associated with each. Are audience members, he asks, second-person addressees or referred to as third-person absentees from the supposed scene of interaction? Bell adds a further category here too. This is the category of 'auditor', which he uses to signal a distinction within what he considers the presently blurred category that covers both clearly targeted addressees and an ever-present but unplanned possibility of eavesdroppers. 'The auditors and overhearers, here in mass communication', he suggests, 'are graded from fully expected to highly unexpected attenders, rather than two distinct groups' (1991: 95–6). Other writers, including Jenny Thomas (1983) and Mary Talbot (2007), have taken Goffman's insights in new directions in investigating the strategic intentions of speakers. So has the applied linguist Anne O'Keeffe.

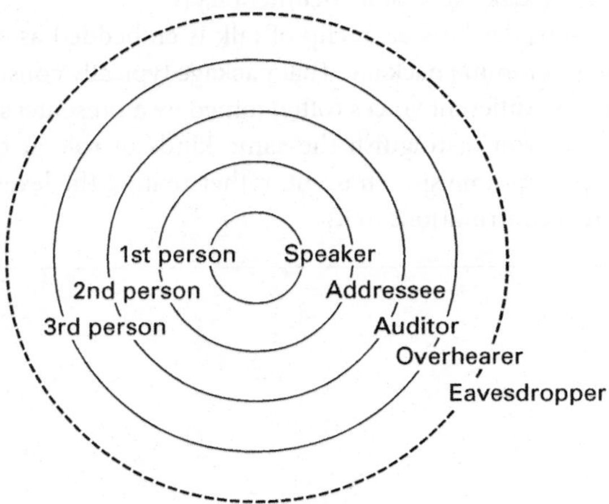

Figure B3.1 Persons and roles in the speech situation (Bell, 1991)

In her research papers and textbook (O'Keeffe, 2006), O'Keeffe extends Goffman's analysis by exploring media interaction between broadcaster, interviewee and audience across a number of genres, including radio phone-ins, political interviews and chat shows. What distinguishes her approach is its concern to identify particular linguistic features in the texture of recorded speech data (e.g. vocatives, markers of shared assumptions, vague terms and categories, hedging, and response tokens) as ways of tracking the 'footing' phenomena identified by Goffman. For O'Keeffe and her co-researchers emphasis is placed on use of corpus linguistic approaches and conversation analysis to investigate the frequency and distribution of particular discourse markers (such as the categories above, or first, second and third person pronouns). Her aim is to test general hypotheses about different kinds of mediated interaction.

Activity

Consider the following anecdote presented by the Italian novelist and essayist Umberto Eco in an article about the complexity of communicative events. (See unit A4 for a different angle on this same extraordinary media utterance.) Eco narrates how, in 1985, during a microphone test before a public speech, US president Ronald Reagan said, 'In a few minutes I'll push the red button and I'll start bombing the Soviet Union'. The microphone happened to be switched on, and a group of news reporters heard – in Goffman's terms, they 'eavesdropped' – and reported the utterance. Asked about what he had meant, Reagan said that he was joking. Being an ex-actor, he might well have been just relaxing during a sound-check ('goofing around', in actors' talk). Severely criticising Reagan's joke, however, some newsmen inferred, according to Eco, that 'the real intention of Reagan was to suggest nonchalantly that he was such a tough guy that, if he wanted, he could have done what he only pretended to do' (1990: 53). In unit A4, we look at the president's utterance from the perspective of expected linguistic register and discourse genre.

1 Which of the two competing explanations do you consider more likely, and why?
2 Is there any way to get to the bottom of a dispute over the significance of a media comment of this kind (even an apparently unintended one)? What is in question, after all, is not the wording but the uncertain 'stance' or 'alignment' of the speaker towards the content of his message.
3 If it isn't possible to be sure about even apparently important utterances – where what is potentially at stake includes death and destruction on a massive scale – does this suggest that it may often be impossible to hold people accountable for what they say? Or can you think of other ways of establishing 'ownership' of the content of someone's utterance in circumstances such as these?

Pseudo-intimacy in media culture

Why do the participation structures of media communicative events matter? We conclude this unit with one widely discussed possibility.

Media discourse often adopts a style that is far more informal than the relationship between participants (who do not know each other at all) appears to warrant. Informality, even a semblance of intimacy, is created by devices such as familiar terms of address and a generally colloquial register. Possible objections, reservations or enthusiasms on the part of the listener are anticipated. Indicators are given of assumed responses or appreciation from listeners whose actual reaction can't be known. Together, such devices construct a kind of 'simulated co-presence' or 'quasi-interaction' (for discussion, see Goffman, 1981: 138). The effect is 'simulated', 'quasi' or 'pseudo' in that it isn't supported by any relationship beyond the style of the communication itself. If participants in a media interaction do know each other at all, it is only a public *persona* that is known, not any particular person. (Indeed the contrast between persona and off-screen personality in celebrities has itself become a media genre, exemplified by the British TV series *Katie and Peter* about the domestic life of Katie Price [aka Jordan] and Peter André.)

Many media commentators feel there are risks with mediated interaction at a distance that adopts an over-personalised style. One early view along these lines was expressed by Richard Hoggart in his influential book *The Uses of Literacy* (1957). Hoggart described a 'false intimacy' in media communication in which personalised, direct address modelled on face-to-face interaction is simulated in order to convey credibility and a sense of belonging. Hoggart was especially concerned about the rapidly developing, US-influenced mass media environment of his day. But wider risks in seeming to be addressed informally and in an over-personal way by someone who appears to know you are also evident in contemporary, including online, media. Examples include telesales techniques, much spam email, and so-called online 'grooming'.

It is also possible, however, to take a more favourable view of 'simulated' styles of media discourse. One view is that simulated media and online identities allow exploration of virtual worlds, or even living simultaneously in multiple worlds in a kind of mental space–time travel. Reinvention of the self is made possible by opportunities to become someone else in an online environment, and to fantasise by playing different roles (including ones that may not be possible for a given individual in real life). Each of these possibilities can be held to be creative and liberating unless shown to be otherwise. In unit C3 we consider the imaginative opportunities (as well as some of the possible dangers) opened up for listeners by such listening relations – as imagined speakers, addressees and overhearers – when listening to song lyrics.

Whatever moral or value judgement you reach, shifts of communication style and technique contribute to a larger restructuring of our social environment. The sociologist John Thompson (1995) sets such changes in how we experience communication in a wider theoretical and historical perspective. He links shifts in the methods and styles of communication to major social changes of lifestyle and opportunity. Thompson develops the notion of 'non-reciprocal intimacy at a distance' to describe how modern communications media have altered our expectations about communication in a public sphere. He notes how media language contrives intimacy and a simulated sense of dialogue that in fact only goes in one direction. Personal contact cannot be returned from any given audience member to the media protagonist. Focusing on the asymmetrical character of such media relations, Thompson explores how increased visibility of political figures and celebrities – who are constantly filmed and recorded, in many different staged and unstaged situations – is linked to ever evolving styles of informal self-exposure and self-presentation. In a more recent book, Thompson (2000) draws on Goffman's work again. This time, he investigates how situations unravel when media self-presentation breaks down in the manoeuvring and deception that accompany major political scandals.

SCHEMA AND GENRE THEORY

B4

This unit extends our discussion of media genres, by looking more closely at the impact on the concept of genre of schema theory and genre theory. Each of these theories enhances our understanding of different text types and how we distinguish one from another. We describe

- a linguistic framework for analysing large-scale schemas in media discourse, and
- various factors that come together in making different genres recognisable, including audience expectations and norms of social interaction.

In unit A4 we saw that the term 'genre' denotes a distinctive type of text that is organised on the basis of recognisable, and therefore potentially classifiable, patterns. Because of their organisation in this way, texts (whether spoken, written, or communicated in some other media form) are more easily memorised and recalled.

Genre as discourse practice

In discourse analysis, 'discourse genre' involves a wide-ranging and varied set of properties. Montgomery (2007) makes the point as follows:

> A genre of discourse is a specific and recognisable configuration of discourse elements realising a particular communicative purpose or set of purposes and usually known amongst a language community by a widely shared label, such as 'advert', 'sermon', 'gossip', 'joke', 'lecture'. 'News' is one such genre. The label is widely understood; and instances of broadcast news are instantly identifiable as such to audiences. Indeed, news has claims to be the most widely dispersed and understood discourse genre of modern times. However, even within this genre, there are generic variations between radio news and TV news and between bulletin news and rolling news. And in any case news as a genre is woven out of subgenres such as the news report, the news interview, or the news headline. Indeed,

> the structural composition of news discourse may be seen in terms of the chaining together of units each of which is realised by a different sub-genre. Like structure, genre as a concept also faces two ways. 'The constructional value of each and every element of a work can be understood only in relation to genre . . . It is genre that gives shape and meaning to . . . a whole entity, and to all the elements of which that entity is comprised' (Medvedev, 1928, quoted in Titunik, 1973).
>
> Genre is both the stabilisation or sedimentation of a particular set of discourse practices and the enabling framework from which discursive change and innovation take place. Indeed, a major source of difficulty in defining and applying the term genre is that some genres, at least, are unstable, in flux, with the boundaries dividing one from another tending to be indeterminate. In print journalism, for example, the notion of a 'news piece' is understood as generically opposed to 'feature'. The latter tends to be longer, less compressed, with less emphasis on current incident, more personal, with more focus on human interest and with greater allowance for the personal viewpoint of the journalist. Despite this there seems to be no contradiction involved in describing hybrid or intermediate cases as a 'news feature'.
>
> So, genre describes more than a patterned, recurrent configuration of elements or units but also encompasses shared understandings between producers and audiences about forms and the purposes they serve. In this sense although genre is textually manifested in discourse it may also be considered a process beyond the discourse itself involving a promise, by producers, and recognition, by audiences, of the type of discursive activity being performed. Genre is a set of generative and interpretative procedures, a 'horizon of expectations' (Todorov, 1990, p. 18) against which any specific generic instance must be set.
>
> While genre is at once the sedimentation and routinisation of a set of practices and a backdrop against which innovation and change can take place, it should also be noted that well-defined discourse genres such as the lecture, the sermon, the debate, legal cross-examination, or the medical consultation are often embedded in strongly institutionalised domains of social life such as medicine, education, law, politics and religion. They derive their purpose from their institutional position, at the same time as being the discursive embodiment of the institution. The productivity of genres, however, also allows for their migration across domains as models for newly discovered communicative purposes. Thus 'the lecture', 'the debate' and 'cross-examination', which have all had a life in broadcasting (Scannell and Cardiff, 1991), sometimes become transformed into new genres such as the studio discussion or the political interview.
>
> (Montgomery, 2007: 26–7)

Central to Montgomery's argument in the quotation above is the idea of 'shared understandings between producers and audiences about forms and the purposes they serve'. One way of thinking further about how we recognise different text types or media discourses – and can distinguish for example, between a television soap and a documentary – is to investigate what Montgomery describes above as 'promises' and 'expectations' in terms of our schematic knowledge. (Note, however, that the term 'schemas' is also introduced in unit B6, in our discussion of narrative structure; in that

discussion, the term 'schemas' is used in a related sense to describe sequential stages in narrative development.)

Schema theory

Bartlett (1932) was one of the first scholars to appreciate the importance of schemas, which he described as high level structures that help memorisation. In his study of memorising and recalling stories, Bartlett outlined a model of *schema theory* that brought together earlier thinking in a number of fields, and gave such work an experimental grounding.

In one experiment, Bartlett found that when participants were asked to recall a story they had been given, they changed parts of the story either by 'flattening', 'sharpening' or 'rationalizing' parts of that story. Bartlett showed how his informants 'used their own schemata as structures of expectation to fill in probable details when recall was partial' (p. 204). From Bartlett's insights, two related implications in relation to genre follow:

1. Schema theory may help us in understanding how people make sense of texts.
2. Schemas may be the psychological basis for our sense of 'promises' and our horizon of 'expectations' when we encounter a text that resembles a type we have encountered previously.

Put more generally, schema theory applied to the area of language processing describes our mental organisation of stereotypical knowledge about patterns in discourse. We rely on such knowledge to help us interpret and understand texts, especially because of our tendency to draw on previous knowledge in comprehension (e.g. using previous understandings of story structure and content when reading a 'new' story, as in Bartlett's experiment). Mostly, our everyday contact with new texts confirms existing schemas, in a process known as 'schema preservation' or 'reinforcing'. Occasionally, our schemas fail to account for our experience of a text, resulting in 'schema disruption' that follows when existing schema knowledge is challenged (Stockwell, 2002). This line of psychological explanation based on schematic knowledge is not confined to text comprehension. It is applied and tested in many other fields of perception and understanding. Here, the model provides a basis for understanding how we recognise texts across the many different and rapidly changing forms of media discourse.

Genre theory

Genre theory, as described in Daniel Chandler's (1997) study of media and communication, builds on schema theory. In his discussion, Chandler argues that the term genre can be problematic, as

> Contemporary theorists tend to describe genres in terms of 'family resemblances' among texts (a notion derived from the philosopher Wittgenstein) rather than

> definitionally (Swales 1990, 49). An individual text within a genre rarely if ever has all of the characteristic features of the genre (Fowler 1989, 215). The family resemblance approaches involves the theorist illustrating similarities between some of the texts within a genre. However, the family resemblance approach has been criticized on the basis that 'no choice of a text for illustrative purposes is innocent' (David Lodge, cited in Swales 1990, 50), and that such theories can make any text seem to resemble any other one (Swales 1990, 51). In addition to the definitional and family resemblance approach, there is another approach to describing genres which is based on the psycholinguistic concept of prototypicality. According to this approach, some texts would be widely regarded as being more typical members of a genre than others. According to this approach certain features would 'identify the extent to which an exemplar is prototypical of a particular genre' (Swales 1990, 52). Genres can therefore be seen as 'fuzzy' categories which cannot be defined by necessary and sufficient conditions [. . .]
>
> The interaction between genres and media can be seen as one of the forces which contributes to changing genres. Some genres are more powerful than others: they differ in the status which is attributed to them by those who produce texts within them and by their audiences. As Tony Thwaites et al. put it, 'in the interaction and conflicts among genres we can see the connections between textuality and power' (Thwaites et al. 1994, 104). The key genres in institutions which are 'primary definers' (such as news reports in the mass media) help to establish the frameworks within which issues are defined. But genre hierarchies also shift over time, with individual genres constantly gaining and losing different groups of users and relative status [. . .]
>
> (Chandler, 1997: 2–3)

Roland Barthes (1975) argued that it is in relation to other texts within a genre rather than in relation to lived experience that we make sense of certain events within a text. There are analogies here with schema theory in psychology, which proposes that we have mental 'scripts' which help us to interpret familiar events in everyday life. John Fiske offers this striking example:

> A representation of a car chase only makes sense in relation to all the others we have seen – after all, we are unlikely to have experienced one in reality, and if we did, we would, according to this model, make sense of it by turning it into another text, which we would also understand intertextually, in terms of what we have seen so often on our screens. There is then a cultural knowledge of the concept 'car chase' that any one text is a prospectus for, and that is used by the viewer to decode it, and by the producer to encode it.
>
> (Fiske, 1987: 115)

In contrast to those of a traditionalist literary bent who tend to present 'artistic' texts as non-generic, it could be argued that it is impossible to produce texts which bear no relationship whatsoever to established genres. Indeed, Jacques Derrida proposed that 'a text cannot belong to no genre, it cannot be without . . . a genre. Every text participates in one or several genres, there is no genreless text' (Derrida, 1981: 61).

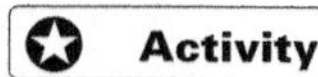

As part of his discussion of genre and genre theory, Chandler (1997) produces a useful 'DIY generic analysis' in the form of a list of questions, primarily for his students. The questions are designed to enable individuals to analyse a text in relation to genre (p. 10), see below. Use Chandler's questions to describe differences between what are commonly understood to be two texts from two different genres (e.g. a song and a poem; a news report and a blog, etc.).

General

1 Why did you choose the text you are analysing?
2 In what context did you encounter it?
3 What influence do you think this context might have had on your interpretation of the text?
4 To what genre did you initially assign the text?
5 What is your experience of this genre?
6 What subject matter and basic themes is the text concerned with?
7 How typical of the genre is this text in terms of content?
8 What expectations do you have about texts in this genre?
9 Have you found any formal generic labels for this particular text (where)?
10 What generic labels have others given the same text?
11 Which conventions of the genre do you recognise in the text?
12 To what extent does this text stretch the conventions of its genre?
13 Where and why does the text depart from the conventions of the genre?
14 Which conventions seem more like those of a different genre (and which genre(s))?
15 What familiar motifs or images are used?
16 Which of the formal/stylistic techniques employed are typical/untypical of the genre?
17 What institutional constraints are reflected in the form of the text?
18 What relationship to 'reality' does the text lay claim to?
19 Whose realities does it reflect?
20 What purposes does the genre serve?
21 In what ways are these purposes embodied in the text?
22 To what extent did your purposes match these when you engaged with the text?
23 What ideological assumptions and values seem to be embedded in the text?
24 What pleasures does this genre offer to you personally?
25 What pleasures does the text appeal to (and how typical of the genre is this)?
26 Did you feel 'critical or accepting, resisting or validating, casual or concentrated, apathetic or motivated' (and why)?
27 Which elements of the text seemed salient because of your knowledge of the genre?

28 What predictions about events did your generic identification of the text lead to (and to what extent did these prove accurate)?
29 What inferences about people and their motivations did your genre identification give rise to (and how far were these confirmed)?
30 How and why did your interpretation of the text differ from the interpretation of the same text by other people?

Mode of address

1 What sort of audience did you feel that the text was aimed at (and how typical was this of the genre)?
2 How does the text address you?
3 What sort of person does it assume you are?
4 What assumptions seem to be made about your class, age, gender and ethnicity?
5 What interests does it assume you have?
6 What relevance does the text actually have for you?
7 What knowledge does it take for granted?
8 To what extent do you resemble the 'ideal reader' that the text seeks to position you as?
9 Are there any notable shifts in the text's mode of address (and if so, what do they involve)?
10 What responses does the text seem to expect from you?
11 How open to negotiation is your response (are you invited, instructed or coerced to respond in particular ways)?
12 Is there any penalty for not responding in the expected ways?
13 To what extent do you find yourself 'reading against the grain' of the text and the genre?
14 Which attempts to position you in this text do you accept, reject or seek to negotiate (and why)?
15 How closely aligned is the way in which the text addresses you with the way in which the genre positions you (Kress, 1988: 107)?

Relationship to other texts

1 What intertextual references are there in the text you are analysing (and to what other texts)?
2 Generically, which other texts does the text you are analysing resemble most closely?
3 What key features are shared by these texts?
4 What major differences do you notice between them?

Analysing genres: Hymes's SPEAKING grid

How do such accounts of genre relate to linguistic frameworks for analysing speech genres in particular?

One framework that brings the two different streams of insight together is known as 'the SPEAKING grid'. This framework was developed in the field of 'the ethnography of speaking', an approach to discourse that analyses regular or predictable communicative patterns in intensively studied bodies of interactional data. Investigation of genre in the ethnography of speaking extends Dell Hymes's (1977) concept of 'communicative competence', or knowledge of a language that includes not only core areas of linguistic form but also appropriate use of language in given situations.

As regards language practice in general, the ethnography of speaking moves from detailed transcription and analysis of data towards theoretical questions, such as what a speaker needs to know to communicate appropriately within a particular speech community. A large part of what 'communicating appropriately' means involves understanding genre, and this in turn relies on schematic knowledge. Hymes (1972) develops a framework of 'components', or characteristics of communication, that can be used in investigating rules of speaking and how such rules are embedded in social understandings and expectations. The name of Hymes's framework takes the form of a mnemonic: the individual letters that make up 'SPEAKING' each represent a component of the scheme (see Table B4.1).

Table B4.1 Hymes's SPEAKING grid (adapted from Hymes, 1972)

S	Setting and scene	Setting = time and place; scene = cultural definition of occasion e.g. Queen's Christmas message
P	Participants	Speaker–listener, sender–receiver, etc. fill socially specified roles e.g. lecturer and students, interviewer and interviewee
E	Ends	Conventionally recognised and expected outcomes of exchange and personal goals, e.g. courtroom trial (although different participants – judge, witnesses, accused, defendant, etc. – will have different personal goals)
A	Act sequence	Actual form and content of what is said; words used, how they are used, etc. Different forms of speaking: party, lecture, casual conversations, gossip
K	Key	Tone and manner, e.g. serious, light-hearted, sarcastic, pompous. Also, non-verbal behaviour
I	Instru-mentalities	Whether spoken or written and form, e.g. language, dialect, code or register. Formal, legal written language is one instrumentality
N	Norms of interaction	Specific behaviours and properties attached to speaking within cultural belief system, e.g. silence, loudness, gaze return
G	Genre	Types of utterance appropriate to an occasion, e.g. prayers, lectures, conversations

Hymes's framework provides a useful descriptive tool for analysing a community's ways of speaking. But how useful is it in analysing media discourse?

Activity 

Try relating the SPEAKING grid to examples we have considered elsewhere in the book. For example,

- ❑ Is the framework likely to be helpful in identifying the various components that make Barack Obama's presidential acceptance speech a distinct genre, for instance, distinguishable from other spoken events and even from other political speeches (see unit C5)?
- ❑ Can the SPEAKING grid be extended to analyse mismatches in media events between social expectations and the style of discourse that is used, as in the political gaffe made by President Reagan about bombing Russia (see units A4 and B3)?

Analyse either Reagan's political gaffe in unit A4 and B3 or Obama's speech in unit C5 using Hymes's SPEAKING grid. 'Analyse', here, means finding evidence in the text under each heading in the classification, then looking across your findings under all the headings for patterns (and also for inconsistencies or apparent irregularities).

- ❑ What difficulties do you encounter in carrying out your analysis?
- ❑ Are you able to identify evidence in relation to all the components of the grid? (You may wish to read unit C5 before undertaking this task. Our discussion of Hymes's grid is broadened there in relation to media interviews in particular.)

B5 PERSUASION AND POWER

This unit explores interaction between information and persuasion in media discourse. It builds on our introduction to information and rhetoric (unit A5). It also connects closely with other units, including our accounts of register (thread 2), media genres (thread 4) and storytelling (thread 6).

Linguistic aspects of how information is presented in persuasive ways are important in many public media forms. Two especially influential fields of media practice in this respect are news and adverts. News appears primarily a matter of information being conveyed, but it can be shown to have a persuasive undercurrent. Advertising seems primarily a matter of persuading consumers to buy, but it also conveys information about the products and services being promoted. We

- ❑ illustrate how presenting information incorporates persuasive or rhetorical techniques, both in news and advertising, and
- ❑ introduce themes in the work of critical discourse analysts and other linguists who investigate power relations in media discourse.

First we consider news and information media, then we look at adverts.

News

News and information media have a long and complicated history, from notices and announcements in public places to contemporary 24-hour rolling satellite news and newsfeeds to your mobile or PC. Any full appreciation of how media news operates would be set in the context of its technological and institutional development.

Throughout most of their history, news formats have been intertwined with kinds of promotional discourse, including messages from sponsors and advertising. We focus here on linguistic dimensions of how news is selected and composed, as well as how it is likely to be interpreted.

News as events or as accounts of events?

If someone asks you 'if there's any news', they are asking whether there have been any recent events, significant developments, or other occurrences in the world that you think they may wish to be informed about. In this sense, 'news' denotes events or actions in the world. The same term 'news', however, is also used in relation to newspaper, magazine or other media news reports and stories. In this context, 'news' means something different. It no longer denotes events themselves but a constructed representation of such events or actions. This is an obvious distinction but also an important one (for discussion, see unit A5). Language in news media structures *how* whatever goes on in the world is represented:

- ❑ how stories are selected,
- ❑ how they are organised, and
- ❑ how they are presented.

Distinguishing the two senses of news leads into a further question that is central to critical linguistics and to critical discourse analysis: how *far*, in appearing to report news, does the process of selecting and representing news shape the news that is reported?

It might seem that 'news' (as media presentation) should simply reflect 'news' (as actions and events). Such reflection would give news objectivity and truthfulness. If, on the other hand, you consider that reported 'news' reshapes news events and actions to a significant extent, then 'news' appears not so much direct reporting of events as the output of a media agenda for news-making. In between the events and reports or stories, there would be a set of creative and editorial processes for giving form to whatever events and actions are depicted. News, in this second view, serves an agenda. It can use its own framing and storytelling techniques to highlight issues, to

campaign, to criticise, to celebrate, to promote forthcoming events, or to attract attention to or distract attention from *other* events. This view of news is essentially that news language serves rhetorical purposes as much as it reflects how things are or what has happened. News, in such a perspective, may even offer only a distorted and distorting account of how the world is. To understand the language of news, accordingly, would be to understand its capability for bias, manipulation and possibly deception as well as its potential to inform.

What constitutes news

Consider the well-known anecdote made by the editor of the *New York Sun*, John Bogart, about what constitutes news: '"Dog bites man" is not news, "man bites dog" is' (quoted in Mott, 1950: 376).

What Bogart implies is that media news is not all the events that *could* be reported. Rather, news involves a selection of those events. So we need to ask how and why some stories are told, and not others. What gives a particular event or action its public interest? This preliminary stage of how 'information' is turned into 'story' is investigated extensively in media and journalism studies, under the heading of news value. We bring together three linguistically relevant aspects of news value, each of which is extensively discussed elsewhere (Bell, 1991; van Dijk, 1988):

- ❑ the conventional topic areas that contribute to a news story's genre characteristics (these fields guide news treatment in an analogous way to subject matter, or field, shaping register),
- ❑ the characteristics or attributes of events and actions that make a story newsworthy (these are highlighted or accentuated in the ways a story is presented), and
- ❑ the sources, or underlying materials (these shape how a story is presented, including in what order, and with what balance between different elements).

Topic areas

Hartley (1982) describes the main kinds of news material or news 'content' typically found across media news outlets:

> Although news is supposed to be about new, unexpected things, it is quite easy to outline its main preoccupations. They are grouped around and within six major topics.
>
> *Politics* Defined as government (Whitehall/White House), parliament (Westminster/Capitol Hill) and the policies, personalities and disputes that make up the context of decision-making.
>
> *The economy* Defined as (a) companies and the City – their performance, their figures and their management; (b) 'government figures out tonight' – the economy as a statistical model of trade figures, imports and exports, unemployment, wages, inflation, prices, etc.
>
> *Foreign affairs* Usually the relations between governments and especially those involved in an issue concerning 'us' (i.e. the British Government); also reports on wars, coups, earthquakes, etc.

Domestic [= national] news Here the range of referents is wide, but the organisation of them is quite tight. They fall into '*hard*' and '*soft*' stories. Hard stories are characterized by *conflict* (violence). Soft stories include *humour* and *human interest* (often defined as having a 'woman's angle'). [. . .]

Occasional stories Stories about disasters, celebrities, the Royal Family and topical talking points of the day [. . .].

Sport Accented towards male, professional, competitive sport; football in winter, cricket in summer, with a league-table of 'other' sport in season.

(excerpted from Hartley, 1982: 38–9)

Hartley's classification serves as a guide to the main fields that news stories cover, and to which they are aligned editorially (i.e. as regards the style adopted in their presentation).

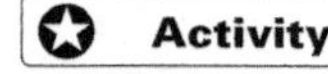

Work through the print version of a newspaper, page by page. *For each page*, write a brief description of what it contains:

- Is the page mainly hard news, soft news, features, opinion/editorial, adverts, etc.? (Don't worry about being too precise here; it's the overall pattern that is significant.)
- What overall style or design is adopted for each page (short or long stories; use of photographs)?

Remember: each page may involve a mix of text types. Your description will only be a simplified account. The point of the task is to help you think about how far a compound media genre can be broken down into more specific categories.

Now consider Hartley's categories again. These categories were first formulated nearly 30 years ago, in the first edition of *Understanding News* in 1982. How adequately do Hartley's categories reflect the news stories you now encounter? Consider a selection of stories in the newspaper you have worked through, or a radio or TV news broadcast. Allocate each story to one of the categories above. Note what page each kind of story is on, in a newspaper, or how far through the running order of a broadcast news programme it is presented. With print media, consider what features of design signal what kind of story it is (e.g. headline size, number of column inches covered, use of photographs and size of photographs, etc.). Are there stories which don't easily fit any of Hartley's categories (or some combination of those categories)? If so, what name would you give to the new category of news story that your example seems to belong to?

Newsworthiness

In unit D5, we reproduce Bell's (1991) commentary on the main characteristics that recommend some stories for coverage in the news and discourage treatment of others. Bell's discussion is based on work by researchers Johan Galtung and Mari Ruge in their 1973 chapter 'Structuring and selecting news'. Bell focuses on the following typical features of news. He proposes that an action or event is likely to be newsworthy if it

- is bad or negative,
- has only just happened,
- took place geographically close to the reader or viewer,
- fits the reader's or viewer's preconceptions or stereotypes about how the world is,
- is relatively clear-cut and unambiguous,
- is rare, unexpected or unpredictable,
- is outstanding or superlative in some respect,
- can be presented as relevant to the audience's own lives or experience,
- can be pictured in personal terms,
- involves news actors who are socially prominent in some respect,
- comes from news sources who carry some kind of socially validated authority, and
- consists of or can be supported by facts and figures.

Characteristics such as these indicate the point of view towards a news story likely to be adopted by the reader or viewer in assessing what is interesting about it, or what merits attention. Note how some of the criteria of newsworthiness are attributes ('is', 'consists of'). Others signify potential to be presented in a certain way ('can be presented', 'can be pictured'). This mix of characteristics raises important questions:

- How far is each aspect an established category of human interest (e.g. people are interested in the prominent figures of their society, they crave information, they are worried about risk, etc.)?
- How far does each aspect reflect an appetite created by the news media themselves?

We can now consider what Bell's list adds to Hartley's classification of subject areas. Any given action or event, in any one of Hartley's areas (e.g. sport), can be evaluated in terms of whether it has the necessary characteristics to warrant coverage as a news story.

Without such characteristics, the event or action is unlikely to be successful in competition for published or broadcast space or time against some other story that has (or has more). For news creators – whether they are journalists or public relations workers – a major challenge in media language is to mould or reshape the raw material of events and actions into stories that have enough conventional news properties to be included in a target media outlet. For readers and viewers, newsworthiness functions a bit like a prism. Many different events and actions that take place pass through the 'newsworthiness' prism, where they are filtered and deflected before being published or broadcast. (See also Palmer, 1998, for a broad discussion of news values and approaches to the criteria of newsworthiness.)

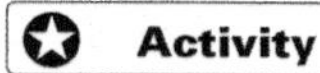

As with Hartley's list, the list of newsworthiness attributes discussed by Bell was devised during a period of primarily print journalism and broadcast news. This was before multimedia, online news sources, and personalised news feeds allowed individual users to shape their own news priorities more actively. Look again at the selection of news stories you used in the previous task. Ask yourself whether Bell's categories match your experience of news media now.

We now have two influential lists of news categories (a list of topic areas and a list of newsworthiness features). The two lists are useful because they represent two dimensions of the genre of a news story: its field (what it's about) and its function (here, the function of gaining attention, having impact, or achieving some other effect such as entertaining, frightening or shocking). A news story is always *about* some particular area. Its language is adapted to expectations associated with that area (e.g. a sport or personal interest story will differ from an international news story not only in its content but in its approach and style). The language of a news story is also adapted to *highlight* its newsworthiness (in this way, it justifies or maximises the attention it will be given).

Sources embedded in the story narration

The third major dimension of news stories that governs their use of language concerns the sources they are created from. News stories are produced by journalists who put them together from raw materials, many of which are already in language form. Bell (1991) offers the following list of sources that go into news stories:

- interviews, either face to face or by telephone,
- public addresses,
- press conferences,
- written text of spoken addresses,
- organisationally produced documents of many kinds: reports, surveys, letters, findings, agendas, minutes, proceedings, research,
- papers, etc.,
- press releases,
- prior stories on a topic, either from own or other media,
- news agency copy,
- the journalist's notes from all the above inputs, especially the spoken ones.

Each of these sources has its own style of language. It also has its own, distinctive storytelling structure. Some of the features of the underlying sources for a story, or at least their general approach, are carried across into the finished article itself. As you read any given news story, you can ask what use has been made of the sources for it in creating each of its paragraphs. You can do the same when you listen to radio news or watch a TV news package. What sources have been drawn on in creating each section

(e.g. of voice-overs, interview dialogue, vox pop, or studio–anchor link)? In some cases, you won't be able to tell. In other cases, there will be clear signs of where information has come from, or whose voice is being echoed.

Bell's list of sources could be extended or modified. Controversially, for instance, it has recently been argued that for cost reasons one of the main sources of published and broadcast news stories is public relations handouts, such as press releases or VNRs (video news releases). Such material (e.g., material related to fuel cost or a fuel shortage produced by the oil industry; research on GM foods sponsored and reported by representatives of the GM food industry) presents a commercial client's point of view on a topic. PR news releases are often designed to be used without the need for much further editing (Davies, 2008).

Analysing the language of a news story – whether in print, online or in broadcast form – involves collecting together evidence in response to quite specific questions, then evaluating that evidence in the light of your own interests, preoccupations or critical standpoint. A list of useful questions to ask in analysing stories is presented in Table B5.1.

Table B5.1 A guide to analysing the language of news stories

	General question	*Evidence to look for*
1	What topic area, or established field of interest, does the story present itself as part of? What area of interest is it expected to be part of, as a reader scans through or decides what to pay attention to?	Key subject-related words and themes Where located in news layout or running order (see Hartley's list above)
2	What claims does the story make, as regards its own newsworthiness (i.e. what are you supposed to think is new or worth your attention?)	Newsworthiness features in Bell's list above
3	How does the story use available materials (e.g. new facts based on documents or interviews, quotations, public statements made by people involved in the events, etc.)?	Quotations, reported speech, and paraphrased utterances Attribution of facts or opinions to particular actors (e.g. 'according to . . .')

	Describing the story's style and way of addressing the reader/listener/viewer	*Evidence to look for*
4	How does the story address its audience?	Use of rhetorical questions Use of second-person pronouns Reference to categories or ways of thinking about topics associated with a particular social group (e.g. 'and that's definitely not what you want to see when you go out on a Monday morning')
5	How are people in news items (either individually, or as groups or organisations) referred to?	Different ways of referring to the protagonist of the story (i.e. the person or group that the story is mainly about). List the different ways that the person (or group or organisation) in question is referred to. Then describe what effect you think is created by the choice of descriptions. (Example: 'Mr Michael Jones', 'a resident of North London', 'the former gambler and convict', 'friendly old man who feeds birds in the local park', 'this harmless eccentric', etc.). If you find this task difficult, try thinking of different descriptions that could have been used to describe the same person, group or organisation that would have created a different effect.
6	What about the register or style of the language used?	Use of an especially formal or colloquial register Density of idioms, reference to proverbs, etc. Amount of wordplay or verbal humour Types of adjective used to describe events or actions ('sudden', 'shocking', 'catastrophic', etc.)
7	Are there other voices embedded in the news story besides that of the journalist or news presenter?	Use of direct quotations, reported speech, or paraphrase Citation of authorities
8	What indicators are there of opinion or feeling towards the topic?	Use of evaluative vocabulary ('outstanding', 'disastrous') Terms of praise or abuse ('political loser') Expressions indicating doubt or reservation ('perhaps', 'might', 'could on balance be')

9	With broadcast media, how are the newscasters used to anchor presentation? How do they hand over to contributing journalists, to contributions from experts, to other opinion-formers, and to each other?	Reference to where news utterances are being made ('here in the studio', 'we have a report from . . .', 'over to our correspondent in . . .', ' live by satellite') Use of first names in addressing journalists contributing to news packages Use of *vox pop* compilations (i.e. quick-fire series of short snapshots of opinion on a topic already discussed, without name captions)
	Locating the news story in its social context	*Evidence to look for*
10	What do you think makes the particular story of interest to the likely audience?	Reference to values, interests or agendas of particular social groups Mention of particular traditions, precedents, or parallels
11	Does the particular way of reporting the story reflect any identifiable set of attitudes, values or opinions in the society?	Mention of different ways the topic might be viewed (e.g. reference to different sensibilities, specific points of view, competing interests, need for balance)
12	Does the story reflect any specific political or commercial interest?	References to particular products or suppliers, or statements encouraging or endorsing some political course of action
13	Is the coverage biased?	Fair representation of opposing sides of issues Under-emphasis or over-emphasis of some aspect of an event Use of hostile interviewing techniques Use of terms or phrases in connection with one party in a dispute, or images and production treatments (e.g. camera angles, music) known to influence audience opinion Emotive vocabulary

14	Could there be a more general, 'campaigning' or 'agenda-setting' dimension of the story: some way it seeks to persuade or influence the viewer or reader towards a different attitude than the one they hold already?	Connection between the story and what you take to be prevailing issues or priorities of government and other social bodies (e.g. big companies, charity sector, etc.)
15	If the story covers something seemingly secret or private, is there a legitimate public interest in, or right to know about, what the story reports?	Indications of the story being treated as an example or illustration of some wider theme, perhaps illuminating a wider social question, rather than being told for interest or entertainment in its own right

This table presents informally many of the key themes investigated in more detail in critical linguistics and critical discourse analysis (CDA). To follow up such questions and topics, see our suggestions for further reading related to this thread. Critical studies of news typically explore what point of view news events are seen from, as well as their susceptibility to bias. Other studies consider how media discourse, including news and documentary, engages with readers and viewers in ways that reflect and promote particular ideological points of view. A number of key themes are illustrated in the readings from Graddol and Fairclough we include in units D5 and D7. News discourse has been an especially important field for such critical approaches. This is because news is where media discourse exerts its greatest influence on our understanding of how the world is, what our place in it is, and where we might look for authoritative information and opinion about the world we live in.

Adverts

Advertising offers a thought-provoking contrast with news. Its main function appears to be to persuade consumers to buy, achieving this partly by differentiating brands from one another in the marketplace that may not have obvious differences. At the same time, advertising conveys information, so that consumers know what is available, who makes it, and where and how they can get it. News and advertising both contain elements of information and of persuasion, or rhetoric. But they do so in very different balances.

In the contemporary media environment, advertising takes many different forms (for discussion, see Myers, 1994., and for a classification of different ways that language relates to products and services, see Durant, 2009). Interaction between information and persuasion cuts across all of them. But such interaction is complicated by the many different styles of discourse that advertising adopts. Advertising space and advertising time are expensive. So people who buy media slots concentrate on value

for money. They select slots where an advertising message will be favourably associated with a genre or format, and will reach an audience considered suitable for the particular product or service. With commercial radio and TV, media purchasers prioritise programmes watched or listened to by large audiences, or alternatively by specialised, 'niche' audiences). They also compete for (and sponsor) results from searches using search engines. As a result, there is a commercial as well as creative logic in advertising styles. That logic requires interpreters to find associations and puzzle out meanings for themselves: to produce a lot of product-related meaning from short, concentrated input of words and images. Many advertisements, and a lot of packaging material, are designed to elicit consumer inferences. Claims about products that are actively constructed by consumers for themselves may be more persuasive than claims stated by the vendor. Advertising styles in many countries – though by no means all – have responded to this extra value of inferred messages by moving towards greater message condensation and indirectness.

Investigating advertising discourse in the contemporary multimedia environment must also take into account complex interaction between images, sounds and written text (see unit A7, and the reading from Kress and van Leeuwen in unit D7). Such investigation needs to connect with wider social questions:

- How are consumer desires created?
- Do consumers react to advertising on a reasoned, logical basis, or are they motivated by other kinds of desire and aspiration?
- Are consumers entertained by advertising, or manipulated by it?

As regards the verbal discourse of advertising, three topics stand out: the register (or language 'style') of advertising; the suggestiveness or connotations created by advertising language; and specific claims about products and services that adverts convey. We look briefly at each, and explore examples further in unit C5.

The register of advertising

A large number of books and articles have focused on the distinctive styles of advertising language (e.g. Cook, 1992; Goddard, 2002; Leech, 1966; O'Donnell and Todd, 1980). Such studies draw attention to different kinds of language that typically make up a promotion: characteristics of the brand name; of the headline, tagline or strapline that often offers memorable endorsement of the product or values associated with it; and other descriptive material (such as price information, safety warnings, or stipulations that terms and conditions apply) that accompanies more obviously rhetorical copy.

Analyses of the language of advertising have often focused on creative use of conventionally poetic devices (see the extract from Myers in unit D5, and Montgomery et al., 2006 for exposition). Such devices include:

- Sound patterning, such as rhyme and consonance ('Beanz Meanz Heinz') and alliteration ('The salon secret for silky shine').
- Parallelism: the creation of meaning by partial similarity coupled with striking contrast. A structure (such as a phrase or sentence type) is repeated with

contrasting elements in prominent positions. An example is the tagline of an advert for Sunny Delight drinks, 'I found a way to be a good mother and still be a great mom'. Here, the parallelism is 'be a [A] [B] . . . be a [C] [D]'. The relatively neutral adjective of approval 'good' contrasts with informal 'great'; and formal and distant 'mother' contrasts with affectionate 'mom'. Overall, the parallelism conveys the idea that it is simultaneously possible to perform the guardian function of a responsible parent and also occupy the position of an approachable friend.

Using the description given in the Sunny Delight example as a template, analyse the following similar examples:

1 'The future's bright, the future's Orange'.
2 'Your pictures. Our passion' (tagline of a UK camera supplier, Jessops).
3 'Too old to fight . . . too proud to beg' (tagline of an advert seeking donations to the Gurkha Welfare Trust, a charity supporting ex-Gurkha (Nepalese) soldiers facing hardship in retirement without a pension despite having served in the British Army).

A summary of the formal characteristics and function of verbal devices in advertising language can be found in the extract from Myers in unit D5.

The suggestiveness of advertising language

Within the overall texture of advertising language, some features of creative copy evoke a world, or lifestyle, that the advertiser wishes to associate with the product or service. Advertising often communicates such messages obliquely. It uses mini-stories or dramas, or exoticised images, irony and indirect humour, rather than directly stating claims about the product. With such language, it is the connotation as much as the stated meaning that has the power to attract and entertain. (The concept of connotation is explained in unit B7, where we discuss how words and images produce meaning together.)

Language used in this way makes no specific claims about the product or service being advertised, such as what it weighs, how much it costs, or what it is capable of. In this respect, it doesn't offer any specific information. It merely conveys or evokes an overall impression of the product's attractiveness.

Specific claims about products and services

Some advertising language *does* make specific claims. It states or directly implies information about the product or service. A 'claim' is a statement that can be substantiated (i.e. shown to be true) or demonstrated to be false, misleading or deceptive. What is known as a 'trade puff', by contrast, states attributes of the product in such a highly favourable light that it is considered to be merely exaggerated praise (it puffs

up, or inflates, the quality of what is being sold with rhetorical praise). Such language is thought typical of anyone engaged in selling, and is considered unlikely to be taken literally or interpreted as a truth-claim by a potential consumer. Examples include 'best ever', 'unique', 'stunning', 'fantastic', 'outstanding' and 'excellent'.

The idea of limiting advertising claims to specific and defensible statements that can be substantiated plays an important part in how advertising is regulated in many countries. The advertiser is held responsible not only for claims that are explicitly stated but also for further claims that might be reasonably inferred by a consumer. The only specific claims for which the advertiser is not held responsible are ones that are obviously false, or which are presented in a joking way. Such claims are considered unlikely to be entertained seriously by any reasonable consumer.

The idea of a specific advertising claim – and the principle that claims can be formulated in a scale of relative strength – can be seen in the following example of a slogan used as part of a newspaper advert for a shampoo (Pantene Pro-V). The advert communicates a carefully worded claim embedded in the wider marketing appeal that consumers will be attracted by a shampoo that can restore hair damage.

> Rewind time. Helps fight the signs of up to two years' hair damage in just one wash.

What exactly is being claimed here? We might say that it is,

> Use of this product 'rewinds time'

This highly general (figurative) claim only becomes something that might be substantiated, however, in the follow-up text:

> One use of this product ('one wash') reverses two years of hair damage

But this is not exactly what is claimed. Rather,

> One use of this product fights to reverse two years of hair damage

Or more exactly, what is communicated is the weaker claim that,

> One use of this product *helps to* fight to reverse two years of hair damage

Yet it is not precisely 'damage' that is fought. Rather, it is 'signs' of damage:

> One use of this product helps to fight to reverse the *signs of* two years of hair damage

And the time period, if we look carefully, is not in fact two years but an indeterminate shorter period:

> One use of this product helps to fight to reverse the signs of *up to* two years of hair damage

In this carefully crafted example of advertising copy, we see a scale of *possible* claims. Advertisers word their claims as strongly as can be substantiated but sufficiently carefully that they avoid misleading or over-claiming. Geis (1982) analyses TV advertising of the 1970s. He shows how many advertising claims are inferred, by explaining them in terms of accounts of inference developed in pragmatics. Preston (1994) shows in great detail how advertisers calculate, substantiate and defend claims of different strengths.

TELLING STORIES

B6

Developing our earlier account of the pervasiveness of story structure in media news, documentaries and public information videos, we discuss work that brings analysis of narrative structures to bear on various kinds of media text. We

- consider conventional story patterns and how their characteristic features influence perceptions of what makes a narrative a 'narrative',
- offer a brief overview of the historical development of models of storytelling, and
- examine two important, functional models of narrative, before applying such models to media examples in unit C6.

Once upon a time . . .

Forster's literary model of narratives, discussed in A6, highlights features commonly associated with narrative structure. It helps us understand how narratives work. But there is another major source of information about story perceptions: formulaic oral narratives in many different cultures provide prototypes of storytelling, and invite investigation of how repeated narrative structures offer a resource for improvisation.

Vladimir Propp's (1928) *Morphology of the Folktale* provides a model of storytelling based on a limited number of actions that can occur in a story. Propp analysed a corpus of 115 Russian fairytales. He paid particular attention to the syntagmatic (or linear, successive) structure of these texts. Propp found that the fairytales he was examining involved permutations of 31 possible actions or 'functions', that develop around seven character types or roles. Permutations of these 'raw materials' account for the inclusion and combination of actions and characters into stories that form the recognisable body of Russian folktales. Here is a list of Propp's possible actions or functions (adapted from Toolan, 2001: 17–18):

1 One of the members of a family absents himself from home. (An extreme exponent of this function of 'absenting' is where the parents have died.)
2 An interdiction is addressed to the hero.
3 The interdiction is violated.
4 The villain makes an attempt at reconnaissance.
5 The villain receives information about his victim.

6 The villain attempts to deceive his victim in order to take possession of him or of his belongings.
7 The victim submits to deception and thereby unwittingly helps his enemy.
8 The villain causes harm or injury to a member of a family (defined as 'villainy').
8a One member of a family either lacks something or desires to have something (defined as 'lack').
9 Misfortune or lack is made known; the hero is approached with a request or command; he is allowed to go or he is despatched.
10 The seeker agrees to or decides upon counteraction.
11 The hero leaves home.
12 The hero is tested, interrogated, attacked, etc., which prepares the way for his receiving either a magical agent or helper.
13 The hero reacts to the actions of the future donor.
14 The hero acquires the use of a magical agent.
15 The hero is transferred, delivered or led to the whereabouts of an object of search.
16 The hero and the villain join in direct combat.
17 The hero is branded.
18 The villain is defeated.
19 The initial misfortune or lack is liquidated.
20 The hero returns.
21 The hero is pursued.
22 The rescue of the hero from pursuit.
23 The hero, unrecognised, arrives home or in another country.
24 A false hero presents unfounded claims.
25 A difficult task is proposed to the hero.
26 The task is resolved.
27 The hero is recognised.
28 The false hero or villain is exposed.
29 The hero is given a new appearance.
30 The villain is punished.
31 The hero is married and ascends the throne.

The seven roles identified by Propp are basic character types or roles involved in folk tales. When compared with stories in very different traditions, such as contemporary films, soaps or documentaries, such persistent characters' types are often thought to provide archetypes or stereotypes of characters, both fictional and factional.

- ❑ villain,
- ❑ donor/provider,
- ❑ hero (seeker or victim),
- ❑ dispatcher,
- ❑ helper,
- ❑ princess (+ father), and
- ❑ false hero.

Think of a soap you are familiar with. It is very likely that you can map its characters, their roles and the unfolding actions of the plot onto Propp's framework. Simpson (2004) discusses Disney's *The Jungle Book* in terms of the Proppian model. He also maps in detail the film version of *Harry Potter and the Philosopher's Stone* in terms of Propp's list of functions. Interestingly, Simpson shows however that not all of Propp's narrative functions are found. Those that are present, he notes, 'are slightly out of kilter with the sequence developed by Propp' (2004: 74).

Many models of how narratives work have developed from Propp's work, in fields ranging from structuralism in anthropology through to literary and media studies. Particularly influential among those models has been Roland Barthes's (1977) account of different 'levels' operating in stories, which acquire meaning in relationship to each other. Barthes outlined the following characteristics as being present in any given story (Barthes, 1977a):

1 a basic sequence of events,
2 a dialectic of enigma followed by reversal, followed by resolution/closure,
3 a set of connections between the story and the world outside the story: realism and representativeness,
4 themes and contrasts which give the story significance (e.g. good and evil; the difficult route to true love; rescuing success out of failure), so that the story takes on a value in explaining things or persuading people about how the world is or how to behave), and
5 symbolic questions of identity and sexuality (Barthes thought that stories have a psychoanalytic dimension in which we play out dramas about ourselves as sexualised beings).

 **Activity**

Media stories can be analysed using Barthes's list of characteristics.

- ❏ Look at a weekly gossip/celebrity magazine (one that is well known for celebrity scandals, for example). Analyse at least three leading stories into the categories provided in Barthes's list. How many of his features are you able to find? Do different amounts of interpretation come into your allocation of various aspects of the story to particular categories?
- ❏ Develop a checklist of your own for each story, based on your experience of using Barthes's list. Include in your list all features that you consider to be common to all three stories. Is there an underlying structure for gossip-type stories? Are they formulaic in how they are presented?
- ❏ Try linking some of the thinking about narrative structure we have introduced here to the criteria of newsworthiness introduced in a different context in unit B5. What is it about gossip-type stories that makes them newsworthy? Could there be a deeper link between newsworthiness and narrative structure?

Personal narratives as storytelling modes

One area of storytelling found throughout public media output is the personal narrative. Part of the power and influence of media, we have pointed out, is an ability to project personal concerns as topics of public interest. Personal narratives encapsulate first-person experiences. In doing so, they provide the human interest condition necessary for reporting events in story form in the first place. (See A6 for discussion of human interest as a necessary condition of narrative in relation to our 'The King died and then the Queen died of grief' example.) Newspapers and magazines pay large sums of money to secure interviews from celebrities and public figures whose private lives are considered of public interest (e.g. the fees paid out by *Hello* magazine). In such cases, the more famous the narrator and the more scandalous, tragic, shocking or damaging the story, the better the story will be in terms of readership and sales. First-person accounts by 'ordinary' people are also deemed to be newsworthy, however, if they can be presented as providing information about events that are of public interest or concern. 'Survivor stories' associated with major world events are a prime case of this. (We consider some examples of survivor stories in C6.)

A personal narrative has the following general properties:

- the narrator is the protagonist,
- the first person pronoun 'I' is used,
- it is spoken – in media this can be reported and found in written forms,
- the events actually happened,
- events are temporally ordered, i.e. they are told in the sequence that they happened: 'this happened then this and then this . . .',
- it uses past tense to record events in the past, and
- it uses the present historic: 'I'm walking down the street and this person comes up to me and says . . .'

But what function do personal narratives serve? What is it that they say? Personal narratives seem intuitively to fulfil a number of functions:

- By making experiences memorable, stories that relate experiences allow them to be passed on. The personal narrative plays a part in our socialisation.
- We construct and reconstruct our identity, and the presumed identities of others, through reported experience (e.g. as victim, hero, etc.). The personal narrative provides scope for identity construction and self-presentation in a desired light (sometimes this function is called 'self-aggrandisement', Labov and Waletzky, 1967).
- In relating an experience, we can confirm our status as a good, funny or entertaining storyteller. The personal narrative displays performance abilities.
- Experiences, especially shocking, tragic or unusually dramatic ones, can be difficult to imagine but are nevertheless of significant human interest. The personal narrative provides insights that would otherwise not be publicly known or felt.
- Telling and exchanging stories is part of the fabric of social life. The personal narrative is a resource to be used in managing personal interaction.

A sociolinguistic model of personal narratives

One influential model of narratives that is widely viewed as providing a useful framework for analysing personal stories was developed by the sociolinguists Labov and Waletzky (1967). Labov and Waletzky developed their model of narratives as part of a study of linguistic variation in Black English Vernacular (BEV) in New York. They asked their informants to recall 'danger of death' and 'fight' stories as a means of collecting large amounts of speech data that they needed for other purposes. Analysis of their informants' personal experience stories, however, revealed structural and linguistic patterns in the story data that they had not anticipated. From this, they developed their narrative model, which consists of six stages or 'schemas' (see Table B6.1). Each schema is said to serve a particular function:

Table B6.1 Labov and Waletzky's narrative schema model (adapted from Labov, 1972; Labov and Waletzky, 1967)

	Schema or stage	*Function*
1	Abstract	signals what the story is about
2	Orientation	provides the who?, what?, when? and where? of the story; usually descriptive
3	Complicating action	provides the what happened? part of the story and is the core narrative category
4	Evaluation	provides the so what? element and highlights what is interesting to narrator or addressee; reveals how participants in the story felt
5	Resolution	provides the what finally happened? element of the story
6	Coda	signals the end of the story and may be in the form of a moral or lesson

In Labov's (1972) later analysis of story corpora, the fourth schema or stage of this model ('evaluation' and evaluative strategies) was found to permeate the narrative as a whole, rather than being found at a single point. A 'fully formed' narrative is nevertheless generally described, according to this model, as one which has evidence of all six schemas in the order presented above. The schemas provide a way of linking formal evidence in the narration itself (e.g. choice of words and different ways of saying things) to higher-order structures in how stories develop and what social functions they serve. On the strength of the degree of structure they perceive in narrative, Labov and Waletzky conclude that narrative is 'one method of recapitulating past experience by matching a verbal sequence of clauses to the sequence of events which actually occurred' (1967: 20).

To illustrate how personal narratives connect these different levels together, a number of examples of first-person accounts of traumatic experiences are presented in unit C6, in the sub-genre of personal experience stories increasingly known as 'survivor stories'.

B7 ANCHORING VISUAL MEANINGS

In this unit we extend our discussion of the meaning-making impact of verbal captions and voice-over on the images they accompany. We

- outline Roland Barthes's concepts of 'relay' and 'anchorage' ('ancrage'), relating these concepts to other ways of understanding how words and images combine with each other, and
- adapt Barthes's (1977b) framework to take account of the fact that captions are kinds of unattributed utterance or speech event.

Captions, images and meaning

Captions serve a general function. They 'anchor' the meaning of an image. Without a caption, an image might be read in many different ways. The meaning of the image may even overspill any specific reading at all, leaving the image with either any meaning or no particular meaning at all. Perhaps we would enjoy images to which we can give almost any meaning. Barthes, by contrast, claimed that captions are pervasive and influential largely because we would be traumatised by images with no directed meaning imposed on them.

Barthes's discussion of *how* captions anchor meaning, in his essay 'Rhetoric of the image' (Barthes, 1977c), has been highly influential in media studies. It has been less discussed in linguistic approaches to media. Here we look at two brief extracts. Early in the essay, Barthes asks if there is 'always textual matter in, under, or around the image?' His answer is this:

> In order to find images given without words, it is doubtless necessary to go back to partially illiterate societies; to a sort of pictographical state of the image. From the moment of the appearance of the book, the linking of text and image is frequent, though it seems to have been little studied from a structural point of view. What is the signifying structure of 'illustration'? Does the image duplicate certain of the informations [sic] given in the text by a phenomenon of redundancy or does the text add fresh information to the image? The problem could be posed historically as regards the classical period with its passion for books with pictures. [. . .] Today, at the level of mass communications, it appears that the linguistic message is indeed present in every image: as title, caption, accompanying press article, film

> dialogue, comic strip balloon. Which shows that it is not very accurate to talk of a civilization of the image – we are still, and more than ever, a civilization of writing, writing and speech continuing to be the full terms of the informational structure. In fact, it is simply the presence of the linguistic message that counts, for neither its position nor its length seem to be pertinent (a long text may only comprise a single global signified, thanks to connotation, and it is this signified which is put in relation with the image). What are the functions of the linguistic message with regard to the (twofold) iconic message?
>
> (Barthes, 1977c: 38)

What Barthes calls a 'signified' here, following the distinction between signifier and signified made by de Saussure (1983), is the concept associated with a particular signifier. Together, signifier and signified make up a sign. 'Signified' is accordingly a broad term for meaning, within which a number of more precise distinctions are drawn in semantics and pragmatics. Barthes's interest in the 'signified' here is that it can be of several different kinds, or can function at several different levels. An image can show something (by depicting it); it can make you feel something (because of associations that surround whatever it shows); and it can say something (by combining what it shows and what it suggests in a way calculated to lead the viewer to an anticipated response). More technically, Barthes identifies

- a denotative level, designating or describing what is visible in the image, and
- a connotative level, which is suggestive or evocative of culturally attached meanings that accumulate around what is shown.

With most photographic images, denotation is fairly straightforward. The image shows particular things that can be recognised, because of visual likeness (the visual image is iconic, in consisting of signs that visually resemble what they mean). Connotation, on the other hand, will vary to some extent from interpreter to interpreter, and from case to case. It depends partly on where you look from, when, with what beliefs and attitudes in mind.

Barthes's main suggestion is that photo captions constrain and direct meaning in two ways: by means of anchorage and relay. Anchorage has been most discussed in media studies, and we look at this concept below. But it is easier to begin with relay.

Barthes suggests that the relay function is most evident in cartoons and comic strips. In these linguistic–pictorial forms, text and image work together as fragments of an overall structure: that of an ongoing story. What is shown happening in the image, and what is said in the words, may differ from each other. But both move the story forwards, hence the term 'relay'. Relay, Barthes suggests, is not particularly common in the fixed image. Story, if it exists at all in a fixed image, is implied. But relay is important in film. Meanings that are not depicted in the image at all may still be introduced by means of the dialogue. Progression in a story depends in this way on an interplay between image and dialogue.

Anchorage has been more discussed but requires more clarification. Barthes suggests that for any image an accompanying linguistic caption serves 'to *fix* the floating

chain of signifieds in such a way as to counter the terror of uncertain signs'. At the level of denotation described above,

> the text replies – in a more or less direct, more or less partial manner – to the question: *what is it*? The text helps to identify purely and simply the elements of the scene and the scene itself; it is a matter of a denoted description of the image . . . Shown a plateful of something (in an *Amieux* advertisement), I may hesitate in identifying the forms and masses; the caption (*'rice and tuna fish with mushrooms'*) helps me to choose the *correct level of perception*, permits me to focus not simply my gaze but also my understanding.
>
> (Barthes, 1977c: 39)

At the level of connotation described above (what Barthes in another context calls the level of the 'symbolic message'), the caption

> no longer guides identification but interpretation, constituting a kind of vice which holds the connoted meanings from proliferating, whether towards excessively individual regions (it limits, that is to say, the projective power of the image) or towards dysphoric values. An advertisement (for *d'Arcy* preserves) shows a few fruits scattered around a ladder; the caption (*'as if from your own garden'*) banishes one possible signified (parsimony, the paucity of the harvest) because of its unpleasantness and orientates the reading towards a more flattering signified (the natural and personal character of fruit from a private garden); it acts here as a counter-taboo, combatting the disagreeable myth of the artificial usually associated with preserves.
>
> (Barthes, 1977c: 39–40)

Put more generally, captions direct the meanings of images away from 'dysphoric values' (i.e. unwanted, potentially distasteful or traumatic meanings) and selectively towards other meanings. The linguistic text

> *directs* the reader through the signifieds of the image, causing him to avoid some and receive others; by means of an often subtle *dispatching*, it remote-controls him towards a meaning chosen in advance. In all these cases of anchorage, language clearly has a function of elucidation, but this elucidation is selective, a metalanguage applied not to the totality of the iconic message but only to certain of its signs. [. . .].
>
> (Barthes, 1977c: 40)

Activity 

Barthes's writing can be dense and allusive; and we have only presented selected points from his thinking about linguistic captions that accompany images. But judging from the account we have offered,

- ❑ Is Barthes right about unaccompanied images being potentially traumatic? What kind of trauma could he have in mind? What would count as evidence of finding an image 'traumatic' because its meaning is uncertain?
- ❑ How is Barthes suggesting that a caption narrows or limits an image's potential for unbridled meaning? What do the words of a caption have to do to achieve this?
- ❑ How close, physically, does accompanying language need to be to what is shown in the image, if it is to be involved in this kind of close interaction with it? For example, is there a significant difference, in terms of 'anchorage', between
    - a caption printed directly under an image;
    - an image printed opposite a story on a facing page;
    - a press article that simply comes out around the same time but seems to be about the same topic that the image depicts?

Captions and speech events

Overall, Barthes suggests that captions help us to pick out a correct level of perception for an image. They direct the range of possible connotations we might access for what is shown towards a particular symbolic interpretation.

Can we be more specific than Barthes is about the possible different forms that verbal text in the caption might take? Barthes himself never said much about what form the anchoring caption takes. More recent developments in language studies, however, might allow us to be more specific about what kind of utterance the caption is.

In many cases, it is not just the image that can seem '*un*-anchored'. The words of the caption also seem unanchored. They are presented in an unattributed way, as a speech event without a speaker, addressee, or context. We should ask:

- ❑ Who do we imagine is saying the words in the caption?
- ❑ Does the imagined speaking voice originate within the image, like a speech or thought bubble in a cartoon? Or,
- ❑ Is the caption an implied voice of a viewer of the image, commenting on what they see in front of them?

In practice, the caption can be either – and creative exploitation of the uncertainty is also possible.

Activity 

Look at the image in Figure B7.1, a photo that could come from any family album. Five captions are given, any one of which could be used in a suitable context to accompany the photograph. Each would create a slightly different meaning for the image. Describe as precisely as you can *how* each of the suggested captions leads a reader/viewer to interpret the picture. You should focus on linguistic features of each caption. Ask yourself: what kind of utterance is this? *Whose* utterance is it? How does register, or the speech act that the caption forms, or pronouns and other deictics affect the likely meaning that a viewer will give to the image?

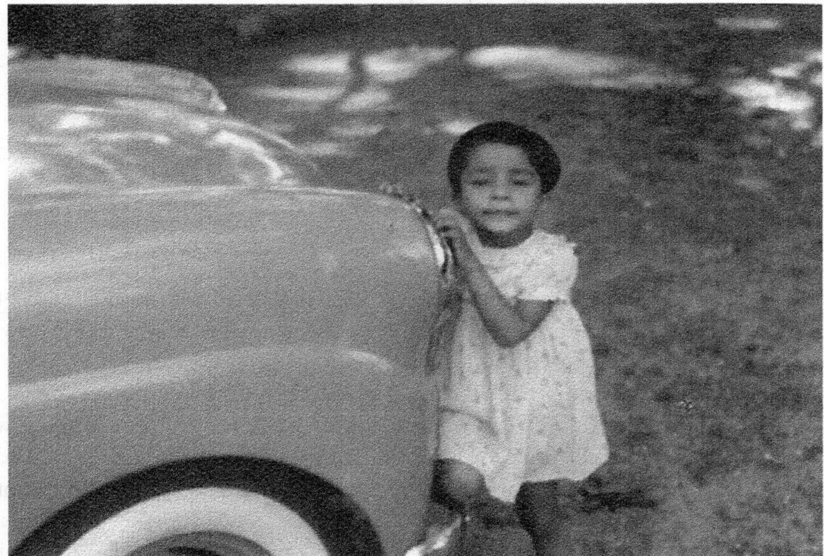

Figure B7.1 'Child and car' image and activity

1 'The photographer's daughter at home in our compound as a young girl'.
2 'Which way do I turn if I want to reverse into the drive?'
3 'Half a century ago not everyone had a car but many people who didn't wished they had'.
4 'Kottayam, Kerala. India, 19 August 1957'.
5 'There's no reverse gear, the past is another country'.

Identify as precisely as you can what object or feature in the image is picked out by particular words in the caption. Where no specific object or feature is identified, decide how what Barthes calls the 'correct level of perception' is achieved by other techniques (e.g. use of a general term that can be connected with something shown in the image; evocation of a particular mood, period or culture, etc.).

Is precise description of captions possible?

The 'speech event' dimension added here to Barthes's description of words and images is not in competition with his overall insight: that captions direct us towards some 'correct' level of perception of verbal–visual meaning. Rather, it opens up the other possibilities as regards description and analysis. There may for instance be a limited number of possibilities as regards *how* the words of a caption narrow down the range of possible interpretations. So far, there is no established model (or simple, semiotic grammar) as regards how captions function.

Activity

Look through a pile of newspapers and/or magazines. Make a selection of photographic images that have captions, and draw up a list of them. The process of giving a name to each photo in creating your list so that you can refer to them (most likely names based on their denotative meaning) will be interesting. Compare the sorts of names you give, for example, with names you tend to find in a clipart folder, or as the search names given to thumbnails online, or prints in a picture-library. Now go through the captions of the photos in their original context and decide which of the major types of caption in Table B7.1 is used in each case.

Table B7.1 Types of caption

1 The caption picks out and labels objects or details in the image. It provides information, disambiguates, and identifies things or people denoted (Barthes's example of the *Amieux* advertisement, above).

2 The caption provides a place and date for *the creation* of the image: where and when it was taken. In this way the caption indicates some sort of 'origin'. It locates the moment of the image being taken. There is one caption of this kind provided for the 'family album' photo above.

3 The caption identifies the genre or function of the image (e.g. as an advert or promotional image; as a document in a given historical archive, etc.). This is an elaboration of origin or source.

4 The caption indicates a *general* phenomenon of which the image presented is a specific case or concrete illustration. There is a caption of this kind provided for the 'family album' photo above.

5 The caption evokes some general quality or value *implied by* the image. It may, for example, convey evaluative associations. In doing so, it puts a positive or negative spin on what can be seen in the image. This is Barthes's example of the advertisement for *d'Arcy* preserves.

6 The caption makes reference to something *else*, not depicted but typically associated with what is shown in the image. The relation between what is shown and the topic of the caption involves a bridging inference.

7 The caption puts words into the mouth of a protagonist depicted within the image (like an implied speech bubble or thought bubble). There is a caption of this kind provided for the 'family album' photo above.

8 The caption offers a response to, explicit comment on, or rebuttal of some 'thought' likely to be triggered by the image in the viewer. In doing this, the caption seems in dialogue with a meaning the viewer is likely already to have attributed to the image. Commonly with photographs this kind of caption comment reflects a kind of wisdom that comes with hindsight. There is a caption of this kind provided for the 'family album' photo above.

The different categories listed on the previous page overlap in various ways, and they might not all be needed in a miniature semiotic grammar of captions. How many – and which – categories would be needed depends largely on how precisely we identify the speaker or utterance of the caption (the photographer, someone in the image, a viewer who has just looked at it, etc.). It also seems to depend on how many sub-divisions we introduce into the idea of interpretive inference.

Because of the important role of inference in interpretation that these examples already begin to show, it would be more precise to describe the categories listed here as the beginnings of not so much a grammar of photographic captions as a framework of pragmatic interpretation.

Activity 

Below we give a checklist of practical questions prepared for students interested in captions by the curator of a museum close to the campus where one of the authors works: the Church Farm Museum, in Hendon, North London (Root, 2008). The list was drawn up as a guide to how captions combine with images in a display that would be practically useful to a trainee curator writing captions for their first exhibition:

1 Is it necessary?
2 What should it be about?
3 Who is it aimed at?
4 How much information should it give?
5 How long should it be?
6 In what typeface should it be?
7 In what format should it be?
8 Where in the display should it be placed?

- ❑ Which categories of caption in the list used in the previous activity seem most suited for use in museum exhibitions?
- ❑ How would using different categories of caption (in the list used in the previous activity) affect the overall seriousness or attitude with which a visitor would be likely to approach an item of displayed material?

COARSENESS AND INCIVILITY IN BROADCAST TALK

B8

This unit widens our discussion of the boundaries of language in the media begun in unit A8. We

- consider historical changes in styles of broadcast talk, especially in the representation of different accents, dialect and speech registers, and
- explore the relationship between increased access to and participation in media and claims of 'coarseness' or 'incivility' in media discourse.

Contrasting voices

We can usefully approach the public circulation of different voices, and objections made to the 'offensiveness' of new or different voices in the media, by considering the traditional idea of broadcasting as a form of 'public address' or 'speaking to the nation' (see unit B1). That style of public discourse contrasts dramatically with more conversational styles of contemporary media talk, such as chat shows and phone-in programmes.

How do we characterise the difference between these contrasting styles? Consider, as a striking example, how a state occasion or ceremonial event is covered on radio or television. If you listen to radio or television coverage of such an event from an earlier period (e.g. in a UK context, from the coronation of Elizabeth II in 1953 until about the funeral of Winston Churchill in 1965), you are transported into a different world of media speech.

On radio and television at least until substantial changes in styles of broadcasting during the 1960s, such coverage tended

- to be framed as being of automatic importance to the media audience. Little obvious effort was made to involve the audience by emphasising angles of personal engagement or interest, or to empathise with the viewer or listener, or to link the audience in to the event.
- to use presenters chosen for their class persona and accent, who spoke a standard form of English ('BBC English'). The media persona of such presenters appeared to reflect the dignity of the occasion and to mediate that occasion for a wide but deferential audience.
- to be narrated at a relatively slow tempo and in a formal style. Where interviews were included in the broadcast coverage, questioning of interviewees would be respectful, even deferential.

Roughly the same speech style was commonly adopted to create seriousness and authority in national news programmes on radio and television, as well as in documentary features.

Systems of state broadcasting differ. But a patrician sense of 'addressing the nation'

in this way has been a common means in radio and television broadcasting of symbolising national identity and authority or (from another point of view) of controlling public discourse. The style persists in some national broadcasting systems.

The style described above relates to a particular period in the development of television and radio (1950s and 1960s). It of course coexisted with other speech styles adopted in drama and light entertainment. Two major forces within the changing media environment, however – in tandem with broader social changes beyond it – have in many societies fundamentally shifted those earlier styles of what we can now see as a distinctive form of 'broadcast talk' (Scannell, 1991). Those two forces are commercial broadcasting and digital media.

Commercial broadcasting

Commercial broadcasting (in the UK, from the 1950s onwards but with a different history in many other countries) was more responsive, for commercial reasons, to audience ratings. Potential consumers had to be delivered to advertisers. Commercial broadcasters, accordingly, made extra efforts to maintain and expand audiences, and in doing so they pursued forms of closer identification with audience tastes, styles and aspirations. Audiences were increasingly conceived as consisting of different categories of consumer in a mixed audience demographic (see Kent, 1994, on measuring media audiences, and unit A3 on related techniques involved in creating media 'pseudo-intimacy'). This overall shift of approach resulted over a period of time in a wider range of programme formats, including (alongside traditional news, documentaries, features, drama and entertainment) many new kinds of quiz show, phone-in, make-over programme, reality TV format, and chat show. Sports coverage was extended with surrounding features. Slots associated with celebrity entertainment were increased. The significance of such shifts, and questions they raise about interaction between conventionally high culture and popular culture, are a major theme of media and cultural studies (Hall, 1997).

Digital media

Digital media, and an increased multichannel supply of broadcast programmes (by cable and satellite, as well as terrestrial broadcasting), has contributed to a further reshaping of approach and style. With more broadcast content available, new categories of people began to appear on radio and television, and no longer only in minor, comic or token roles. Alongside the established categories of newscaster, actor, politician, etc., more extensive opportunities became available for participation: as personality interviewees, quiz and game contestants, studio audiences, chat show contributors, video diary recordists, interviewees in documentaries and features, and others. The contemporary broadcast media environment as a result gives space to a far wider range of different voices than in previous periods. Media participants come from most walks of life, not only from a professional media establishment or class (though a small number of media professionals and celebrities continues to play a central role in broadcast output).

The fundamental shifts of broadcasting style brought about by these two cultural forces have enlarged the range of language varieties that must now be included as

'media discourse', or 'the language of media'. There are still, of course, especially 'authorised' voices (such as those of continuity announcers, newscasters, chat show hosts and others). At the same time, there are many other media participants, whose dialect, accent and preferred speech styles are *also* kinds of media discourse.

Understanding 'media discourse' is partly a matter of understanding how these various different voices interact with one another (O'Keeffe, 2006; Montgomery, 2007). It is also important to investigate how various voices and speech styles are distributed across the media environment at large, which is a symbolic field with its own language-variety hierarchies, preferred styles, and exclusions of certain styles of language from particular roles or positions (Bourdieu, 1991).

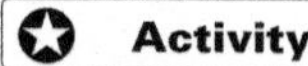

One mini-format that offers a test case of how different media voices interact with one another is the 'vox pop'. This audio or audio-visual genre (short for *vox populi*, or voice of the people) consists of a series of short speech clips inserted into a longer (usually news or documentary) feature. The package is compiled to illustrate the range of opinion on a particular topic. The vox pop can now appear to be a slightly old-fashioned style, given our comments above. It controls, and may even look down on, the participant voices it presents, putting them 'in brackets' as merely an embellishment of a dominant discourse (consisting of presenter and major interviewees) within which the vox pop is merely an interlude.

❑ Record several vox pop items from television or radio. Now construct an editorial justification for the following features of the 'vox pop' style:

  Vox pop contributors are not captioned, in the way that contributing media experts and correspondents are
  Each person's contribution is kept short and undeveloped
  Sometimes utterances are cut at a point of rising intonation, where it is likely that the comment being made actually continued
  Views represented by contributors seem chosen to be representative of a range of alternative positions, rather than to present each individual viewpoint or opinion coherently.

❑ What does a vox pop item constructed along these lines contribute to media treatment of a given topic or issue? What problems, if any, attach to using people's recorded utterances in this way?

Finally, note any further contrasts that you observe between the cluster of voices presented in the 'vox pop' and the surrounding, anchoring voice (of presenter, announcer, etc.).

Media representation of accent and dialect

The general fact of change in relation to participant roles in the media describes only the surface of a more complicated history.

Consider, for example, media representation of accent and dialect. In unit A2, we described how the 19th-century notion of 'standard pronunciation' of English (known as Received Pronunciation or RP) gave way in the course of the 20th century to a stronger perceived connection between standard pronunciation of English speech and broadcasting: so-called 'BBC English' in the UK and (with a rather different earlier history) 'Network Standard' in the US. We can now extend our account by highlighting a process through which the wider range of voices referred to above began to appear in British broadcasting.

Prominent roles in media output continued to be occupied by speakers whose accent approximated to RP for more than a generation. Gradual change as regards the range of accents represented in media discourse followed a similar historical path to representations of accent and dialect in literary fiction (Blake, 1981; Montgomery et al., 2006). In early novels, marked regional or class accents were typically presented only as the voices of minor characters, often for comic effect. This is paralleled in broadcast talk by the prevalence of marked regional class accents initially only in comedy and light entertainment. Over time, in literary works major (including sympathetic) characters and narrators (including reliable narrators) began to be presented who used non-standard varieties. On radio and television, the range of accents and dialects to be heard widened in a similar process between the 1950s and the turn of the century. The role of newscaster, except for regional news, survived longest as a preserve of more standardised forms of pronunciation. With the widening range of media formats, however, has come a far wider range of accents and dialects, across all genres. This shift – in which many or perhaps most UK youth programme presenters, children's programme presenters, and radio DJs now have marked class, regional or ethnic accents – partly reflects the changing make-up of the population. It also reflects a shifting sense of national identity and a social agenda of media inclusion. Media speech, at least in the UK, is no longer expected to provide a singular model of cultural authority. Rather, it now reflects the varied voices of a wide range of media participants and users.

Activity 

Compare the situation described here regarding the range of accents heard in UK broadcasting with broadcasting in another national language. Is there a similar range of accents typically heard in broadcast media in that language? Are there roles which are always occupied by a 'standard' accent? With languages that have a significant international reach, you will need to allow for other aspects of the historical and political relationship between the countries which use the same language (Jenkins, 2003).

Voices in a public conversation

Across broadcast output overall, the shift of style described above, from standardised varieties and formal register towards accent and dialect representation and informal registers, contributes to what has been called 'conversationalisation' (Fairclough, 1994, 1995a). Features of conversational style (including first names and an informal mode of address rather than honorifics, as well as a generally informal register) are adopted even where there is no actual conversation, either between speakers in the studio setting itself (e.g. with news and features) or between a media speaker and the listening or watching audience.

Contemporary styles of much broadcast talk function partly to level out hierarchical difference between media speakers and their audiences. The more informal register style and low-distance mode of address displace status differences with a model of interaction apparently between more equal conversational participants. In previous eras of broadcasting, presenters in many radio and TV formats would have adopted what amounts to a mediator or diplomat persona, bridging between different kinds of conversation or explaining points made in one conversation to participants in another. Presenters in equivalent roles now, by contrast, frequently position themselves as a sort of people's representative, asking questions that an audience might want asked and saying out loud what the audience privately thinks. The contemporary interviewing agenda is often one of puncturing pomposity, simplifying technicality, and trying to cut to the chase through circumlocution and deception.

For further discussion of interviewing styles, it is worth looking at examples of research on broadcast interviews in a Conversation Analysis framework (including the extract we present from Clayman and Heritage in D4). The shifts of interactional strategy described in this unit are partly changes of preferred register. But they can also have editorial implications. It is now more difficult, for example, to define borderlines between what should and shouldn't be said, and how.

Conflicting standards and attitudes

Complaints are often made about standards of broadcast talk. Some are about editorial judgement (e.g. whether a different line of questioning should have been taken by an interviewer, or whether too much time was spent discussing one particular topic). Many other complaints are couched in terms of incivility and coarseness.

What are complaints about incivility and coarseness actually about? They can sometimes sound like a straightforward case of resistance to language variation and change. You might therefore expect to find at least two contrasting responses to them, for and against:

- A general position urging acknowledgement of and acquiescence in use of new words, idioms and styles of discourse as a natural part of language change (cf. arguments frequently presented in radio interviews by the linguist David Crystal).
- Positions that advocate trying to control and resist language variation and change by prescribing and seeking to maintain established norms of usage, as attempted

by exponents of what Deborah Cameron has critiqued as 'verbal hygiene' (Cameron, 1995).

In some cases, this is how debate unfolds. But cultural controversies about media incivility and coarseness sometimes go in at least one major respect beyond this traditional complaint-type. They bring together questions about language change and questions about directions of social and political change.

Controversies about incivility and coarseness are certainly about what is called 'bad language'. As we note in unit C8, however, the folk category of 'bad language' is very broad. It runs from slang, swearing (taboo words) and poor grammar through to allegedly rough or outlandish accents. In unit C8, we look at issues surrounding swearing in particular. Sometimes controversy about bad language involves a more specific sense of what is bad, however: a general view of social conduct – 'verbal offensiveness' – which is not reducible to swearing, slang or getting your grammar wrong.

Controversy of this kind is no longer mainly about words, accents or constructions. It is concerned with complicated relations between admissible *words* (such as swear words) and admissible *voices* (e.g. what sort of speech style, and so what kind of person, is suitable for presenting or being part of a broadcast programme). Arguably, the problem of words and voices is also connected with a further boundary: that of admissible *ideas* (e.g. what opinions or views should be listened to and taken seriously).

There is a complicated relationship between these aspects of incivility. Without simplification to either of the two language change positions stated above, the US linguist Robin Lakoff (2003) has analysed the issues closely.

Media shouting in the marketplace of ideas

Lakoff begins by noting that two words figure prominently in talk about verbal behaviour in the public sphere: politeness and civility. These two words are often treated as if they mean the same, she suggests. She argues instead that there are important differences between them. 'Politeness', she notes, has been much discussed by linguists and other social scientists. 'Civility', on the other hand, has not really been examined.

'Polite', Lakoff suggests, involves positive consideration of others. 'Civil', by contrast, merely suggests mutual tolerance in a shared space, or observance of accepted social custom. Lakoff's distinction is important because, she notes, commentators often talk about a contemporary 'coarsening' of public discourse and behaviour – but without it ever being clear exactly what they feel is at stake.

'Incivility', for Lakoff, involves several different elements. It consists of claims for respectful naming of minorities and historically subordinated groups, by challenging negative or stereotypical names and replacing them with more respectful terms such as 'African American' rather than 'Negro'; 'woman' rather than 'girl' or 'lady'; 'Asian' rather than 'Oriental'; 'disabled' rather than 'handicapped'; and others. Paradoxically, it also involves extensive use of swearing, especially use of abusive epithets about other people and casual hate speech. Drawing on the idea of 'Agonism', as defined by Deborah Tannen (Tannen, 1998), Lakoff also notes a combative manner or pose that people frequently adopt and an increased tendency to escalate hostility towards one another

rapidly. What makes such behaviour significant, Lakoff suggests, is that it exacerbates social debate not only in day-to-day interaction but also inside major civil institutions (e.g. in government, law and the media). Such styles bring into high cultural situations apparently inappropriate vernacular terms of description and abuse (e.g. public use by politicians or lawyers of terms like 'bitch' and 'whore' towards one another).

Having described practices that she considers constitute coarseness and incivility, Lakoff puts such behaviour in a historical perspective. She suggests that 'fears of a new incivility reflect a persistent myth of a past golden age, a prelapsarian Eden where everyone was cordial to everyone' (Lakoff, 2003: 40). Any such period is a myth, she suggests. Rather, perceptions of emergent incivility – which seems to banish society from its imagined golden age – go hand-in-hand with increased diversity and social pluralism. Such perceptions are therefore related, though in complex ways, to democratic traditions and potentially to social progress. Drawing on a comparison she makes between the US and classical Rome, Lakoff illustrates her wider point by suggesting that

> For the Romans, as for us, incivility grew as differences developed between political factions, and as the previously disenfranchized gained political power (p. 41).

The opposite of diversity is homogeneity, and Lakoff argues that

> Geniality and consensus tend to flourish in societies that are homogeneous and in which all members share common interests; or, failing that, where only one group, itself homogeneous, has the ability or right to control public discourse (p. 41).

Given these points, the recent rise of incivility and coarseness that Lakoff notes might be because, for the US,

> the last thirty-five years have been a period when those who had for so long unilaterally controlled the language of public discourse – because they were the only ones with automatic access to that discourse, namely white middle- to upper-class men – have been gradually forced to cede that unilateral right and begin sharing language control and meaning-making with others: blacks, women, members of other classes. The 'political correctness' critiques of the late 1980s represent their dismay at this change and their attempt to keep it in check. The extension of meaning-making power leads to what is perceived as 'coarsening' (p. 42).

Lakoff considers that it is the present social settlement of acknowledged cultural diversity that is reflected in the new discourse styles. She argues that non-standard dialects, obscenities, and sometimes shocking traditions of narrative are all part of a new and necessary kind of 'shouting', because

> many of the groups achieving discourse power have never had it before. There are centuries, if not millennia, of resentment, for being shut out and shut up: can anyone blame the newly voiced if they shout, if they aren't totally willing to let bygones be bygones? Until women, blacks, and others begin to feel that the public

> floor is really, permanently theirs, the heat will not subside, nor, I suggest, should it. [. . .] The debate will become more heated as it gets more complicated. There is more to debate – issues that were formerly not even raised because they were not what the Old Guard was interested in (p. 42).

In the face of such challenges to conventional standards of public discourse, Lakoff confesses to mixed feelings. She doesn't retreat into either of the two general views of language change described at the beginning of this unit. She acknowledges that a golden age of mutual civility would be pleasant and reassuring. But she also recognises that a certain amount of abrasiveness is inevitable, and concludes:

> Abrasiveness is in part the result of the novelty of language rights for many of us. Once everyone gets used to having a stall in the marketplace of ideas, they will feel less of a need to be belligerent about demanding it (p. 43).

Activity 

As with our other summarised material and extracts, Lakoff's argument is more detailed than the points made here can reflect adequately. On the basis of what you have read, however, consider the following questions about her position:

- ❑ Are there social perspectives on this 'language and culture' debate that Lakoff fails to represent at all, or which in your view she fails to give due weight to?
- ❑ What counter-arguments might be made to Lakoff's points (and what examples could you give to support those counter-arguments)? For example, is there an argument to be made that tolerance of such verbal behaviour may even work against social integration or progress?
- ❑ The style of Lakoff's argument is that of an essay, perhaps even a polemical essay, rather than of reported research. Can you formulate specific linguistic claims based on what she says and some ways to investigate them further?

Semantic change and challenge

In the argument we have just discussed, Lakoff relates offensiveness, and a coarsening of discourse style in the media and public sphere, to new discourse roles occupied by participants in public and media debate. She relates the styles adopted by these participants to the emergence of new and sometimes difficult ideas in what she refers to, using a common metaphor from traditions of debating freedom of expression, as 'the marketplace of ideas'. She also puts the emergence of such discourse styles in a historical perspective.

At any given historical stage in a process of social change of the kind Lakoff refers to, abstract questions of language use are tangled with the powerful impact of

historically inherited words and styles. People get hurt by what others say to them, or about them, and are sometimes caught in a crossfire of verbal histories and loaded meanings. Different people can say the same words but with different meanings, and with very different social impact. One person's routine pause filler, or vocabulary item unconsciously acquired from peers and parents, is another person's gross obscenity. In unit 8, we take up the issue of obscenity and verbal offensiveness more directly.

LOOKING INTO THE FUTURE

B9

This unit examines alternative visions of our media language future, and how we can evaluate them. We

- introduce the idea of utopian and dystopian predictions about language and media,
- consider the idea of in-built progress associated with the impact of technological innovations on verbal communication, and
- encourage ways of thinking about media futures that take into account specific combinations of technology, language functions and cultural values.

Contrasting visions of media discourse futures

Analysing the past and the present, we have suggested in unit A9, offers a useful (and sometimes also cautionary) guide in making forecasts about the future. Such analyses provide historical parallels and indicate long-term directions of travel. Controversies regarding discourse, such as those surrounding taste, decency, accuracy and impartiality, can signal underlying forces and repeated points of tension, which may be projected forwards into as yet unknown future circumstances.

But what about predictions we already have (e.g. about our own rapidly changing 'information society' (Castells, 2000) or about the distinctiveness of Netspeak (Crystal, 2006)? Each of these is a frequent topic of discussion, even if predictions are often overtaken by events because of the rapidity of change.

Two contrasting emphases are worth identifying in predictions of the future. One emphasis is on progressive or evolutionary, including utopian, forecasts. In such accounts, communication technologies constantly provide stories of social improvement and human fulfilment. (The term 'Utopia' is the title of a speculative political essay, written by Sir Thomas More in the 16th century, describing a 'Utopia' or 'nowhere land' characterised by shared ownership of property, ready access to education, and religious tolerance; there has been a long tradition of works since, in many media, that imagine present desires as achieved in a future or hypothetical society.) A contrasting emphasis is that of dystopian visions. Such visions accentuate dangers or abhorrent characteristics of the present, projecting them forward into imagined future societies. As regards language and communication in particular, in such

dystopian visions communication machines typically displace the human and subjective dimensions of communication and social interaction. They may even take control of human interaction, like virtual-world avatars that no longer respond to mouse control.

Popular utopian visions often take as their point of departure the rapid growth and almost immeasurable potential of the internet (for discussion, see Crystal, 2006, including the extract given below in D9). Other prominent features of present communication accentuated in such accounts include multi-channel global entertainment by satellite, 24-hour rolling news, the popularity of wikis and blogging, social networking sites, and synchronous messaging. Such features, of course, are technological capabilities first of all, but they are open-ended in their social applications – hence the potential for speculation. What makes visions of the future that extend such features of contemporary communication 'utopian' is often some link they make between technological capabilities and social benefits related to one or more of the following:

- access to infinite amounts of information (information riches),
- ease of social interaction, including across time and at a distance (telecommunication blended with time travel),
- liberation of the self into creative, alternative online identities (virtual-world avatars), and
- freedom of expression and opinion (unrestricted free speech).

Dystopian visions take many different forms. They magnify risks and dangers in verbal communication as presently understood (e.g. the power of propaganda to mislead, or intrusions into the personal sphere by means of different kinds of surveillance), and they distort those risks and dangers into grotesque nightmares.

In George Orwell's *1984* (a dystopian vision of the future written in 1948, with the numbers of the year reversed), language is distorted into 'Newspeak'. As Orwell explains in a note at the end of the novel, Newspeak is

> the official language of Oceania and had been devised to meet the ideological needs of IngSoc, or English Socialism [. . .]. The purpose of Newspeak was not only to provide a medium of expression for the worldview and mental habits proper to the devotees of IngSoc, but to make all other modes of thought impossible. It was intended that when Newspeak had been adopted once and for all and Oldspeak forgotten, a heretical thought – that is, a thought diverging from the principles of IngSoc – should be literally unthinkable, at least so far as thought is dependent on words.
>
> (Orwell, 1949: 241)

Another classic dystopian vision in relation to language can be found in Ray Bradbury's novel *Fahrenheit 451* (1953). In Bradbury's novel, books (and so the record of human experience they contain) are at risk. The paper of which books consist is systematically set on fire by the state authorities, leaving citizens with no access to the mental worlds that books make possible. Instead, citizens of Bradbury's imagined

world have only instructional spoken messages emitted by a screen on the wall. The only form of resistance that Bradbury visualises is that of isolated pockets of citizens preserving human 'writing' as sections from books that individuals are able to memorise and repeat as speech.

Numerous other dystopian visions exist – and many others again are possible. You can imagine one, for example, based on the alienation of lives ruled by impenetrable or inflexible bureaucratic discourse. Another might be based on the pollution of social interaction by junk mail and spam (in 2004, it was estimated that 80 per cent of email communication was spam). Another again could be based on the consequences of a loss of public trust brought about by propaganda and calculated deception on the part of those who hold power, or by online scams and fraud.

Utopian and dystopian visions share some underlying features. In each type of vision, the benefits – or alternatively the obstacles standing in the way of such benefits – operate at different levels. They may involve an abstract or ideal philosophical value (such as access to pure truth, or what constitutes ideal 'mutual understanding' in communication). Or they may involve a celebration or criticism of already historically constructed social values, such as 'free speech' or the emergent value of open access to an archive of digitised information. Or they may involve opportunities and risks felt to exist in styles of behaviour (such as the advantages and disadvantages of adopting different identities online, or of never having any privacy, because of the reach of mobile, global communication technologies).

- ❑ Think of as many different aspects of verbal communication as you can (for this activity, it is probably best to think in terms of functions to begin with). Draw up a list of those aspects of communicative behaviour that might provide a basis – if suitably exaggerated – for a utopian or dystopian account.
- ❑ It is fairly easy to think of dystopias in which verbal communication is hijacked, controlled or restricted. It can be difficult, by contrast, to think of novels or films that explore a specifically communication utopia, rather than an imagined society that is ideal primarily in some other respect (e.g. in terms of wider human values or a political order of some new kind). Can you think of some?
- ❑ Try experimenting with an aspect of communication that might, for one group of language users, encourage a utopian view if exaggerated but for another group of users a dystopian view. You could start by imagining some exaggerated version of a stereotypically gendered aspect of language, e.g. use of media as information source versus use of media as networking and support channel.

Social progress and information revolutions

Irving Fang's *A History of Mass Communication: Six Information Revolutions* (Fang, 1997: xvii–xix) describes a series of periods in Western history that fit his description of an information revolution. Fang's periods range in time from the 8th century BC to the near future.

Here we list Fang's six revolutions and the main historical claim he makes for each. Then we describe the main values underlying each revolution that Fang views as evidence of social progress. By implication, these or similar values will underlie 'progressive' revolutions of the future.

Fang's six revolutions are:

- the Writing Revolution ('with writing used to store knowledge, the human mind would no longer be constrained by the limits of memory. Knowledge would be boundless'),
- the Printing Revolution ('with printing, information spread through many layers of society . . . printing lent itself to massive political, religious, economic, educational, and personal alterations'),
- the Mass Media Revolution ('for the first time, newspapers and magazines reached out to the common man with news about events near and far, and packaged goods for sale. For the masses, literacy came within reach'),
- the Entertainment Revolution ('entertainment could now be infinitely replicated and canned . . . the whole world would come to love the entertainment products'),
- the Communication Toolshed Home ('transforming the home into the central location for receiving information and entertainment, thanks to the telephone, broadcasting, recording, improvements in print technologies, and cheap, universal mail service'),
- the Information Highway ('communication is shaking off transportation for work, study, and play').

(adapted from Fang, 1997: xvii)

Reflecting on this long history, Fang argues that the pace of information revolutions is speeding up. 'The second revolution', he points out, 'arrived 1,700 years after the first crested. The last four, each quite distinct, have overlapped during the last two centuries' (Fang, 1997: xviii; for further discussion see Briggs and Burke, 2005). In each period that Fang considers to be an information revolution, he suggests that there are shared characteristics. Fang identifies nineteen such characteristics. The characteristics which are especially relevant to verbal communication in particular are listed here (adapted from Fang, 1997: xviii–xix):

- The need for physical transportation to send information has been reduced as communication replaced transportation of messages.
- Information revolutions tended toward some levelling of conditions for those who participated in them. Their results tended to be egalitarian. They pointed toward a greater degree of democratisation or sharing of influence than previously

existed. Where the use of the tools has been limited, both in ancient times and now, human beings have been less free.

- New literacies have arisen to accommodate the new communication technologies, from the phonetic alphabet of the first information revolution to the computer codes of the latest. With each new language has come a new class of experts fully aware of the advantage emanating from the hoarding of their knowledge.
- The changes wrought by these dispersions led toward a greater sharing and more specialisation of knowledge than previously existed. They also led to an overloading of information and to an increase in misinformation.
- The spread of media production, emanating from a multiplicity of independent thought, led to [. . .] a widening of the expression of points of view, frames of reference, experiences and histories.
- Each new communication technology has displaced some other means of communication or behaviour that had been satisfactory until the new technology became available. When something was gained, something of value may have been lost.
- Changes in communication encountered opposition from those who, for political or financial reasons, disliked the changes taking place. Reaction was inevitable from those who must surrender a share of influence and power.
- Heavy personal use of the tools of communication has been accompanied by less social activity. The more time spent with mass communication, the less time has remained for face-to-face communication and group activity. In extreme cases, a social dysfunction has resulted.

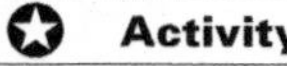

In most of the social generalisations Fang puts forward in his list, technological advances in communication media are accompanied by substantial improvement in the quality of personal and social life. Based on your reading of other sections of this book, and other sources of information and opinion about verbal communication and media, do you think Fang is justified in this assertion?

- What kinds of evidence support Fang's suggestion? Is that evidence mainly linguistic? sociological? political?
- What relevant evidence can you point to that Fang omits, or which might be interpreted differently, to challenge his view that media innovation leads to an improved social availability and circulation of information?

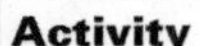

Although Fang's long-term historical view is one of social progress, he does acknowledge setbacks, risks and impediments to progress in his list. What are the main difficulties he identifies?

- ❑ How would you account for each of the following in Fang's general framework: political propaganda, centrally held personal information (e.g. health records, mobile phone records, data on recent purchases, state secrets)?
- ❑ The internet is often celebrated as a zone or virtual environment ('cyber-space') which has so far remained unrestricted by regulation or censorship. Yet in some countries access to particular websites is routinely blocked. Sometimes, even in countries that claim unfettered access to the internet, service providers are persuaded to withdraw internet services from whole classes of users (e.g. spammers, pornographers). How far do such restrictions undermine Fang's claims above? Or could such forms of selective restriction confirm a larger model of social progress?

C

Section C
Exploration
ANALYSING MEDIA LANGUAGE

C1

MESSAGES AND MEDIA

The *Dictionary of Media Studies* (2006), published by A. & C. Black, defines 'media' as 'the various means of mass communication considered as a whole, including television, radio, magazines, together with the people involved in their production' (p. 143). In units A1 and D1, we consider complexity in use of this term that extends beyond mass communication and its producers. In this unit we look at patterns of media use involving the 'various means' available to different people, at different times and for different functions.

The media and I

Recently I – one of the co-authors – was asked which period I would choose if I could go back to any period in history, and why. I immediately responded that I wouldn't. I would stay right here in this time, please. Part of my response was to do with available media. As someone living in a mediated age, surrounded by computers, the internet and email, MSN and Facebook, and someone who has witnessed the development of videos, DVDs, CDs and MP3s, as well as the emergence of mobile phones and texting, I couldn't possibly imagine being without all of those technologies. This is a reaction I know many people would share. As a lecturer, researcher and author, too, computers and the internet have become essential tools of my trade. To put my reasoning in context, I looked back at my use of media technologies today, since I got up this morning:

- played radio and listened to music and news,
- switched on laptop computer and read news online while eating breakfast,
- read a magazine in the doctor's waiting room,
- stopped off at a supermarket on the way home and shopped; read lots of food labels and adverts promoting a range of products,
- played radio in car,
- read advertising hoardings when car was at traffic lights,
- switched on computer again and read, wrote and sent emails,
- opened several Word files to continue drafting this chapter,
- searched the internet for Ron Scollon's definition of 'mediated discourse',
- received and sent several texts from my mobile phone,
- received and made several phone calls from both my mobile phone and landline,
- printed off several photos of a close friend from picture files on my computer,
- played a CD,
- helped a friend draft a report on my laptop,
- watched TV including news headlines, and
- read TV guide for tomorrow.

Imagine that you had *not* been told that one of the authors wrote the above list. Would you have been able to guess what sort of person is reporting their media use here? Using the grid in Table C1.1, see how far you can establish a person's social characteristics from the information given. What is the evidence for each judgement that you feel confident in making? Use the grid to record your answers.

Table C1.1 Social characteristics of a media user

Social characteristic	*Your guess*	*Evidence?*
Age		
Gender		
Social class		
Where the person lives, roughly (what sort of place: town/suburb/countryside, etc.)		
Any other relevant information		

- ❑ Now consider a more general question: Is it possible in principle to identify someone's social characteristics or identity from their patterns of communication and media use? If so, what makes this possible? If not, why not? What aspects of contemporary communication and media might make such guesses or generalisations unreasonable?
- ❑ Does your response to the previous question – how far media use may not be a good predictor of social characteristics – have implications for audience researchers, market researchers, advertisers and/or media policy planners?

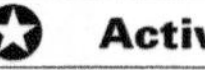

We can now list some different kinds of mediated discourse to help us think about choice of medium for a given function. The question we are now asking is whether one medium tends, in the present media environment, to be preferred over another. To start, construct two lists in the grid shown in Table C1.2.

Column A is a list of different uses of language (what you're using language for). Draw on the notion of speech acts described in unit C3. Examples of speech acts include promising, warning, congratulating, demanding, inviting, etc. If thinking of speech acts doesn't help, then try other ways in

which you might classify your communicative behaviour, but note that some descriptions, like 'write a letter' already shift you from the left column towards the right column.

Column B is a list of different mediated communication formats (i.e. uses of specific machines or technologies) that you would be likely to use for some particular communicative purpose.

You should end up with two lists, ten entries in each. The first three rows have been filled in with examples to help you get started:

Table C1.2 Mediated discourse: function and form

	A Use of language	*B Communication format (or technological medium: kind of 'mediation')*
1	Thank someone	Text message
2	Issue notice of a legal summons	Write a letter
3	Keep in touch with family	Write an email
4		
5		
6		
7		
8		
9		
10		

- ❑ How clear or fixed is the boundary between your two lists? Think again about 'write an email'. Does this activity already contain a suggestion of content, or style, or relationship with the addressee, as well as an indication of the technology used?
- ❑ Are there uses of language that are so closely linked to a particular technology that you can't think of them apart from the technology they use (e.g. 'we were MSNing')?

If in doubt, fill in column A with some of the following: marriage proposal, course essay, advertisement to sell a car. Now, link each item in column A to

an item potentially suited to it in column B (e.g. if 'birthday greeting' is in column A, you might want to say this function can be achieved by means of fax, card sent by post, text message, etc.).

Try reversing the process. Link each item in column B across to suitable speech acts or communication functions in column A.

- ❑ Are there uses of language that don't seem especially strongly linked to a particular technology but could be achieved across almost any number of different technological platforms? Note the word 'platform' here, which means a support for something to be placed on. This word is commonly used in relation to digital media as a way of capturing the idea that content is transferable across 'platforms', or particular media formats, in an age of digital media convergence.
- ❑ How much choice do you have, as regards which technology to use for any given communicative purpose? And what are the main constraints on choosing (e.g. availability of the technology, cost of use, time it takes to use, time it takes for the communication to be delivered/downloaded, etc.)?
- ❑ Finally, discuss entries that seem to complicate the distinction between what we might call function or use and what we are calling the form of 'mediation' or 'technological medium' of communication (see Scollon, 1999) . If you can't think of any problematic cases, consider 'television'.
- ❑ Is 'television' a piece of electrical hardware you buy and switch on? Or is it a form of entertainment that you watch? Or is it some complicated combination of the two? (See Williams, 1974 for detailed historical analysis.)

Media communication audits

A communication audit is an analysis of how much and what kind of communication takes place. (The grids above offer a glimpse of what such audits are like.) Large businesses and organisations often conduct them. They are interested in the flow of information and opinion that takes place, both in terms of the channels that are selected and the content that is communicated. Particular interest centres on 'horizontal' communication (for example, between peers by means of task-related talk or gossip between co-workers) and 'vertical' communication (between different levels of the organisation's hierarchy, for example by means of newsletters and emails). Whether horizontal or vertical, communication is also audited in terms of whether the flow is merely transmissive, passing messages in one direction, or whether it is a two-way process offering dialogue and feedback. The direction-of-flow dimension of organisational communication is felt to be important as regards management style. Content of communication refers to considerations such as what kinds of information, instruction, comment and opinion flow through the channels. And the channels themselves are analysed not only in terms of what technologies and formats are available but

– as in this unit – in terms of which channel is preferred, for which purpose, and by whom.

It is less common for individuals to conduct a 'personal communication audit' than for organisations to audit their corporate communication. But it is equally possible. It can be illuminating to do so, especially where attention is given to the different kinds of 'mediation' of communication that are chosen by different people.

Activity 

Reflect on your use or experience of media *by type* to complete the grid in Table C1.3. There is no need to do this in the sequence of any given day, as above. Instead, think of a general set of habits. You can do this from memory, because we are interested in general features and comparisons – and in complications that arise – not especially in exact details or proportions. (If you want to develop this procedure further, then you will need to think more carefully about method: keeping a diary; recording what media you have been involved with every thirty minutes; getting someone to observe you, etc.)

In order to widen our discussion, we've added two extra features to the process of reporting used above: medium/delivery system, and function.

To help you complete your personal communication audit, here is an explanation of each column that you will need to fill in:

A General description: here you should put the communicative activity (e.g. have a conversation, compose a text message, watch drama, listen to music, etc.).

B Medium/delivery system: here you should indicate what technical means are involved (e.g. speech, writing, computer software, TV, fax, mobile phone, etc.).

C Language: people don't necessarily do all their communicating or access media in the same language. Sometimes there are patterns in combinations of type of use and particular language (e.g. pray in one language and watch TV in another, talk to relatives on the phone in one language, browse the internet in another). Also, think of the use of emoticons in texts and email). Indicate here which language you communicate or receive media in.

D Function or social role: indicate here what function in your life, as you see it, each communication-plus-media type combination plays. There can be no fixed categories here. But you may wish to use such terms as relaxation, search for information, small talk, escapism, networking, problem-solving, etc. This is likely to be the hardest column to fill in, with perhaps the most impressionistic answers. Think about what sorts of category we typically use to describe the different roles that communication and media play in our lives. The first two rows have been filled in to give you an idea of how to get started.

Table C1.3 My personal media and communication audit

	A General description	*B In what medium or from what delivery system?*	*C In what language?*	*D Function or type of use*
1	Drama	Computer, DVD player, TV	English	Relaxation, escapism
2	Advertising	Computer pop-ups, magazines, newspapers, posters in an Underground station, advertising hoardings	English, but depends on product e.g. *Vorsprung durch technik* (German strapline used to advertise Audi cars since the 1980s, meaning 'advancement through technology'), etc.	Sometimes noting information about products I'm interested in Sometimes just unsolicited amusement and entertainment Sometimes annoying distraction from what I was doing
3				
4				
5				
6				
7				
8				
9				
10				

Use difficulties that arise with filling in this grid as a source of questions to ask in re-reading this thread and in preparation for other threads in the book.

Media for life

Finally, we return to the scenario we started with: time travel. What would it be like to inhabit a different media environment? We can know something about this from travel. Media technologies are unevenly distributed across the globe, as well as between different social groups occupying the same place. In one country there may

be a television set in nearly every room of the house; in another country there may be places where everyone gathers around a single television set in the middle of a village. And even though it may not seem like it, not everyone has a mobile phone or writes emails. To travel, or put yourself in a different social position from a situation you're familiar with, can show up how differently people are connected up or wired into rapidly changing global media (Castells, 2000).

Activity 

- Compare your experience – as reflected in the grids in this unit – with how you think the same grids would be (or would have been) completed by each of the following:
  - One of your grandparents
  - One of your parents
  - Someone you know who lives in a different country from the one you live in.
- What are the main differences? More importantly, what is the significance of those differences, in terms of people's individual lives and the general ways of life of the societies in which they live or have lived? In what terms should we explain those differences, especially as regards the structures and uses of language they involve?

C2 THE CASE OF THE BLOG

In this unit, we examine the medium of blogs and look at several examples. These include a blog where political content appears to be articulated in a humorous style. We also consider the idea that individuals have membership of a range of different 'discourse communities' (Swales, 1990), in which groups of individuals share goals and purposes and use communication to achieve those goals. We would expect that people who participate in blogging will be familiar with the genre or shared set of communicative practices of the blogging discourse community and that they will use appropriate terminology or jargon and adhere to some kind of code of conduct when communicating. However, while factors such as what language is acceptable may be understood, occasionally a need is felt to reinforce what is suitable and non-offensive language when boundaries of acceptable style and register are breached. This point is discussed in the 'Civility Enforced: O'Reilly's draft code' section below. The code sets out to address this general problem.

An example of a blog . . . or is it?

PermaBlog

The following example (Figure C2.1) of the weekly *PermaBlog* appeared in *The Guardian* newspaper supplement called *G2* on a Wednesday. It begins by presenting a comment on a piece of news and is followed by responses to that comment in the form of a blog, a sort of blog on a blog. In fact, *PermaBlog* is not an authentic blog but a spoof

Figure C2.1 Tim Dowling's *PermaBlog* (*The Guardian*, 25 April 2007)

PermaBlog

'Non-stop comment for a non-stop planet!'

Yeltsin: The wave of murder continues

The assassination of Boris Yeltsin by former elements of the KGB is just the latest in a rash of killings aimed at crushing dissent in Putin's increasingly totalitarian Russia. In the west we have too long taken for . . . *[read more]*
Posted by MorganWClist at 0931 on 25.04.07
Morgan W Clist is the author of Project Katrina: The Hurricane That Never Happened

Comments

JaneT at 0942 today	**I didn't realise Yeltsin was murdered.**
SixKindsOfChris at 0949 today	**He wasn't. This is just another one of those crackpot conspiracy theories for which the blogosphere is justifiably ridiculed.**
liberati at 0957 today	**I didn't even know Yeltsin was dead until today.**
ElSmell at 1006 today	**I didn't know Yeltsin was still alive until yesterday.**
MegaDave at 1015 today	**I never heard of Boris Yeltsin until just now.**
SixKindsOfChris at 1021 today	**That's not so odd. Yeltsin disappeared from public life in 2000, and almost nothing has appeared about him in the press since. Someone under the age of 20 might easily have not heard of him.**
MegaDave at 1026 today	**I'm 36, but thanks for trying.**
JaneT at 1032 today	**So what did he die of?**
MorganWClist at 1045 today	**My contacts think he was possibly sent an email containing thallium.**

SixKindsOfChris at 1047 today	**Nonsense. Why would anyone bother to kill Yeltsin? He was at Death's door for over a decade.**
liberati at 1058 today	**With his forehead resting against Death's doorbell.**
MorganWClist at 1109 today	**Simple: the oligarchs who owe their billions to Yeltsin were planning to have him canonised as a Russian orthodox saint so they could form a quasi-religious political movement based around his cult. He is in suspended animation until his miracles could be independently verified by the Pope.**
MegaDave at 1112 today	**MorganW's theory is so unlikely that it absolutely has to be true. Is there a website?**
MorganWClist at 1117 today	**Just a domain name so far – www.stboriscult.org – but watch this space.**
SixKindsOfChris at 1126 today	**I think we should be concerning ourselves with Yeltsin's legacy – Russia's transition to a market economy and Putin's premiership.**
liberati at 1128 today	**& getting really drunk all the time.**
MorganWClist at 1133 today	**Yeltsin was teetotal – he only pretended to be drunk in order to keep his enemies guessing.**
liberati at 1151 today	**I guess the only thing we can all agree on is that Boris Yeltsin is dead.**
ParanoidBob at 1156 today	**That's exactly what they want to you think.**
ElSmell at 1208 today	**Hi ParanoidBob. Left the house at all this week?**
ParanoidBob at 1213 today	**No.**

You must be registered to comment. Offensive? Unsuitable? Email us

(or parody) written by the journalist Tim Dowling. *PermaBlog* appears convincing for a number of reasons. For example, comments are generated from a topical piece of news, which is also a spoof, and follow the style of the blog genre. They also appear to be written by a mix of people/characters that you might expect to find taking part in this kind of online discourse community. As would be expected in a blog, the bloggers also respond not only to the original comment but also to each other. One feature that the weekly *PermaBlogs* have in common is their thread of humour, which attempts to undermine the topic being discussed and even to undermine the spoof bloggers themselves.

Activity 

Read the article 'Yeltsin: the wave of murder continues' *PermaBlog, The Guardian* (Figure C2.1).

- ❑ How is group membership or an online discourse community established in this piece? How are online identities maintained or upheld?
- ❑ Identify the language and grammatical structures associated with the blog genre.
- ❑ Describe the range of features that in your view make this blog convincing.
- ❑ How is humour used to undermine the supposed serious and political content of the news item?
- ❑ After reading *PermaBlog*, go on to read the authentic blog that follows the article 'Civility Enforced: O'Reilly's draft code', below. Consider how it compares with Dowling's *PermaBlog* in terms of format, language, grammatical structure, interaction among participants and use of humour.

A code for bloggers and blogging

Recently the blogging world has faced criticism, from without and within, concerning the low standard and tone of cyberdebate. Online discourse, it is said, is characterised by personal insult, childish mudslinging, meaningless feuds, self-serving digression, pranksterish vandalism and empty threats. Two blogging pioneers, Tim O'Reilly (who coined the phrase 'Web 2.0') and Jimmy Wales (the founder of Wikipedia), proposed a code of conduct which would, among other things, exhort bloggers not to say anything online 'that we wouldn't say in person' (Tim Dowling, *The Guardian*, 14 April 2007, p. 25 of the Saturday section).

Activity

- ❑ Begin by describing what kinds of language you would consider inappropriate on a web forum. Such language could include use of capital letters, for example, which is seen as 'shouting'.
- ❑ Read 'Civility Enforced: O'Reilly's draft code' (*The Guardian*, 14 April 2007, reprinted below) and decide if you agree or disagree with this code of conduct. Are there further unstated arguments to add?
- ❑ Comment on the six principles listed – indicate whether you agree or disagree with each and say why.
- ❑ If you were adding a seventh principle of conduct, what would it be?
- ❑ Read the comments in the online blog responding to the article. How do bloggers create different discourse community 'identities' to fill a communicative goal? How do they respond to each other's comments?

Civility Enforced: O'Reilly's draft code

We celebrate the blogosphere because it embraces frank and open conversation. But frankness does not have to mean lack of civility. We present this Blogger Code of Conduct in hopes that it helps create a culture that encourages both personal expression and constructive conversation.

1 We take responsibility for our own words and for the comments we allow on our blog.

We are committed to the 'Civility Enforced' standard: we will not post unacceptable content, and we'll delete comments that contain it.
We define unacceptable content as anything included or linked to that:

is being used to abuse, harass, stalk, or threaten others
is libelous, knowingly false, *ad hominem*, or misrepresents another person,
infringes upon a copyright or trademark
violates an obligation of confidentiality
violates the privacy of others.

We define and determine what is 'unacceptable content' on a case-by-case basis, and our definitions are not limited to this list. If we delete a comment or link, we will say so and explain why. [We reserve the right to change these standards at any time with no notice.]

2 We won't say anything online that we wouldn't say in person.

3 We connect privately before we respond publicly.

When we encounter conflicts and misrepresentation in the blogosphere, we make every effort to talk privately and directly to the person(s) involved – or find an intermediary who can do so – before we publish any posts or comments about the issue.

4 When we believe someone is unfairly attacking another, we take action.
When someone who is publishing comments or blog postings that are offensive, we'll tell them so (privately, if possible – see above) and ask them to publicly make amends.
If those published comments could be construed as a threat, and the perpetrator doesn't withdraw them and apologise, we will cooperate with law enforcement to protect the target of the threat.

5 We do not allow anonymous comments.
We require commenters to supply a valid email address before they can post, though we allow commenters to identify themselves with an alias, rather than their real name.

6 We ignore the trolls.
We prefer not to respond to nasty comments about us or our blog, as long as they don't veer into abuse or libel. We believe that feeding the trolls only encourages them – 'Never wrestle with a pig. You both get dirty, but the pig likes it'. Ignoring public attacks is often the best way to contain them.
or
This is an open, uncensored forum. We are not responsible for the comments of any poster, and when discussions get heated, crude language, insults and other 'off colour' comments may be encountered. Participate in this site at your own risk.

The following comments present a sample of postings in response to the above.

Comments

RoyA1
April 14, 2007 5:06 AM
I completely agree. Comments of the type you quote from Jonathan Freedland's article earlier this week are all too common, even on CiF [*The Guardian*'s Comment is Free blog]. Blogs should encourage debate and discussion, not abuse. They seem to attract those who see people with different views to their own as an enemy, who should be ridiculed and abused. It is like football fans who hurl vicious abuse at players during games, sometimes from a distance of a few yards, yet who would never behave like that if they met the player in the street. They feel protected by their anonymity as part of a crowd. In the same way, people commenting on blogs hide behind anonymity. They should behave as if they were talking face-to-face.
Roy Allen

Offensive? Unsuitable? Email us

philiph35
April 14, 2007 6:20 AM
Speaking only of CIF, I do not see so much personal abuse. More shocking is the level of hatred displayed against the Jews. But I am quite grateful to have seen it and would not like it checked, even though the Guardian apparently maintains some level of censorship and perhaps really evil things are not getting through. As a result of several months of reading, I am emigrating.

Offensive? Unsuitable? Email us

seriousleftfoot
April 14, 2007 10:02 AM
Interesting article, but there is an easy way to put a stop to the blogosphere nonsense: Don't respond to abuse, ever. It encourages the people who post it. Abusive bloggers are lonely people who feel unloved, bless them. Ignore them, and they'll go and vent somewhere else.

Offensive? Unsuitable? Email us

BornFree
April 14, 2007 2:42 PM
My experience is hardly a demographic study, but an interesting anecdote. I am a 64-year-old woman who comments on a number of US and English-speaking technical and feminist blogs. I have the credentials to post technical commentary and am partly to blame for the battles women have had to face in various engineering and technical arenas, because I am pretty pig-headed and refuse to be run out of town. So the responses to my posts are interesting.

If I use a gender-neutral or potentially male name to sign off, I am either ignored or disagreed with relatively respectfully.

If I use my own name or a potentially female handle, a whole range of responses are posted, from date offers at the local bar, to invitations to f— either myself or the poster, to ignorant rants against feminists, to professional responses that end with comments about how misguided I am, to (very few) legitimate professional conversations.

My rationalization for the gender difference is this: there is a surfeit of horny, teenage (in spirit, if not in fact), under-socialized males with internet access with nothing better to do with their time than flame. They are uncreative, at best, and bordering on psychopathic, at worst.

Ranting against them just makes the various forums (fora?) unusable. Making rules is patronizing and doomed to eventually shut down the few forums that are intelligently member-monitored. Lack of self-discipline seems to be a rising global norm that is often confused with 'freedom', and the only remedy I see is to keep doing what I am doing.

Offensive? Unsuitable? Email us

TheNuclearOption
April 14, 2007 7:42 PM
I tend to moderate my behaviour based on that of the original commenter and what they stand for. If your denigrating others and pushing a narrow agenda from the start or if in past posts you've been insulting to others then as far as I'm concerned you're fair game especially if you are simply using CiF as a propaganda organ rather than as a forum for genuine debate and discussion.

Offensive? Unsuitable? Email us

clbcz
April 14, 2007 10:43 PM
I agree with BornFree when she says that 'there is a surfeit of horny, teenage (in spirit, if not in fact), under-socialized males with internet access with nothing better to do with their time than flame. They are uncreative, at best, and bordering on psychopathic, at worst'. A few people responding to the original comment have affirmed this.

Offensive? Unsuitable? Email us

sanuk8
April 14, 2007 10:58 PM
Can anyone be bothered to read this verbose shit?

Offensive? Unsuitable? Email us

adam6am
April 14, 2007 11:09 PM
'Only a fool writes for anything but money'. – Dr. Johnson

C3 LISTENING TO POP LYRICS

Pop lyrics are an influential use of language in media. For many foreign-language learners (certainly of English), pop lyrics are an important source of language data and of language-learning motivation. But they can also be strange data. Someone listening to pop music in a crowded hall, or to a radio that is on in the background, may wonder whether they are even supposed to be able to make coherent sense of the words – or possibly even to hear the lyrics at all. This is partly because pop lyrics are sung rather than spoken. Some of the phonological features of speech are adapted to requirements of the music. For example, syllables are drawn out, and speech sounds sometimes accommodate to other sounds around them (by elision and assimilation).

The natural intonation of speech is also made to fit the song's melodic contour. None of that is surprising. The voice is functioning as a musical instrument in compositions that evoke feeling and mood musically as well as by depicting some real or imagined situation through the meanings of the words.

Over several decades, radio DJs (and more recently bloggers and chatroom contributors) have drawn attention in a light-hearted way to one consequence of this blending of speech with singing: how easy it is to mishear song lyrics. The words of even people's favourite songs are sometimes imprinted forever in their minds in a contorted, misheard form. This can create complete nonsense or sometimes incongruous, usually trivial alternative wordings. Some examples of such misheard lyrics can be read in an article 'Police top misheard lyrics chart' (http://news.bbc.co.uk/1/hi/entertainment/7574541.stm) (20 November 2008).

Words, singing and meaning

When you *can* hear what is being said, the fact that pop lyrics come to us in a mediated, electronic audio form has several significant effects that we focus on in this unit.

- We encounter lyrics in precisely recorded spoken, rather than written form. In this respect, song lyrics differ from poems on the page. Vocals (as singing is often called) are superimposed on the usual patterns of the speaking voice. We have already noted how speaking then merges with other dimensions of the music. The 'spokenness', rather than written quality, of pop lyrics also gives pop songs, across all their different genres and styles, a characteristic conversational directness.
- Mass distribution of music files, CDs, MTV videos and radio airplay give sudden, mass exposure to the particular words and idioms used in some songs. One day's dialect term on a local housing estate (or a novel euphemism for sex, drugs or some other aspect of lifestyle – think of examples here) can be catapulted next day into international, even global circulation. Yet the lyrics of some songs seem calculated to be private. They circulate as a kind of anti-language, having been devised precisely so as to exclude anyone outside a given sub-culture. Some listeners are nevertheless so intrigued by this sense of special secrecy that they will try anything – slowing tracks down, playing them backwards – in an effort to disclose a song's 'real' meaning.
- Songs broadcast on the radio, or reproduced as MP3s or on CD, are detached from any particular situation, or any social context beyond the situation in which they are listened to. Pop lyrics as a result are made sense of by listeners in many different contexts. They can be used for different purposes than may have been foreseen for them. Lyrics are given a new context. They are turned into 'borrowed' or imagined speech events.

This last effect is especially worth investigating. In this unit we raise some questions about how pop lyrics work that go beyond phonological questions (i.e. questions

about how the words that are sung are articulated) and beyond sociolinguistic questions (i.e. questions about what kind of words, idioms, grammatical constructions and registers the lyrics contain). We ask what sort of speech event, or imagined speech event, pop lyrics enact. How far, for example, do we construe song lyrics by filling in vaguely implied information as a way of creating intelligible situations and stories of our own?

We begin exploring these questions by looking at one particular song: James Blunt's *You're Beautiful*, from his bestselling 2005 album *Back to Bedlam*. As authors, we have no particular liking for this song – it is one among many possible examples of how some key aspects of pop lyrics work.

You're Beautiful opens with a contrast between the different channels of musical arrangement and voice. The musical accompaniment consists of sparse guitar notes and chords, played in a slow and melancholic vein (with the result that at least one available parody of the song is called *You're Pitiful*). By contrast, the words begin 'My life is brilliant . . .'. 'Brilliant', however, we discover means brightness rather than approval, as the word leads on to 'pure' and then to 'saw an angel'. The other available sense in a conversational style ('My life is fantastic') is squeezed out.

What has mainly led to this song being widely discussed by listeners is how its lyrics report a central, slightly mysterious incident. The singer describes seeing (a female) someone (her) 'on the subway' with 'another man'. Recollection of this incident in the first verse switches in the chorus from reporting mode (she) to addressing mode, 'you're beautiful'. The change is signalled by a contrast made between first and second person pronouns (I, me, you) and third person pronouns (she, her). First and second person pronouns refer to people present and interacting: they are the pronouns of 'talking to'. Third person pronouns (he, she, it, him, her, his, her, its, they, them, their) refer to people or entities absent from the conversational situation: they are the pronouns of 'talking about'. Despite the switch, we infer that the person talked about and the person talked to are the same person. This is what makes the song narrative coherent. Later in the song, the pattern of switching between recollection and imagined interaction is repeated (from 'yeah, she caught my eye' to a repeated further chorus and the closing lines 'But it's time to face the truth / I will never be with you').

So what is the mystery? The song lyric gives apparently great personal significance to a minor incident (a momentary sighting of someone in the Underground). On more than one occasion, Blunt himself has described how he wrote the song about seeing his ex-girlfriend with a new man he didn't know about on a train in the London Underground (note, however, how Blunt refers to the London Underground with an American-English term, 'subway' – why?). The singer says he and the woman shared a lifetime in their brief eye contact. The song words came to him all at once.

We have laid out this 'reading' of the song lyrics in order to go on to explore the difference between a fairly standard interpretation like this – rather like reading a poem – and seeing the lyrics as what we have described in this thread as a mediated communication event. To open up a more media-sensitive way of listening to pop lyrics, we need to consider how the song is actually heard.

To explore this question, we now consider the words of *You're Beautiful* alongside another widely known song, *Every Breath You Take* by The Police. Again, this

second song is purely an example. It was written and first recorded in 1983, but is often played on radio and TV as part of adverts and programme soundtracks. It is also familiar from cover versions by other performers and has been sampled by performers such as Puff Daddy in his hit *I'll Be Missing You*. For our purposes, the choice of song is not important, beyond the fact that it should be familiar or at least accessible.

Listen to *You're Beautiful* and *Every Breath You Take*. The key aspects of the lyrics of The Police song can be seen in the following extracts.

Verse 1:

> Every breath you take, and every move you make,
> Every bond you break, every step you take,
> I'll be watching you

Middle 8 (i.e. conventional 8-bar section in related key to harmonic structure of verse):

> Oh can't you see, you belong to me;
> How my poor heart aches, at every step you take.

Other main interlude (different harmonic structure from either verse or middle 8):

> Since you've been gone I've been lost without a trace,
> I dream at night, I can only see your face.
> I look around but it's you I can't replace,
> I feel so cold and I long for your embrace,
> I keep calling, baby, baby, please.

Remember: what we are interested in is how the words project an imagined speech event, with imagined participants and context. So we need to ask:

- ❏ Who is understood to be 'talking'? (i.e. who is 'I')?
- ❏ Who to? (i.e. who, in the Police song, is 'you' and 'baby')?
- ❏ What kind of new, or 'borrowed', speech event is created?

If the song is going to appeal to you, the scenario or speech event constructed needs to offer pleasure. What we will explore is whether structures of listening, and related structures of pleasure, may be common across the two songs we have taken as examples – and perhaps by implication common to others.

Activity 

Look at Table C3.1. Assign a number from 5 through to 1 to each of the alternative possible interpretations of each of the two songs. How close does each gloss come to your intuition about how you hear the words? Use 5 for 'very close'; 1 for 'not at all close'.

Table C3.1 Interpreting two songs grid

	Description	Grade
A	1 This is a personal, autobiographical song. As James Blunt has commented in a press interview: 'it's a really personal song about a moment which meant a great deal to me. And I'm sure plenty of guys have seen their ex-girlfriend with a new man at some stage. It bites into you and I captured that in a really honest song'. The 'I' in the song is James Blunt; the 'you' is his ex-girlfriend, someone reportedly called Dixie Chassay.	5 4 3 2 1
	2 This is a personal, autobiographical song. As Sting has acknowledged in press interviews, he is exposing paranoid feelings during a difficult period in his relationship with his ex-wife, actress Frances Tomelty. The 'I' in the song is Sting; the 'you' is his ex-wife.	5 4 3 2 1
B	1 The power of this song is how James Blunt addresses the listener so directly and personally; when I listen to it I can imagine that James Blunt is talking to *me*. The 'I' of the song is James Blunt; the 'you' is me, the listener – or anyone else who is willing to entertain the idea of being told they're beautiful, and missed, by a pop performer.	5 4 3 2 1
	2 The power of this song is how Sting addresses the listener so directly and personally. When I listen to it I can imagine that Sting is actually talking to me. The 'I' of the song is Sting; the 'you' is me, the listener – or anyone else who is willing to entertain the idea of being told they're missed, and jealously sought after, by a pop performer.	5 4 3 2 1
C	1 This song sums it up. I'm a melancholic, reflective guy too, and it says exactly what I've felt myself. The song says something on my behalf. The 'I' in the song is me; the 'you' in this case is X (someone specific in my own life).	5 4 3 2 1
	2 This song sums it up. It says just what I've felt myself. The song says something on my behalf. It's what I would like to say (should say, etc.) to X. The 'I' in the song is me; the 'you' in this case is X (someone specific in my own life).	5 4 3 2 1

D	1 It's just a song. So many songs are about love, or failed love, and this is one more. It's all convention. James Blunt's song is a classic mix of reporting something that happened and imagining a conversation you never had – all very conventional, especially when you feel nostalgic or jealous. When I listen, I just appreciate the words in terms of the song-writing conventions being followed. The words themselves don't really mean anything. The 'I' in the song is just some random made-up person; the 'you' likewise.	5 4 3 2 1
	2 It's just a song. So many songs are about love, or failed love, and this is just one of them. Sting's words are all convention. When I listen, I just appreciate the words in terms of the song-writing conventions being followed. The words themselves don't really mean anything. The 'I' in the song is just some random made-up person; the 'you' likewise.	5 4 3 2 1

A–D in the above grid represent, in a somewhat simplified form, a series of alternative listening scenarios. They are different ways you might fill in participant roles for a media speech event that has been separated from any particular interactional event, other than the listening situation itself.

Now look at Table C3.2 and consider some kinds of cultural behaviour that can accompany listening to pop music. How well does each kind of behaviour serve as evidence in support of (or against) the alternative interpretive possibilities A–D listed above? Circle the letter or letters in the right-hand column which represent(s) interpretation(s) suggested by the behaviour.

Table C3.2 Listening to pop music and acting it out

	Listener behaviour	*Goes with . . .*
4.1	Singing along with records you like.	A B C D
4.2	Miming and playing an imaginary guitar ('air guitar'), maybe in front of a mirror (mainly, though not only, men).	A B C D
4.3	Putting up posters of attractive pop performers on the wall.	A B C D
4.4	Having favourite songs linked to specific events or relationships in your own life.	A B C D
4.5	Considering a song an 'anthem' for a whole generation or a particular lifestyle.	A B C D

In our experience, in classes there are always students who acknowledge each kind of listening presented in the grid here. Sometimes they confess to an awkwardness or embarrassment in doing so. The private realm has suddenly become public. Equally common, however, is that some people find one or more of the modelled forms of listening almost impossible to imagine, even when linked to visible signs of behaviour presented in the second grid.

To investigate further how far the different forms of listening may have wider consequences in the world, or raise unresolved issues, consider two more complicated cases:

1 Stevie Wonder's famous song *Happy Birthday to You* was written as part of a campaign for a public holiday in the US in honour of Martin Luther King. The lyrics of the verses are clearly about Martin Luther King. In context, the repeated chorus words *happy birthday to you* are also clearly addressed to him. But the song has come to do frequent service as an easily playable, recorded substitute for the other *Happy Birthday* at children's birthday parties. Can this use of the song be explained in any other way than as a result of its pronouns ('we' and 'you') being re-addressed to new and different people in each playback situation?

2 In recent years, the ex-Wham singer George Michael has openly discussed his homosexuality in many media interviews. His single *I Want Your Sex*, which charted in 1987, was banned by BBC Radio 1 because of its possible encouragement to listeners to be sexually promiscuous. This was at a time when HIV/AIDS-awareness was being especially strongly urged in the broadcast media. The radio ban was enforced despite a label attached to each disc declaring 'Explore monogamy'. An accompanying video simulated heterosexual, 'monogamous' sex between Michael and his supposed girlfriend of the time, make-up artist Cathy Leung. Little discussion took place in the media about exactly *how* the song advocated more extensive sexual activity than many other depictions of sex in song lyrics. How do you think people were considered to be hearing these song lyrics in such a way that their sexual values or behaviour might be more at risk than they would be as a result of listening to other songs?

Activity 

- To follow up whether mode of address works differently in different styles of music, examine the lyrics of a number of songs from different periods and genres. (Don't only choose songs in musical styles you like.) Look particularly at their use of pronouns. You might start by examining each of the 'perfect' pop songs reported as someone's definitive list for the genre in unit A4, for example.
- Examine the lyrics of songs, as above, but this time work with a narrower research question. All four songs referred to in this unit were written and performed by men. Would you expect mode of address, and related structures of listening, to be different with songs composed and/or performed by women? Or what about if the song in question was originally composed and/or performed by a man, but then adapted and covered by a female performer? Or vice versa?

- If you know another language, consider how similarly or how differently mode of address in pop lyrics works in different languages (e.g. with 'tu' and 'vous' forms in French, which distinguish relationship as well as distinguishing singular/plural).
- We have looked at 'I' and 'you' on the assumption that pop lyrics frequently use first- and second-person pronouns. Such use, we have suggested, opens up a range of interpretive possibilities once these pronouns are floated free from the anchors of a given situation of utterance. But what about first-person plural: 'we' and 'us'? In English, 'we' has an exclusive and an inclusive use. Exclusive 'we' refers to the speaker and others but not the addressee. Inclusive 'we' means the speaker and the addressee as well as possibly others. In many pop lyrics, 'we' is a repeated and emphasised term, for example, in the charity single *We Are the World* released in 1985 to raise funds to help famine-relief efforts in Ethiopia. Who exactly are 'we'? Take account of inclusive and exclusive uses of 'we' in following up this unit. Look at how 'we' works in a sample of pop songs, again from different genres and periods.

To explore the issues raised in this unit further, there is another line of speculation that it may be interesting to pursue. At the beginning of the unit, we suggested that pop lyrics are commonly misheard – and that many people find a strange pleasure in alternative lyrics thrown up by such mishearing. The mishearing of lyrics is not some pathological or dysfunctional failure of listening but an inevitable side-effect of the fragmentation and selective hearing that take place in how we hear words sung as part of a musical composition (rather than as part of a spoken utterance). We should therefore look directly at this phenomenon, and not just assume it is some minor effect in the margins of 'proper' listening.

The modes of listening outlined above all involve efforts to produce coherence by reconstructing fairly stable, alternative modes of address. How could we research more fleeting and evanescent patterns of hearing, where sense comes into focus and then disperses at different times in listening to any given song?

COMPARING KINDS OF STUDIO TALK

C4

In unit B4 we looked at Hymes's (1972) SPEAKING grid and considered whether it could be extended, as a framework for analysing a community's way of speaking, to media discourse such as a radio broadcast. We also raised the question whether the framework provides all the necessary components to describe different genres of media discourse adequately, or whether the model has limits in this respect.

In this unit, we examine the media interview as a type of speech event. We look at its different components, such as specific discourse strategies, the structure of

interaction and the relationship between the participants involved. Our assumption is that analysing media interviews using Hymes's SPEAKING grid (whether those interviews are in a news or chat show format) will reveal a distinctive combination of discourse features. How far is this the case?

We can test our assumption on a small scale by looking at two interviews: a political news interview and a chat show interview. Below are two excerpts to illustrate this:

1 an excerpt from a well-known interview between Jeremy Paxman and Michael Howard. Paxman asks the same paraphrased question six times (he asks 13 times in the interview as a whole) and Howard evades the question each time (taken from Clayman and Heritage, 2002: 256), and
2 an excerpt from an interview between Oprah Winfrey, a popular American chat show host, and a guest (taken from Clayman and Heritage, 2002: 109). A transcription key is provided in Table C4.1.

A political news interview

Jeremy Paxman, a news journalist with the BBC and known for his confrontational interview style on BBC's *Newsnight* programme, is particularly known for an interview in 1997 with Michael Howard, the former Home Secretary and at the time a candidate for the Conservative party leadership. Paxman questioned Howard about his role in events leading to the firing of a prison official (which related to events involving a prison escape). Howard had previously denied any involvement in operational matters. So any response in the interview that would contradict his earlier statement would have serious implications as regards his credibility and standing as a politician. Despite Howard avoiding answering the question, Paxman pursued his goal by asking the same question 13 times. The following excerpt (Clayman and Heritage, 2002: 256) contains the first few rounds of this remarkable line of questioning:

BBC *Newsnight* 13 May 1997: Michael Howard
IR: Jeremy Paxman, IE: Michael Howard

IR: Did you threaten [to overrule
IE: [I – I was <u>not</u> entitled
to instruct Derek Lewis and I did not instruct
him .hh [an the
IR: [Did you threaten to overrule [(him)
IE: [>The<
the truth of the matter i:s thet (.) Mister
Marriott was not suspende[d. I did not-
IR: [Did you threaten to
overrule him.
IE: I did <u>not</u> overrule Der[ek (Lewis).
IR: [Did you <u>threa</u>ten to
overrule h[im.

IE: [I took advice on what I could or
could not d[o::
IR: [Did you threat[en to overrule him=
IE: [and I acted=
IR: =Mister Howard.
IE: =scrupulously in accordance with that advice=I
did not overrule D[erek
IR: [Did you threaten to
overrule him

A chat show interview

A comparable pattern emerges in the modern chat show, despite this format being designed to simulate a more conversational style of interaction. In the following sequence from the *Oprah Winfrey Show* (Clayman and Heritage, 2002: 109–10), the guest describes how a colleague simulated illness as part of a campaign against the smokers in her office building:

ABC *Oprah Winfrey Show*: April 1991: Passive Smoking
IR: Oprah Winfrey IE: Lenora

IR: =Uh you: uh::: (.) say she fakes it?
(.)
IR: Lenora she fakes it, she faked a heart attack.
IE: Yeah she faked a heart attack.
IR: Uh huh. Faked it.
(0.2)
IE: Faked it.
IR: How. Fell out on the floor: the whole d- deal?
(.)
IR: Fa[ked it.
IE: [No she: (0.4) said she was havin' uh:: (.)
hard time abreathin'.=She was uh: havin'
palpitation of the heart,
IR: Mmhm?=
IE: =Called paramedic, they came down. .hhh They
examine her but she refused to go to
th'hospital.
IR: Mmhm.
(0.5)
IE: So: then: (0.2) next week she did the same
thing.
IR: Mmhm.
(0.5)
IE: Then: (.) she didn't go to th'hospital.

IR: Mmhm.
IE: Then she went to: .hh the fire department, and
had them atake her a (.) bou- (0.2) mm (.) three
weeks later.
(1.0)
IR: [To:
IE: [But they didn't f- (.) to the hospital. [.hhhh
IR: [For
the heart attack?
(0.2)
IE: Yes::.
IR: Mmhm.

Here [. . .] Oprah Winfrey acknowledges the overwhelming majority of the statements that this guest makes.

Table C4.1 **Transcription key (adapted from Clayman and Heritage, 2002)**

[square brackets]	Overlap
= equal sign	One sound follows the other sound with no silence or pause or continuous utterance
underlined	Stressed word or part of word
:	Elongated sound
< >	Talk is rushed
(.)	Micropause
(0.2)	Silence in tenths of a second
(word)	Transcriber's uncertainty but likely possibility
- hyphen	Glottal stop

The interaction in both texts is reproduced using low-level transcription conventions. This is because the researcher is mainly interested in the sequence of turn-taking, type of interaction and form and content of what is being said. Nevertheless, a comparison of the two interviews shows a marked difference in interactional style, despite both belonging to the same, overall interview genre. There is the expected question–answer, turn-taking format expected in interviews, with the host asking the questions. However, the Paxman vs Howard interview displays a higher involvement style. This is shown by the greater number of overlaps or simultaneous speech, which can also be interpreted as interruptions. This contrasts with Oprah's less confrontational interview style. Oprah 'allows' her guest time to finish her turn before taking the floor to ask another question, making a comment and moving the interview along. Oprah's style can be described as more conversational, highlighted by the use of

minimal responses 'Mmhm' in lines 14, 18 and 22 (for example) to indicate her engagement. Where overlaps occur, this seems unlikely to be interpreted as confrontational, and is more likely to be viewed as a sign of eagerness to participate in the discussion.

Activity

Use Hymes's SPEAKING grid (Table B4.1 on p. 83) to make a closer analysis of the two interviews. Part of the grid has been completed for you in Table C4.2. Fill in the missing components.

Table C4.2 Analysing discourse in two media interviews

	1 Paxman vs Howard interview	*2 Oprah interview*
S	TV studio; evening; UK; serious news and current affairs programme; no audience present	TV studio with studio audience present; daytime; USA; popular chat show
P	Interviewer–interviewee; news journalist–politician; TV audience at home; TV film crew; (newspaper journalists hoping for a scoop?)	Interviewer–interviewee; chat show host–guest; studio audience and TV audience; TV film crew
E		
A		
K		
I		
N		
G	(Political news) interview	(Chat show) interview

- ❑ How useful do you find the SPEAKING grid in analysing the two interview extracts?
- ❑ Can you identify different as well as common features across the two interviews? Which component of the grid shows the greatest difference, e.g. the Act sequence, Ends, Participants, etc.?
- ❑ Do you think the two interviews are good representations of what you would expect to find in an interview speech event? (Think about norms of interaction.) Do the two interview extracts reflect or challenge your expectations of the interview genre?
- ❑ Would you add any components to Hymes's SPEAKING grid, or remove any particular component from it? Would it be preferable, in general, to strip the model back to a simpler framework?

C5 PURPOSES OF PERSUASION

In unit B5 we explore how persuasive techniques run through information media, such as news and documentary, and also through advertising. In this unit, we look in more detail at examples of each. First, we look at a historic political speech broadcast to many millions worldwide while we were writing this unit: a presidential acceptance speech. Then we consider an advert. The advert we have chosen is not for a retailer or commercial service provider. Like the political speech, it also comes from the world of government, but in this case regional government in the UK. With both texts, we highlight *how* it is possible to go about investigating rhetorical patterns in a piece of discourse.

Rhetoric in a political speech

Political speeches perform a number of rhetorical functions. For example, they can inform, persuade, manipulate, influence and control, while also serving to place the speaker in the best possible light. Where the speaker is a political leader and spokesperson for a nation's government, the content of a political speech can make a major difference to public opinion. It can also affect the speaker's popularity, so the language is carefully chosen. Use of persuasive discourse is rarely if ever more important than during political campaigns. In such circumstances, choice of language is fundamental not only to encouraging the public to vote, but also in persuading them to vote a particular way. Rhetoric can also play a part in celebrating political victory.

Perhaps one of the most historic moments in recent global politics has been the election of Barack Obama, who became the first African American to be elected President of the United States on 4 November 2008. An appreciation of President Obama's victory address on 5 November to crowds in Chicago, Illinois, carried by *The Sunday Times* newspaper in London (8 November 2008), described the speech as 'one of the finest speeches in modern politics, delivered by a master', and as a speech which delivered 'a powerful mixture of classically trained cool and the heat of the traditional African-American church'.

President Barack Obama's acceptance speech

An abridged version of President Barack Obama's acceptance speech is given in Figure C5.1 (opposite). An estimated crowd of 240,000 were in the audience when Obama gave the speech. The speech was also carried live by broadcasters globally and recorded for later transmission. Videos and transcripts of the event are widely available on the internet. (Because of lack of space, the original text has been edited here, but in a way that ensures that certain rhetorical features are retained. What is presented below is most of the first half of the speech plus the final three paragraphs.)

Figure C5.1 Acceptance speech by the new president-elect of the United States of America, Barack Obama (guardian.co.uk, Wednesday, 5 November 2008, 05.24 GMT)

If there is anyone out there who still doubts that America is a place where all things are possible; who still wonders if the dream of our founders is alive in our time; who still questions the power of our democracy, tonight is your answer.

It's the answer told by lines that stretched around schools and churches in numbers this nation has never seen; by people who waited three hours and four hours, many for the very first time in their lives, because they believed that this time must be different; that their voice could be that difference.

It's the answer spoken by young and old, rich and poor, Democrat and Republican, black, white, Latino, Asian, Native American, gay, straight, disabled and not disabled – Americans who sent a message to the world that we have never been a collection of Red States and Blue States: we are, and always will be, the United States of America.

It's the answer that led those who have been told for so long by so many to be cynical, and fearful, and doubtful of what we can achieve to put their hands on the arc of history and bend it once more toward the hope of a better day.

It's been a long time coming, but tonight, because of what we did on this day, in this election, at this defining moment, change has come to America.

I just received a very gracious call from Senator McCain. He fought long and hard in this campaign, and he's fought even longer and harder for the country he loves. He has endured sacrifices for America that most of us cannot begin to imagine, and we are better off for the service rendered by this brave and selfless leader. I congratulate him and Governor Palin for all they have achieved, and I look forward to working with them to renew this nation's promise in the months ahead.

I would not be standing here tonight without the unyielding support of my best friend for the last sixteen years, the rock of our family and the love of my life, our nation's next First Lady, Michelle Obama. Sasha and Malia, I love you both so much, and you have earned the new puppy that's coming with us to the White House. And while she's no longer with us, I know my grandmother is watching, along with the family that made me who I am. I miss them tonight, and know that my debt to them is beyond measure.

But above all, I will never forget who this victory truly belongs to – it belongs to you.

I was never the likeliest candidate for this office. We didn't start with much money or many endorsements. Our campaign was not hatched in the halls of Washington – it began in the backyards of Des Moines and the living rooms of Concord and the front porches of Charleston.

It was built by working men and women who dug into what little savings they had to give five dollars and ten dollars and twenty dollars to this cause. It grew strength from the young people who rejected the myth of their generation's apathy; who left their homes and their families for jobs that offered little pay and less sleep; from the not-so-young people who braved the bitter cold and scorching heat to knock on the doors of perfect strangers; from the millions of Americans who volunteered, and organized, and proved that more than two centuries later, a government of the people, by the people and for the people has not perished from this Earth. This is your victory.

I know you didn't do this just to win an election and I know you didn't do it for me. You did it because you understand the enormity of the task that lies ahead. For even as we celebrate tonight, we know the challenges that tomorrow will bring are the greatest of our lifetime – two wars, a planet in peril, the worst financial crisis in a century. Even as we stand here tonight, we know there are brave Americans waking up in the deserts of Iraq and the mountains of Afghanistan to risk their lives for us. There are mothers and fathers who will lie awake after their children fall asleep and wonder how they'll make the mortgage, or pay their doctor's bills, or save enough for college. There is new energy to harness and new jobs to be created; new schools to build and threats to meet and alliances to repair.

The road ahead will be long. Our climb will be steep. We may not get there in one year or even one term, but America – I have never been more hopeful than I am tonight that we will get there. I promise you – we as a people will get there. [. . .]

America, we have come so far. We have seen so much. But there is so much more to do. So tonight, let us ask ourselves – if our children should live to see the next century; if my daughters should be so lucky to live as long as Ann Nixon Cooper, what change will they see? What progress will we have made?

This is our chance to answer that call. This is our moment. This is our time – to put our people back to work and open doors of opportunity for our kids; to restore prosperity and promote the cause of peace; to reclaim the American Dream and reaffirm that fundamental truth – that out of many, we are one; that while we breathe, we hope, and where we are met with cynicism, and doubt, and those who tell us that we can't, we will respond with that timeless creed that sums up the spirit of a people:

Yes We Can. Thank you, God bless you, and may God Bless the United States of America.

Overall, the speech summons up the ideals of the US Declaration of Independence. It also refers in its language to earlier presidential visions associated with John F. Kennedy and at other points, Ronald Reagan. Most distinctive, however, is its echo of the civil rights campaigner Martin Luther King, whose well-known 'I have a dream' speech evoked a dream of equality. In *The Sunday Times*'s appreciation of the speech mentioned above, the linguist David Crystal calls the speech 'a Martin Luther King sandwich'. Obama, he suggests, 'starts and ends with a reference to the dream. He doesn't mention King by name, but . . . there's an over-arching structure to this: begin, dream and question; end, dream and answer'. Crystal also points out that Obama deploys classic rhythms and structures: 'One of the most famous rhetorical devices in the English language is the rule of three. Everybody who wants to be a successful speaker does it . . . For example, in the paragraph about his wife, he says she is "the rock of our family, the love of my life, the nation's next first lady – Michelle Obama". This triptych effect works because it allows for steady climax, then applause.'

Obama's oratory style also won praise from Jonathan Sacks, Chief Rabbi of the United Kingdom and writer for *The Times*. In *The Times*, Sacks admires 'Obama's long, perfectly balanced sentences, his ability to shift pitch and perspective without losing narrative flow'. Obama's subtle evocations of Lincoln and Martin Luther King, whom Sacks describes as 'two masters of the genre', were seen as 'demonstrations of the power of public speech to move imaginations and lift hearts'. As Sacks put it, 'Words are essential to democracy, where the power of persuasion must always defeat the threat of coercion . . . victory goes to the leader who can speak to the anxieties of the age, constructing for a generation a compelling narrative of hope'. That could be why Obama won.

In this activity we look more closely at different rhetorical devices deployed in Obama's speech.

- ❑ Look for examples of figurative language, such as metaphor and metonymy, sound patterning, as well as repetition, list of three, and alliteration, etc. (as outlined in units A5 and B5).
- ❑ Identify any other rhetorical features in this speech that you associate with political oratory styles. Widen your commentary on the political language used here by describing the function and effectiveness of each device in the context of the speech and in relation to speaker intent. Some of your descriptions of function will be highly general, such as 'being memorable' or 'sounding religious'. Others are likely to be quite specific, relating to the particular topic or theme being presented.

Feedback/commentary on tasks and activities

The results from an analysis of Barack Obama's presidential acceptance speech are shown in Table C5.1. (This is not a comprehensive list; the points under 'Function' present one interpretation of the meaning of the text and are open to discussion.)

Table C5.1 Analysis of Barack Obama's presidential acceptance speech

Rhetorical device	*Form (with line numbers)*	*Function*
Figurative language		
Metaphor	'to put their hands on the arc of history and bend it once more toward the hope of a better day' (15–17)	History is something that can be grasped, shaped and manipulated rather than something that happens (i.e. humans are active agents rather than passive)
	'It's been a long time coming . . . change has come to America' (18–19)	'change' is used as a noun (as opposed to verb) to suggest that it has been on a journey and has finally arrived
	'the rock of our family' (28)	Solid and stable
	'my debt to them is beyond measure' (33)	Debt is seen as something that is quantifiable and therefore measurable
	'I will never forget who this victory truly belongs to' (34)	'victory' is something that can be possessed
	'Our campaign was not hatched in the halls of Washington' (37)	While 'hatched' could suggest the idea of giving life to something, it is more likely to imply a plot
	'The road ahead will be long. Our climb will be steep. We may not get there in one year . . .' (60)	Life and the future is a difficult journey
Metonymy	'our nation's next First Lady' (29)	Wife of America's next President
	'the White House' (31)	Usually a metonym for the Government and President, but here, literally their home
	'this office' (36)	Presidency
	'America' (1, 19, 61, 64)	Government, politicians, citizens and voters
	'American Dream' (72)	Pursuit and achievement of wealth, success, happiness, equality, etc. regardless of status, colour, etc.

Rhetorical device	*Form (with line numbers)*	*Function*
Sound patterning		
Repetition	'so long by so many' (14–15) 'He fought long and hard in this campaign, and he's fought even longer and harder for the country' (20–1)	Repetition of words and clauses offers lyrical patterning to what is being said which can sound poetic and even mesmerising; repetition is also emphatic and memorable
	'victory . . . This is your victory' (34, 38)	Also, see Lexis: Pronouns
	'I know you didn't do . . . I know you didn't do . . . You did it' (49–50)	
	'if our children . . . if my daughters' (65, 66)	*If*-clause mimics the opening clause of the speech
List of three	'who still doubts . . . who still wonders . . . who still questions' (1–3) 'It's the answer told . . . It's the answer spoken . . . It's the answer that led . . .' (5–14) 'cynical, and fearful, and doubtful' (15) 'on this day, in this election, at this defining moment' (18–19) 'five dollars and ten dollars and twenty dollars' (41) 'It grew strength from the young people . . . from the not-so-young people . . . from the millions of Americans' (42–6) 'volunteered, and organized, and proved' (46) 'a government of the people, by the people and for the people' (47–8) 'This is our chance . . . This is our moment. This is our time' (69–70) 'to put . . . to restore . . . to reclaim' (70–1)	Similar to repetition in sounding poetic and being emphatic, it is also attractive to the listener as it provides a sense of unity
Alliteration	'planet in peril' (52)	Provides rhythm

Rhetorical device	*Form (with line numbers)*	*Function*
Lexis		
Pronouns	'because of what we did' (18)	Use of 'we' signals inclusion and personalisation – Obama acknowledges his victory being due to the people of America
	'I congratulate him . . . I look forward to' (24–5)	Return to 1st person pronoun shows command and power
	'this victory truly belongs to – it belongs to you . . . This is your victory' (34–5)	Use and repetition of 'victory' and 2nd person pronouns 'you' and 'your', emphatically credits the voters for election success
	'We may not get there in one year' (60–1)	Inclusive 'we' – everyone is on the same journey along the same road
Other marked examples	'. . . what change . . .? What progress . . .?' (67)	Rhetorical questions with What?
	'Ann Nixon Cooper' (67)	An American activist for African-American people's rights, aged 106 and supporter of Obama
	'Yes We Can' (76)	A catch-phrase that became Obama's campaign chant

Activity ✪

- ❏ Can you identify other examples of rhetoric or creative use of lexis in this speech?
- ❏ Analyse another political speech that you are familiar with. How many of the above rhetorical devices do you also find there?

Rhetoric and figurative language in an advert

Our second example is from a one-page advert for Cheshire County Council, a regional authority in the UK (Figure C5.2). The advert was placed in a free magazine distributed on trains belonging to a well-known national rail company in Britain, between January and March 2008.

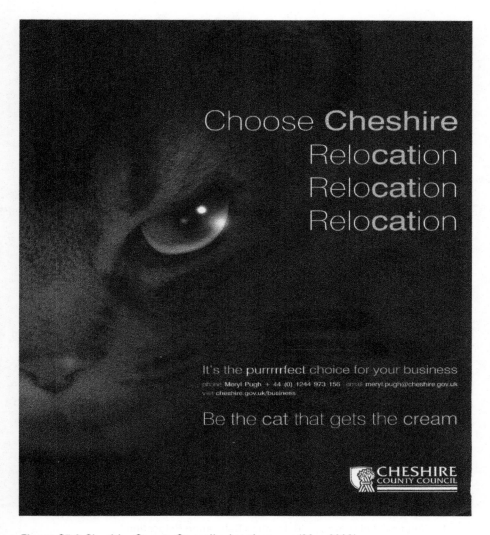

Figure C5.2 **Cheshire County Council advertisement (May 2008)**

There is very little verbal material in the advert. But it nevertheless uses a number of rhetorical devices outlined in unit A5, including *metaphor*, *repetition*, *onomatopoeia* and *the list of three*. Additionally, pragmatic inferencing is needed to make sense of the 'Cheshire cat' link. The reading processes involved show how, in some adverts, understanding requires more than narrowly linguistic knowledge. There is a need for cultural and pragmatic knowledge that underpins a process of interpretive problem-solving.

Activity 

Examine the advertisement for its range of rhetorical devices and write a brief response to each of the tasks given in Table C5.2.

Table C5.2 Analysis of Cheshire County Council advert (tasks grid)

	Task	*Response*
1	Find a list of three	
2	Find an example of onomatopoeia	
3	Find an example of alliteration	
4	Find an example of an idiom or proverb, and explain what it means	
5	Identify some features of design that show wordplay	
6	Is there any specific connection that links the cat imagery to Cheshire, rather than to any other county?	

Now read some responses to these questions that we would offer ourselves (see Table C5.3). Our responses are not the only ones possible. They are simply one way of getting started and/or checking your ideas.

Table C5.3 Analysis of Cheshire County Council advert (possible answers grid)

	Task	*Response*
1	Find a list of three	'Relocation Relocation Relocation'
2	Find an example of onomatopoeia	'purrrrrfect' (a marginal example, because 'perfect' is the usual word form, and this form doesn't echo the sound made by the cat – it only does when the form of the word is modified)
3	Find an example of alliteration	'Choose Cheshire'; 'cat . . . cream' (both highlighted in yellow in original)
4	Find an example of an idiom or proverb, and explain what it means	'cat that gets the cream' (An English idiom 'the cat that got the cream' means someone who is pleased with himself or herself because they have done something well or been very lucky.)

5	Identify some features of design that show wordplay	The word 'cat' highlighted in the middle of 'Re-location'. (Interestingly, in the original advert the font colours are white and yellow on a black back-ground, mimicking the colours of a tabby cat.)
6	Is there any specific connection that links the cat imagery to Cheshire in particular, rather than to any other county?	There is a character in *Alice in Wonderland* called the Cheshire Cat, who is able to disappear and reappear at will and is famous for its grin. In one episode, the cat's body disappears so only the head is visible, similar to the cat in this advert. Incidentally, there is no special breed of cat indigenous to the English county of Cheshire.

Now consider a wider question. The points made above are isolated observations. How do they relate to each other? And how can an interpretive response be developed from such isolated insights to produce a coherent reading of the advert as something persuasive and memorable?

Consider an example of how a reading of the text might develop. We noted in unit A5 how Tony Blair's celebrated mantra, 'Education, Education, Education', is a three-part list, but uses the same word in all three positions. This has the effect, we suggested, of making the three topmost priorities one and the same: a 'super' priority. Blair was emphasising rhetorically that, for him, 'education' was not just one of three priorities; it stood alone as the single, topmost priority – to be insisted on and not diverted from. In this advert, 'relocation' (for the council, inward investment and new jobs as a result of businesses moving into the area) is similarly used as the repeated, sole term in a three-term list. In this case, however, there is an additional considera-tion to note. An audience reading 'Relocation, Relocation, Relocation' is likely already to know 'Education, Education, Education'. So the relocation three-term list is now also an *allusion*, or reference, to the Blair use. The copywriters could expect this refer-ence to be picked up by most of their UK readers. What significance those readers will attribute to that reference is less certain. They might see it as merely emphatic repeti-tion, used to attract as much attention as possible, like a market trader calling out 'new potatoes, new potatoes, new potatoes' (this is, after all, an advert). Or they might see it as underscoring the single-mindedness with which the council proposes to pursue its priority of encouraging 'relocation'. Or they might consider it a comical self-reference, mimicking how politicians talk (it is, after all, an advert for a council). The effect of the 'relocation' three-part list is accordingly:

- a rhetorical figure (the three-part list),
- an allusion (to Blair's political style), and
- a visual device embedding the word 'cat' within the word.

In examining rhetoric in different kinds of discourse, we suggest that it is generally pos-sible to start from any observation of the kind listed in Table C5.2 and work outwards into an overall reading of what gives the advert its impact. Such linking of observation and interpretation forms the basis of what would be a stylistic reading of the advert.

Promotional culture

The advert we chose to look at in this unit is an advert for a political body, a regional county council. It is not for goods or services provided by a commercial company. Why should such a body be advertising using persuasive, rhetorical devices, rather than working to achieve its purposes through a more neutral information campaign, or by means of other political or civil channels?

Persuasive media techniques, we suggest, play a part in presenting information and viewpoint across a wide variety of fields. Those fields range from commercial advertising, through promotion of charities, NGOs and other not-for-profit organisations, to celebrity and entertainment PR. We also suggest that rhetorical techniques and persuasion play a significant part in the design of information campaigns and news. Rhetorical techniques can serve the purpose of promotion and advocacy for anything from a purchase to a political campaign. In making this point we are not judging the suitability or morality of such techniques. For instance, we are not suggesting that persuasion is automatically biased, misleading or deceptive. We are simply recognising that communication often achieves its effects – especially in a saturated media environment – by heightening memorability and impact in how language is used.

Wernick (1991) describes this enlarged field of 'promotional culture' in some detail. He looks at how an 'enterprise', commercial model of social action is now adopted by many different kinds of public institution as well as by companies. Myers (1999), in analysing 'ad worlds' or the overall advertising environment, links these wider themes of promotional culture to the language of advertising in particular. He reflects on the boundary between advertising and broader strategies of promotion as follows:

> The wider effects of advertising are hard to see because it is set in a wider promotional culture, and it is hard to tell where advertising stops and other forms of promotion begin. So, for instance, there are elements of promotion in job application letters, hospital statistics, university course descriptions, brochures from military research labs, covers of textbooks, charity fundraising events, interviews with authors on talk shows, concerts of classical music, lonely hearts ads, and the building of municipal sports facilities. We know that promotion is everywhere, trust ourselves to discount the hype, and are only surprised when we find promotion in an area where we thought decisions were made on other grounds than images. [. . .] Promotional culture can be seen moving the other way as well, as advertisements take more and more of a role in areas of life that had previously been associated with other forms of communication. For instance [. . .]:
>
> - how an ad for a bank affects concepts of civic responsibility and human rights;
> - how an ad for a detergent deals with concepts of the private and the public;
> - how advertisements shape the timing of TV comedy;
> - how news images are incorporated into advertising;
> - how national images are tied up with consumer products;

- how ads try to intervene to reduce consumption;
- how broadcast ads project sincerity.

> Other institutions have taken on promotion, and advertising has taken on the roles of other institutions.
>
> (Myers, 1999: 5)

In the sort of 'ad world' or promotional culture that Myers describes here, disentangling information and persuasion becomes increasingly important. For any given piece of discourse we do well, therefore, to pay close attention to what is being claimed to be true, what devices are being used to persuade, and what overall outcome or impact is sought. In the third reading in unit D5, Norman Fairclough presents a checklist of questions that it is useful to ask in trying to do this.

MEDIA FICTION AND FACT

C6

This unit brings together themes in our earlier discussion of media narratives, story structures and story functions by presenting accounts of first-person experiences. As a sub-category of the storytelling genre, personal narratives provide the most subjective and emotive accounts of events. Yet at the same time they can seem authoritative bearers of truth, closest to what has happened and as a result 'authentic' in a way that other kinds of report or commentary cannot be. This is particularly the case with accounts of survival related to events of global significance and interest. Storytelling permeates everyday discourse. In mediated form, it also offers a conduit for emotion-laden experiences that influence public opinion and highlight events that have damaging and tragic consequences.

Personal narratives as news: survivor stories

Presented below are several personal accounts of the same event. The stories are presented as told by survivors of the Indian Ocean tsunami (also referred to by the media as the Asian tsunami, the Boxing Day tsunami and the Great Sumatra–Andaman earthquake). The survivor stories presented here invite comparison as regards how personal experiences are told and structured.

The event in question happened on 26 December 2004 (Boxing Day in the UK). An undersea earthquake with a magnitude of 9.2 – the second largest ever recorded on a seismograph – struck the Indian Ocean. The earthquake set in motion a series of tsunamis that devastated the coastal regions of countries in the Indian Ocean. About 225,000 people are thought to have lost their lives, with many, many thousands made homeless. The countries hardest hit were Indonesia, Sri Lanka, India and Thailand. In Indonesia alone, the country closest to the earthquake's epicentre, about 130,000 people died and 37,000 others remain missing.

Activity 

Consider the following questions about the tragic events described above.

- ❏ The Indian Ocean tsunami was covered by all media news channels. In what circumstances, and through what channel, did you first hear the news?
- ❏ Which media format did you use to find out more: newspaper, radio, the internet? What determined your choice of media format for this purpose?
- ❏ What aspect of the reporting did you find the most informative, engaging, or compelling: a journalist reporting events; eyewitness reports and personal accounts; the visual images?

If you are not familiar with this event, think of a differnt event that is memorable to you (e.g. the Chinese earthquake in 2008; the 9/11 terrorist attacks in America, 2001; the Madrid bombings in 2004; the 7/7 London bombings in 2005; the 2008 terrorist attacks in Mumbai).

Below, we present four personal accounts which all appeared online but not all in the same media format: one account was reported by the BBC as a news report; the other three originated as emails to CNN.

Activity 

- ❏ Begin by reading the news report entitled 'Mother in photos survived tsunami' (Figure C6.1). Analyse the news story of Karin Svaerd's personal experience, focusing on the structure of the story. Use Labov and Waletzky's (1967) model of narrative outlined in B6 (Table B6.1) to identify the different stages or schemas of the story (i.e abstract, orientation, complicating action, evaluation, resolution, coda). You may want to construct a grid with the six schemas to help you analyse the story. Try to identify where each of the six stages begins and ends. Are all the components of a typical narrative present? How does Karin Svaerd evaluate her experience? (Think of the formal devices that signal the process of evaluation, rather than the content of her evaluation.)
- ❏ Read the emails (A–C) from tsunami survivors (p. 162). Again, analyse these personal experiences using Labov and Waletzky's model.
- ❏ As a consumer of media discourse, which of the two news formats for reporting a personal experience do you consider more authentic and/or authoritative: a news report incorporating photos and direct quotes, or a series of first-person emails? Which aspects of the format do you consider more authentic or authoritative? Which create the effect you are particularly responding to?

Figure C6.1 'Mother in photos survived tsunami' (http://news.bbc.co.uk/1/hi/world/europe/4141733.stm) Sunday, 2 January 2005, 18:21 GMT

A Swedish tourist who was pictured running into the Asian tsunami to save her family survived the catastrophe, as did her children, it has been revealed.

Swedish tourist Karin Svaerd (right) saw the pictures on her return home

Newspapers around the world showed a desperate Karin Svaerd heading into the waves as other tourists fled.

On Sunday the 37-year-old policewoman told the press she survived by grabbing hold of a palm tree on the Thai beach.

But it was an agonising 10 minutes before she discovered that her husband and three children had also escaped.

"I can remember the white foam, how the surf took them up and they disappeared," she told Britain's *News of the World* in an interview published on Sunday.

Witnesses said she screamed: "Oh my God, not my children!"

"I could hear people shouting at me 'Get off the beach' as I ran past them – but I ignored them," she said.

"I had to try and save my children, nothing was going to stop me."

"I had to try and save my children, nothing was going to stop me" Karin Svaerd

She said she thought she would die as she was engulfed by the tide, but in fact it swept her onto higher ground at the resort of Krabi.

Then she feared for her husband Lars, her sons Anton, 14, Filip, 11, and Viktor, 10, and her brother, Per.

She found them together 10 minutes later.

They flew back to Sweden, arriving on 30 December, and then seeing the pictures in the press, under headlines like: "No one knows if they survived."

"Now, our family is closer than ever before," Mrs Svaerd said. "We came so close to death that we realise how valuable life is."

Tsunami tragedy: your emails

Monday, January 24, 2005, posted: 11:01 AM EST (1601 GMT)

London, England (CNN) – Here are a selection of eyewitness accounts from people who e-mailed us with their experiences of the devastation. Please note our message boards are now closed.

A I went to Pondicherry, on the coast, with my wife and two sons for the weekend. I was playing in the sea with my sons when we first noticed the water coming in higher than usual. I wasn't alarmed as the sea was so calm that day. As the seconds passed, we saw the waves picking up momentum. By that time, my boys and I were walking back. When I turned and saw the waves gaining speed and height, I knew there was something wrong. I just screamed at both my sons to run. We saw another couple by the beach taking photographs and they were much slower in reacting. As we ran into the dining area of the resort the water had climbed to a height of 8–10 feet and was coming on like a wall. I shouted at the restaurant manager that the sea was coming in and ran to the first floor. From there, I saw the sea crash into the restaurant. I ran to our room and pulled my wife out. Just then we saw the water had come around the resort and we were surrounded. Just as I was expecting the water to crash into the first floor, the water started to subside. By that time, a lot of people at the resort had come to the lobby, some even without their clothes on, thinking that it was the end. There was a tourist who passed a remark that he was not told that this kind of thing happens in India.
Karthik, Chennai, India

B I was on holiday near Phuket on Koh Surin. It was my third visit there and everything seemed totally normal. I went kayaking in the morning and reached the shore before the wave struck but was still washed away by the wave. I grabbed the kayak, which was wedged between two trees. I managed to climb off and walked up a nearby hill. It was so devastating to watch.
Charavee Bunyasiri Deer, Bangkok

C I was at the Selaka Shopping Complex at Galle. There was a great hissing sound from the sea and the sea seemed to be caving in. Within seconds, a great wave came rushing in to the shore, destroying everything and sweeping away everybody who was in the way. Everyone vanished in a second. The whole town was destroyed, along with people at the bus stand and vehicles on the road within few seconds. It is like a dream. I have never seen anything like it.
Deepa, Galle, Sri Lanka

Write or audio record a personal narrative reporting an experience (you may wish to choose a far less traumatic topic) in a similar format to Karin's story. Your narrative should include:

- a headline,
- contextual information, and
- actual quotes from the protagonist of the experience which will form the basis of what Labov and Waletzky (1967) describe as the 'complicating action' that is essential to the 'narrative events'. (See Table B6.1.)

SOUNDTRACK AND MULTIMODAL DISCOURSE

In units A7 and B7, we focus on fixed images, typically photographs, and on captions that are used to accompany them. Such captions, we suggest, narrow the meaning of the images. In this unit, we

- widen discussion in order to take account of different kinds of speech on a TV soundtrack or online video clip;
- raise the question whether interaction between words and images in multimodal discourse (such as web pages) calls for repeated, if more complex, kinds of essentially the same approach to analysis – or whether multimodal discourse requires a fundamentally new approach.

Voices on the soundtrack

If you watch a clip of narrative television, most of the speech you hear can be linked back to speakers visible in the image. In unit B7, we describe such talk as diegetic speech. Exceptions (i.e. non-diegetic speech) include voicemail messages played back from machines shown in the image; speech emanating from radios that are visible or implied as part of the situation being depicted; and public announcements at coach and rail stations, signalled by the thinner audio quality characteristic of a PA system. Notice that the sounds of diegetic speech are precisely synchronised with the moving image. This creates a sense of simultaneous movement and paralinguistic gesture (such as kinds of facial expression) along with the sound of speech itself. If you watch online video content reproduced at low quality, such synchronisation is often inexact. The resulting effect shows up how much we rely on precise synchronisation for a sense of co-ordinated verbal action and gesture.

By contrast, if you watch a clip of news, documentary or features television, much of the speech you hear will take the form of voice-overs. This is another kind of non-diegetic speech, since there is no speaker visible in the image to trace the speech back to. There will usually also be kinds of talking in vision, sometimes called 'talking

heads' TV, because emphasis is given by means of the selected camera angles to the head and shoulders of respective speakers. Where there is relatively little visual interest in the images that accompany the talking, sometimes this style of television is dismissively referred to as 'radio with pictures'. A number of features of this televised talk are noticeable.

- The tempo of the talking may vary with genre or format (horse-racing commentary, for instance, represents an extreme of tempo and acceleration, while some styles of reflective documentary linger on pauses and painfully articulated personal comment).
- Periodically the image cuts away from any given speaker, even in the middle of a stretch of otherwise apparently continuous discourse. Such cuts are sometimes referred to as cutaways, or 'noddies'. They allow a segment of spoken discourse to be deleted without an apparent jump in the image by inserting either a detail – the speaker's hands or some other part of the body – or the separately recorded nodding reaction of an interviewer where there is one, hence the informal term 'noddy'.
- Sometimes a picture cut and an audio cut from one speaking voice to another are inserted at slightly different points. This creates what is called a 'split edit'. Mostly the new voice starts ahead of the image of the speaker, creating an effect of voice-over before the identity of the speaker is revealed in vision.

Each of these features of media style is an important device in constructing speech-based television or online audio-visual content. Such features often also tell us something about the raw recorded materials ('the rushes') from which the audio-visual discourse has been constructed. Such stylistic details can act as a guide, for example, to whether the talk being presented was originally continuous or whether it has been edited into an appearance of continuity (and possibly greater coherence).

More important as regards the interaction between sound and image, however, are techniques used in the writing and delivery of voice-over commentary. Such commentary, which is typically switched intermittently with diegetic speech, binds together a mix of synchronised video, rostrum photography, graphics, and other materials that make up the programme.

Voice-over techniques combine the different categories of caption work outlined in unit B7. In the flow of a script, references of different kinds are made to objects and people depicted in accompanying images. Sometimes connections work directly, at the level of what is denoted. At other times they work obliquely, in ways that require inference to connect the thought expressed in the voice-over with what the audience is shown in the image. Functionally, the combination of voice-over and diegetic speech works to achieve both of Barthes's concepts of relay and anchorage outlined in unit B7.

We can explore these distinctions by analysing a short stretch of TV documentary. Below, we illustrate the working of voice-over in combination with diegetic speech by presenting a short section from a documentary television script (Figure C7.1). In the left column, we present a series of screen-grab images to illustrate what is shown in vision in each shot (though remember that shots are not static in TV – each

shot typically contains movement and action). In the centre column, we offer a brief note on what is shown in the image. In the right-hand column, we provide a transcription of what is said on the soundtrack.

The documentary from which the extract below is taken is called *Big Words . . . Small Worlds* (Broken English Productions for Channel 4 television, UK, 1987), written and narrated by the novelist David Lodge. Copyright permitting (one of the authors was producer of this programme), other documentaries and features could have been chosen for the same purpose – though they would have been unlikely to have such a distinguished scriptwriter. The programme is about a linguistics conference which the novelist attends as both an academic speaker and as what he calls a 'conference watcher'. Lodge thus reports in television form on an actual conference, counterpointing how he had previously observed and commented on conferences in fiction.

The extract in Figure C7.1 is from near the beginning of the programme. Lodge comments on his role and reflects on what academics do at conferences. The clip combines first-person narration-to-camera with voice-over commentary. It also contains two moments of transition between the two modes but involving the same speaker, in S4/5 and S6/7 (i.e. shots 4/5 and 6/7).

Figure C7.1 Extract from *Big Words . . . Small Worlds* (Broken English Productions for Channel 4 television, UK, 1987)

S1		Footage of participants entering lecture hall	[*Voice-over*] This behaviour, which might seem mystifying or perverse to an outsider, is in fact a very common feature of academic life.
S2	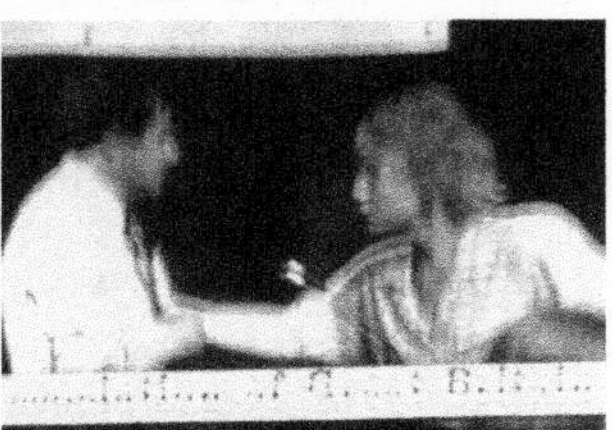	David Lodge and Jane Tompkins in conversation at lectern	As an academic myself . . .
S3		DL in close-up, walks sideways, talking to camera	. . . I've attended a fair number of conferences. I've also published a novel, called *Small World*, . . .

S4

Rostrum shot of novel front cover

Dissolve to speech-to-camera, autocued

. . . which takes a rather irreverent look at the conference phenomenon.

[*Switch from voice-over to recorded speech from conference*]
'My working title . . .

S5

DL addresses audience in lecture hall from lectern

. . . for the novel that's been referred to already several times today was not actually *Small World*. But as we . . .

S6

Sequence of short shots, from different angles, of conference audience sitting in rows

. . . assemble for the sixth time, it seems just as appropriate to this phenomenon. It was called . . .

S7

DL addresses audience from lectern

. . . *We Can't Go on Meeting Like This*'.

[*Laughter. Dip sound and cross-fade to voice-over*]
So I attended this one in a dual capacity – as one of the principal speakers, . . .

S8

Dissolve to DL sitting on settee in conference foyer and beginning to open envelope

. . . but also as what Desmond Morris might have called a 'conference watcher'.

All conferences . . .

S9

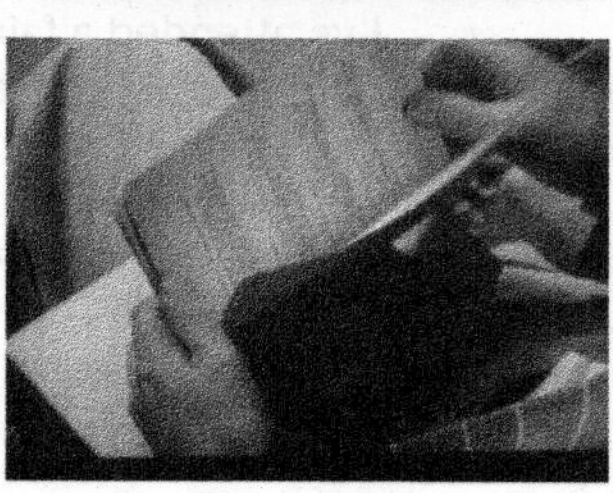

Close-up of DL's lap; DL opens envelope containing conference brochure

. . . have a family resemblance to each other. But each one has its own plot, one might say . . .

S10		Close-up of DL reading names in conference brochure	And of course its own cast of characters.
S11		Close-up of conference brochure listing participants	Most of the people attending this conference fell in two broad categories. Either they were linguists, primarily interested in language as a system . . .
S12		Dissolve to mid-shot of speaker (Mary Louise Pratt) at lectern	. . . or they were literary critics, primarily interested . . .
S13		Dissolve to mid-shot of speaker (John Hollander) at lectern	. . . in the meanings of texts. These two groups, though they work . . .
S14		Dissolve to mid-shot of speaker (Paul Kiparsky) at lectern	. . . side-by-side in universities, seldom engage in public debate with each other.
S15		Dissolve to shot from back of hall of speaker (Stanley Fish) at lectern	The aim of the Strathclyde conference was to arrange just such a confrontation.

Activity 

- ❑ Compare the three columns. Look for points at which reference is made in the voice-over commentary to what is being shown simultaneously in the image, or references which trail (or foreshadow) what will be shown next. To get started, consider the following words and phrases in the script: 'this behaviour' (S1), 'myself' (S2), 'conferences' (S3), 'Small World' (S3 and S4).
- ❑ Now start an equivalent process in the other direction. Begin with what is shown in-vision, rather than with what is referred to in the script. Look through the sequence of screen-grab photos and offer a short explanation of the basis on which each inserted shot might be justified as a suitable accompaniment to the voice-over commentary.
- ❑ Decide, as far as you can on the limited evidence presented here, which shots are superfluous to the progress of the action, and so do not contribute to Barthes's 'relay' function (which is introduced in unit B7).
- ❑ The voice-over commentary extract selected here ends with the phrase 'just such a confrontation'. What sort of shot or sequence of shots do you expect to come next? Why?

Activity 

Record approximately two minutes of news or documentary from broadcast TV (or from a site like YouTube, if you can find a suitable clip that has both speech in vision and voice-over). Two minutes may seem a very short time to record but it is a long time to analyse. Select a genre and topic quite different from the 'arts programme' strand in which the documentary *Big Words* appeared. Go through the clip (probably repeatedly), writing down details of the relation between word and image at each stage. You may find it helpful to set out your analysis in the grid format adopted for the clip above.

1. Distinguish stretches that have speech-in-vision (characters talking). Such speech largely serves Barthes's relay function, and the central interest of the image is likely to be the speaker speaking.
   Is the speaker talking to one or more other people who are also shown in the image? (placing us as overhearers, as outlined in unit A3)
   Is the speaker talking directly to camera? (making us addressees, as discussed in relation to pop lyrics and kinds of contrived pseudo-intimacy in unit C3)
   If there are shifts between these two main lines of sight (sometimes talking to characters in scene, at other moments talking to the audience), why?
   What considerations prompt speech-to-camera, if there is any?
2. How does the language of the clip serve the relay function? What aspects of the language work most to push the story forward?

3 Now consider voice(s) not in vision: i.e. voice-over. Pause where necessary and write down each time a word or phrase in the voice-over script refers directly to something you can see in the image. Obvious made-up examples would include, 'The weather is fine' (with a scene of a sunny day); 'John is driving to work' (image shows person in car), etc. How frequently does this type of link occur? Are there moments when words in the commentary appear connected with the image but not in a directly referring relationship to what is shown?

4 Do the directly referring links to what you can see come mostly at the beginning of a scene, working to 'establish' it? This would be rather like an introduction to a written story or play, guiding you into a pictured world.

5 Listen carefully for deictic terms: 'here', 'now', 'tomorrow', etc. Do such terms relate to a moment of speaking in the image (characters talking about what was happening when the images were recorded)? Or do they relate to a later moment: the moment of recording the commentary? (e.g. 'now' = as we watch, not as it happened). Are there cases where time deictics seem to relate neither to the moment of recorded action, nor to the moment of recorded voice-over, but to a different moment: the moment of viewing?

6 Finally, choose a different genre altogether, such as a sports commentary. Does verbal discourse work in roughly the same way? Use the questions listed above to help you explore this aspect of media genre.

Analysing multimodal discourse

When you look at a web page, you are likely in many cases to be faced with a combination of written text, photographs and other visual imagery. Sometimes the screen view will also show small-screen video content displays embedded in the large screen. Some semioticians argue that such multimodal discourse calls for a fundamentally new kind of analysis, if we are to take proper account of interaction between the different component media forms and styles of design. Some of our discussion above seems to support this view. Our extract from Kress and van Leeuwen in unit D7 sets out such a view in detail. The extract forms part of their introduction to a study they undertake of relations between different elements that make up multimodal discourse (Kress and van Leeuwen, 2001).

An alternative view is that no fundamentally new form of analysis may be needed. Where there are points of interaction between the various kinds of discourse, analysis is needed. But in other respects what is happening may be more a matter of juxtaposition than of mixed-mode synthesis or integration. The idea of constrained inference might offer a more suitable line of enquiry. This second view – which prioritises examining points of contact and interaction between modes, rather than offering an analysis of everything synthesised together – has parallels with other situations. It is a little like saying that analysing someone talking in a room may potentially require

analysis of the social situation, the room décor, the interactants' clothing, their styles of movement and gesture, and what they say. But while such an analysis of the whole-situation-together *may* in the end be needed, little is lost in an analysis that views each element as separate initially, then combines them in the course of a particular interpretation. This second view seems to be, in essence, the point of view that Barthes puts forward in his investigation of photographs (see unit A7). There, he emphasises complementary roles for semiological and sociological lines of investigation, for instance, rather than the need for a unified overall theory.

Activity 

We have presented two possible models of research into multimodal discourse.

- ❑ Which of the two approaches do you find more convincing? Why?
- ❑ What kinds of interaction between the various elements of web pages should we expect to find? And what kinds of concept are likely to be needed in order to describe them?
- ❑ Is the analogy with Barthes's separation of semiology and sociology made above a fair one? For instance, is interaction between different elements shown in a web browser screen really comparable with interaction between analysing signs and analysing social structures?
- ❑ Describe, in as much detail as possible, the different modes of communication in, first, a single screen from a website, and then the combination of various pages you can access by navigating between them (choose a small site to make this task practicable!).
- ❑ When you have undertaken your analysis, read the Kress and van Leeuwen extract presented in unit D7. Assess how far their general framework and indicative concepts allow you to develop your analysis.

C8 MEDIA LANGUAGE AND ACCEPTABILITY

Before we can begin to think about bad or offensive language it is important to establish some kinds of definition. The subject is inevitably a highly subjective one at various levels.

Sociolinguistic research typically investigates, under the heading of 'bad language' judgements, anything from slang, swearing (taboo words), 'sort of' phrases, poor grammar and over-use of 'like', through to allegedly outlandish accents. It also extends through to obscene and derogatory epithets (descriptions and name-calling), and other kinds of insult, slur and invective. The latter categories of 'bad language' can cause grave offence. In certain situations, such language can amount to what in US legal traditions is known as 'speech plus' and as 'fighting words' (Greenawalt, 1989, 1996; Neu, 2008).

According to Andersson and Trudgill (1992), swear words refer to some topic that is taboo, or stigmatised in the particular culture. Such words may be classified into three major groups on the basis of their semantic fields:

1 'dirty' words to do with sex and excrement, e.g bugger, fuck and shit,
2 words to do with the Christian religion, in historically Christian countries (and with parallels in other religions), e.g. Christ, Jesus, God's sake, bloody (by our Lady, i.e. Virgin Mary), and
3 calling a person by the name of an animal, e.g. bitch, cow.

Commonly, what is in question is not purely a taboo in relation to a particular subject matter. Swear words upset social conventions governing situations by combining transgression of taboo content (e.g. they are about sexuality or bodily functions) with slang or low register. Equivalent terms exist for each swear word in other (middle or technical) registers; and slang terms exist for many other, non-taboo referents. It is the combination of slang with taboo – with a resulting pejorative impact – that produces the stylistic distinctiveness of swearing.

Note, too, that the traditional categories referred to above omit a further category, less frequently included in classifications but pervasive in most societies: words that involve racial abuse (Hughes, 1998). Particular issues raised by media use of powerful racially abusive words are considered below.

Activity

Refer to our discussion of offensive verbal behaviour in A8 and B8.

- ❑ Why do people swear? Are there obvious main social functions?
- ❑ Apart from the three traditional categories indicated above, plus racially abusive words, can you think of other major categories of swear word, either in English or in other languages or cultures that you are familiar with?
- ❑ Are some whole classes of swear word, rather than particular individual words, more offensive than others? What would be likely to make one category more offensive than another?

A swearing top ten

The force of particular swear words, and also of swear word categories, changes over time. What was offensive in everyday usage 20 years ago, as well as more specifically in public *media* usage, differs from today's conventional thresholds of acceptability. Media institutions accordingly need to keep track of changes in the public climate of acceptability.

Because many complaints to broadcasting regulators are about 'bad language', surveys of the relative offensiveness of different swear words are periodically undertaken. In the UK, such surveys are reported by the media regulator Ofcom (the Office

of Communications), and previously by the Broadcasting Standards Commission (BSC). Research on the relative force of different swear words was also undertaken in the UK jointly, in 2000, by the Advertising Standards Authority (ASA), the British Broadcasting Corporation (BBC), the Broadcasting Standards Commission (BSC) and the – now defunct – Independent Television Commission (ITC). That research is published online as 'Delete expletives?' (Millwood-Hargrave, 2000). Similar research studies are conducted in many other countries. Figure C8.1 shows in simplified form how data from the BSC survey of 1997 were subsequently reported.

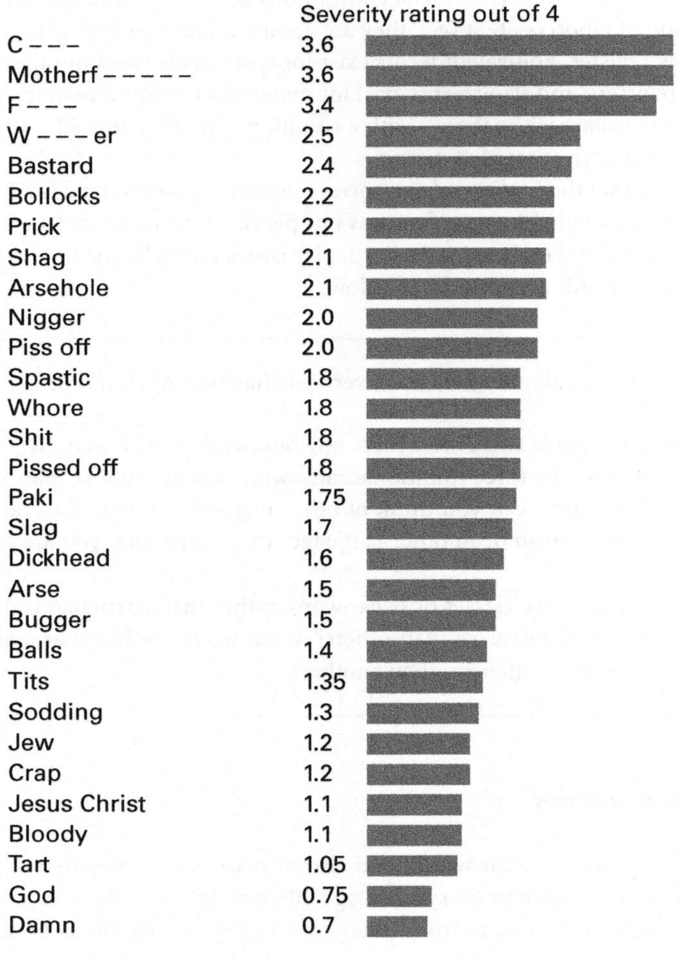

Figure C8.1 Offensiveness of swear words and insults on TV (based on a survey of television viewers by the Broadcasting Standards Commission, 1997)

Activity

1 Are the findings reported here what you would have expected to see in a survey of this kind? If not, what would you have anticipated as being the top five most offensive words? Why those in particular?
2 Are there words that you think (a) should be in the list but are not; (b) should not be in the list but are; (c) are in the list but are far too low down or too high up?
3 If you are from a country other than the UK (where this survey was conducted), consider a comparable recent survey of offensive words if there is one. If not, is there a different source of research data on swear words and their use that you can find for the media in your usual media environment?
4 Draw up a list of complications likely to arise in conducting research leading to this sort of data about media swearing.

In UK research conducted in 2000, the top four most offensive swear words, as rated by informants, remained the same as in the 1997 BSC study above: 'cunt', 'motherfucker', 'fuck' and then 'wanker'. There were signs of movement lower down the list. The highly controversial word 'nigger', which we look at more closely below, rose from only 11 in 1997 to 5 in the 2000 table. The racial epithet 'Paki' rose from 17 to 10. Another change is 'shag', which dropped from 8 to 11. It would be easy to read too much significance into such small shifts. But it is worth considering, as a follow-up to this section, what sorts of hypothesis *would* be worth pursuing in further research, starting from the movements in the table indicated here.

In a more recent UK survey again (November 2008, conducted by the polling organisation YouGov in the midst of a furore about on-screen swearing and offensiveness), almost 40 per cent of viewers claimed to support a total ban on swearing on television. 30 per cent felt that 'fuck' should be banned, and 55 per cent thought that 'cunt' should not be permitted in any circumstances. On the other hand, just under half felt that there *is* a place for some swearing in programmes – mild swear words only – on the grounds that broadcasting should reflect standards of language use even if this means saying things that offend some viewers. The timing of the YouGov poll suggests that it was designed to influence policy thinking, either directly or indirectly. But can conflicting patterns of public feeling be reconciled on this subject? For any individual editor, as well as for broadcasting policy makers, the question is not only a theoretical one: the option does not exist of avoiding specific decisions, and, once made, decisions often have to be publicly defended.

 **Activity**

- As a follow-up to this account of general issues, consider what use should be made of evidence of the kind summarised above. And what *non*-evidential considerations need also to be taken into account in making policy decisions in this field?

Two offensive words

With this general context in place, we now look at two especially controversial words: 'fuck' and 'nigger'.

'Fuck'

Being first to say 'fuck' on television in Britain was a significant act. Theatre critic and writer Kenneth Tynan used the word on TV in 1965. Four motions in Parliament were tabled. In 1976 Steve Jones, guitarist of the group the Sex Pistols, used the same word on a teatime show. They were banned from further appearances but there were no Parliamentary questions or major public outcry. In 2004, an audience of more than ten million watched John Lydon (formerly Johnny Rotten of the same group) say 'cunt' on TV. Fewer than 100 people complained. The power of taboo changes. 'Fuck' is now commonly permitted in evening viewing in Britain, in a number of different genres, though the word is still bleeped out in some programmes and can certainly still cause offence.

Why the change? The word 'fuck' is not a new word in English. It has origins in the mediaeval period and close relatives in other European languages (Hughes, 1998). Over past centuries as well as in the present century, hundreds of millions of speakers of English must have used the word frequently throughout their lives, in many different contexts.

The changing level of sensitivity surrounding media use of the word, therefore, must lie in patterns of language change that reflect shifts of social structure, behaviour and expectation – including about what verbal behaviour in public media should be like. The word 'fuck' is more common in conversational face-to-face usage, including middle-class professional usage, than forty years ago; and it is perhaps unsurprising that media should reflect this change. More importantly, in 1965 the word was symbolic for a media audience operating within a much narrower UK media environment (three terrestrial TV channels, far fewer radio stations, no email and no internet). That media environment was inevitably a more focused public forum for affirming or contesting notions of public identity and standards. Broadcasting styles also tended to be far more formal. In such circumstances, the power of verbal taboo was inevitably much greater.

With current publishing and broadcasting, guidance on use of the word 'fuck' is more complicated. The persistence of complaint suggests that the word still has considerable power to offend and embarrass. Sometimes 'fuck' is still bleeped, or presented in written publications as 'f***', when there is felt to be special sensitivity about a particular audience or related to a specific, restrictive publication or programming policy (e.g. with children's programmes or hospital radio). In the James Blunt song we discuss in unit C3, for example, the line 'I was f–king high' was replaced for the radio edit with 'I was flying high'. Except in reaction to specific panics or public outcries, however, UK editorial policies are concerned more with grounds *why* a particular text or programme should or shouldn't include swearing, rather than with a general rule governing particular words. In practice, what is in question is editorial judgement linked to time watersheds, audience demographics and programme styles.

Editorial judgements are more difficult where the form of the swear word is altered, and so arguably no swearing takes place. The company name FCUK, for

instance (French Connection UK), caused controversy when an application was made to register the name as a trademark (because taboo and offensive words are not eligible for trademark registration). Yet no offensive word is actually used. Leaving aside technical aspects of trademark law, how would you argue a case for (or against) eligibility for trademark registration of FCUK in the face of the objection that the name is offensive? Also consider that in March 2003, in the UK, a juror was dismissed by a judge for wearing an FCUK T-shirt. Was the judge correct to do this if no offensive word is actually used?

Now consider the advert reproduced in Figure C8.2, which raises related issues. The advert appeared in *The Observer* newspaper, a national Sunday quality or broadsheet paper, sister to *The Guardian*. The product being advertised is cheap tickets from Ryanair, an Irish, low-cost airline operating flights across Europe and to North Africa. The advert was printed in the issue of the newspaper for 26 October 2003, timed to coincide broadly with Guy Fawkes Night (or Bonfire Night). Guy Fawkes was the central conspirator of the Gunpowder Plot of 1605. He tried unsuccessfully to blow up the Protestant King James I and the Houses of Parliament in London, and was later executed. Guy Fawkes Night is an annually celebrated festival on 5 November involving fireworks and burning effigies of Guy Fawkes.

Figure C8.2 Ryanair advert (*The Observer*, 26 October 2003)

Activity

When you look at the Ryanair advert, are you:

- ❑ amused and impressed at the creative use of the word 'FAWKING', which involves playful association with a swear word that sounds similar (so that the replacement word functions in combination with 'GREAT' to pre-modify 'OFFERS')?
- ❑ offended that an advert containing such a potentially distasteful verbal trick has been allowed to be printed, especially in what would normally be considered a quality newspaper?

On what lines would you construct a formal complaint about, or a defence of, this advert on behalf of a complainant who felt either one response or the other?

'Nigger'

Many of the core issues to do with swearing have been recently discussed by the US linguist Stephen Pinker (2008). Pinker focuses on the broad issue of desensitisation by offensive words over time (a process that psycholinguists call semantic satiation). Pinker looks in particular at how some speakers, rather than seeking to change a group name applied to them, prefer to confront the negative meanings and associations of the existing name. In doing so, they seek to reclaim the negative name used about them for their own, more assertive or affirmative use. For instance, Pinker describes how

> campaigns have been aimed at epithets for women and minorities, who often try to 'reclaim' the words by using them conspicuously among themselves. Thus we have NWA (Niggaz with Attitude, a hip hop group); Queer Nation, queer studies, and *Queer Eye for the Straight Guy*; Dykes on Bikes (a cycling group for lesbians) and www.classicdykes.com; and the Phunky Bitches, a 'real-time community of women (and men) who are into live music, travel, and a host of other interests'. I have never heard of a temple brotherhood meeting at which the attendees greet each other with 'What's happenin', kike!' but in the 1970s the novelist Kinky Friedman led a country band called the Texas Jewboys, and there is a hip magazine for young Jewish readers called *Heeb*. At the same time, these terms have not been neutralized so much as flaunted as a sign of defiance and solidarity, precisely because they are still offensive in the language community at large. Woe betide the outsider who misunderstands this, like the Hong Kong detective played by Jackie Chan in *Rush Hour* who innocently follows the lead of his African American partner and greets the black patrons of a Los Angeles bar with 'Whassup, my nigger,' thereby starting a small riot.
>
> (Pinker, 2008: 329)

Pinker's discussion here illustrates how reclaiming racially and sexually offensive terms can be seen as an act of empowerment, as well as an act of defiance pending social changes being campaigned for in other ways.

In context, the example of the character played by Jackie Chan that Pinker cites is supposed to be humorous. But it highlights an immediate, practical issue: who, in a situation of simultaneously pejorative and reclaimed affirmative names, has a speaker's right to use certain terms? This is especially problematic where the term is felt to be profoundly offensive or abusive if used by one group, but empowering if used by another. (Note that the wider notion introduced here, that language choice is linked to identity and that certain usages are exclusive, is not new. See, for example, work by the sociolinguist William Labov on overt and covert prestige in his studies of linguistic variables (Labov, 1966).

We conclude this unit with discussion of a UK media controversy over use of the word 'nigger', fuelled by all the issues Pinker refers to. There is always immense sensitivity surrounding use of this word, both because of its accumulated negative history and also on account of its continuing pejorative connotations. Despite its relatively low position in the UK top ten swear words as reported in the BSC survey above, the word appears to be one of the most offensive words in the English language internationally. A comparison between relevant UK and US data would be especially interesting here. It is also unlikely that the term will become neutralised or acceptable in everyday vernacular soon. Sometimes, it is even argued that the word is too offensive to be published even in quotation marks, as an example (as here).

 **Activity**

Consider each of the following general questions raised by our discussion above:

- Given the explosiveness of this word, what happens when the word 'nigger' is used in public media discourse?
- How far are the effects of use of this word dependent on a particular narrative context (as what some given character would say)?
- How far is use of this word dependent on its context in a particular genre or format (e.g. documentary, soap, reality TV)?
- How far is use of this word dependent on the speaker who uses it (e.g. use by members of the African-American or Black-British community, as a resistant term of solidarity)?
- Is media use of the word ever acceptable?

Issues of the kind explored in the activity above were raised directly by an interchange that took place in the UK reality TV show *Big Brother* (Channel 4, 2007). In *Big Brother*, contestants live together in a house and are continuously videoed over a period of weeks; they are gradually 'evicted' until there is one person left, the winner. In the 2007 series, what was widely described as a 'race row' broke out when one of the contestants, Emily, a 19-year-old white middle-class girl, uttered the words, 'You pushing it out, you nigger' as she was dancing with two other female contestants: Charley, who is black, and Nicky, who is Indian. Within the context of the show, the three contestants were friends. Channel 4 immediately removed Emily from the

house for 'breaking house rules'. The TV company claimed that she had caused 'serious offence to other housemates or members of the public'. Axing the contestant on these grounds was welcomed by the Commission for Racial Equality (CRE), whose Director of Policy, Nick Johnson, stated that, 'The n-word is offensive. This will show everyone that racism must never be tolerated in any way, shape or form. There is no stereotype' (*The Guardian*, August 2007).

Discussion in newspapers and on many internet sites following Emily's removal, however (including some sites which posted a transcript of the relevant section of dialogue), suggested that Emily's use of the word wasn't felt by many people to have been racist. It was widely suggested that Emily had been 'chronically naïve' rather than racist. She had used the term in some misguided sense of solidarity with her two housemates. Indeed, *The Guardian* headline for the article from which we quote above was: 'She might have thought it was cool. She might have been naïve. But housemate pays price for race word'.

Activity 

Read the account below of the relevant section of conversation between Emily, Charley and Nicky. Then consider the questions we pose based on that account.

> The controversial utterance begins with Emily's words, 'You pushing it out you nigger'. Emily addresses these words to Charley, who is dancing and pushing her hips forward. Nicky, who is not the person addressed, responds with shocked laughter and the comment, 'Em, I can't believe you said that.' Charlie suggests that Emily will now be 'in trouble', to which Emily replies, 'Don't make a big thing out of it then. I was joking.' Charlie accepts this explanation with the words, 'I know you were', but adds that 'that's some serious shit, sorry.' A series of conversational turns then follows in which Emily queries why it should be 'serious shit'. Charley appears not to want to go into this, and says only, 'Oh my God. I'm not even saying it.' Nicky also advises, 'Just don't talk about it anymore.' Emily, however, insists that she was only joking; but Charlie asks, 'Do you know how many viewers would watch that?' The three *Big Brother* contestants then take up slightly different stances on what has happened. Nikki wants not to 'make a big deal out of it'; Charley expresses astonishment at what Emily has said, with the words, 'Fancy you saying that. I can't believe you said that'. Emily maintains that someone has already used the same word in the *Big Brother* house. After flatly discounting this possibility with the words 'No way', Charley then recognises (after a pause) that she herself may have used the word: 'Yeah, me. I'm a nigger'. At this, Nicky laughs. Charley continues, 'I am one. Fancy you saying it. I know maybe you see it in a rap song. Maybe you and your friends sit there saying it.' Amid continuing expressions of shock (e.g. Charley's, 'I'm fucking in shock'), Emily offers by way of explanation that, 'I'm friendly with plenty of black people'. To the ensuing question from Nicky, 'And you call them niggers?', Emily continues, 'Yeah and they call

me nigger. They call me wiggers as well.' Faced with recognition that, in TV terms, the whole conversation is likely to be explosive, Emily asks of the others, 'It's not a big deal though is it?' and Charley, who was the original addressee of the remark, responds, 'Not for us it ain't. Fuck me.'

Consider the following issues raised by our brief account of this controversial *Big Brother* conversation:

- ❑ Was Emily a racist for using the n-word? If so, what does such racism consist of? Alternatively, how was she 'naïve' (as suggested above) in thinking it might be 'cool' to use the word in the company of her two peers (especially in the knowledge that conversations in the Big Brother house are recorded and broadcast)?
- ❑ Should Channel 4 have removed Emily from the house on the grounds it did (i.e. that, as reported above, she had caused 'serious offence to other housemates or members of the public')? What arguments would you expect television company executives to have gone through in arriving at this judgement?
- ❑ Do you think Channel 4's reaction, and wider public reaction, would have been the same if it had been Charley, rather than Emily, who had uttered the phrase 'You pushing it out you nigger'?

Our account of this controversial conversation raises some further questions about how discussion of such issues should (and can) be presented:

- ❑ Is your interpretation of what happened in this episode affected (or even distorted) by the fact that our account consists largely of paraphrase and summary (e.g. we attribute speech act categories and explanations of the significance of particular conversational turns by means of such words as 'insists', 'maintains', 'advises', etc.)?
- ❑ Would you have been able to judge the issues of public interest in this controversy better if you had been provided with a transcription (see unit C4 for discussion and examples) rather than a summary of the language used? (A TV audience counted in millions had access to the original words, gestures and accompanying actions that make up the conversational interchange on-air (and no doubt in many cases in recorded form); and a transcript of the relevant section can also be found on websites including that of *The Daily Telegraph* newspaper, at http://www.telegraph.co.uk/news/uknews/1553807/Channel-4-hit-by-new-racism-controversy.html, 8 June 2007.)
- ❑ Whose interest (or what public interest) is served by a copyright holder legitimately choosing not to permit publication, as in this case, of a transcript of broadcast material? (The television production company Endamol refused us permission to reproduce an already published transcript in this discussion, even on payment.)

When you have considered these questions, follow up your responses to the two main examples in this unit (the Ryanair advert and the *Big Brother* controversy) in more general terms:

- ❏ How far should considerations of where and when an utterance is made, or where a text is published, be a factor in deciding whether to restrict or ban it, or whether to express strong disapproval of or complain about it?
- ❏ Does the editorial question of whether an utterance or text should be restricted (or even prohibited altogether) depend on what form or style it is in – whether, for instance, it appears calculated to be: descriptive or analytical? fictional? polemical? satirical? dismissive? politically motivated?
- ❏ How can a line be drawn that limits offensive language but still allows for creative and playful use of language as well as for critical and educational analysis of such language?

Issues of language taboo raised in this unit can be followed up in Greenawalt (1996), Neu (2008) and Durant (2009), from which the extract related to this thread is taken. Issues of transcription can be followed up by, for example, taking a transcription offered elsewhere in this book (e.g. in unit C4), re-writing it in the summary form used above to present the controversial *Big Brother* conversation, and then evaluating the interpretation you have imposed on the language data in front of you by adding your own voice as a sort of intervening layer of commentary. The need to present the *Big Brother* conversation in summary form has in this way been for us an opportunity as well as a restriction. It not only draws attention to issues of language data, transcription and summary, but serves as encouragement to explore another boundary of permissible media language introduced in A8: copyright. Copyright law protection of financial reward (and reputation by means of moral rights), as well as arrangements for 'fair dealing' (or permissible use of short extracts from works for critical purposes where publication would be in the public interest), can be followed up in Quinn (2007) and MacQueen, Waelde and Laurie (2008).

C9 MEDIA CHANGE IN THE FUTURE

This unit raises questions about how far language and media combinations may lead to or accelerate particular directions of language change. In this unit we present two short illustrations in which different types of explanation may be called for in accounting for claimed directions of language change. We ask how understanding media language, as part of wider media literacy, relates to what is typically understood as verbal literacy.

Relating our discussion in this unit to topics elsewhere in the book, we encourage you to build predictions about how language and media may develop in your lifetime. Whatever hopes and concerns you formulate, we also urge you to consider how far the views you express can be supported with relevant evidence.

Wonders of the small screen

With screens, size matters. Film has always been considered to have a special magic as a result of its exhibition on the big screen. Currently, home cinema systems and flat-screen digital TVs compete commercially on picture size (as well as on resolution, convergence with other domestic technologies, and price). At the other end of the size scale, the small size and until recently relatively poor resolution of mobile phone screens has sometimes been considered a key factor in determining aspects of language change associated with SMS messaging (and so the rise of the distinctive variety of text language).

Deciding how far screen size plays a part in shaping text language allows us to explore the difference between two ways of viewing language and media change:

- as a kind of technological determinism (i.e. capabilities of the machine cause the change), and
- as a phenomenon that requires wider social explanation, or many different levels of explanation.

Crystal (2006) suggests that the small screen of a particular generation of mobile phones played a major part in shaping the highly condensed language styles of SMS texting: 'gr8' = 'great', '4 u' = 'for you', etc. Such an explanation is an example of technological determinism to the extent that properties of the technology are taken to determine the change of language style. The explanation is this: for a particular generation of mobiles, only a relatively small number of characters were visible on-screen in any single view. So, leaving out characters such as vowels (and using abbreviating features of text language such as numbers and icons to replace phonemes or words) allowed more 'message' to be displayed in a single screen view. This facilitated reading without having to scroll so much.

An alternative explanation of the same change is that the emergence of the same, condensed texting style reflected convenience to the text message *writer*, irrespective of screen size. The alternative explanation is this. Messages can be entered more quickly, with fewer keystrokes, where features of text language are used to replace sounds or words. This offers a user-benefit to the message writer. Screen size and resolution play no part in the explanation. This alternative explanation prioritises convenience to the writer in entering characters over how screen quality may have affected the reader and the act of reading.

There is also a third line of possible explanation. It might be that the popularity of mobile phones among young people during the period of their rapid increase in use led many users to adopt a kind of anti-language: a style that marks some (mostly young generation) users off from others on account of their preferred language

variety, on-screen as well as face-to-face. The attraction of the style was accordingly its stylistic edge, or novelty, and its unattractiveness to outsiders.

Which of these explanations is correct? And how can we decide on the relative contribution made by each to the emergence of this influential media-derived language variety?

Activity 

Evaluate the following possibilities as regards method for researching the questions outlined above:

- We could compare texting styles adopted in corpora of text messages stored on (or originally composed on) mobile phones with different quality screens.
- We could compare texting styles used by people who started texting using different generations of mobile phone (in case users continue with their original style as a matter of habit, despite successive phone upgrades).
- We could look at differences between texting style on small-screen phones and PC-based synchronous messaging. In the latter case, speed and convenience are still desirable. But the screens involved are typically large rather than small.

In practice, of course, such research would be complicated by many variables. Consider how you might improve on each of the three basic research designs suggested above (for further ideas about research method and project design, see Wray and Bloomer, 2006).

- How could you undertake such studies? What practical and ethical problems might arise if you try to conduct each study?
- Do the challenges presented in understanding this recent change tell us anything about how successful we are likely to be in predicting future directions of change?

Listening to whoever shouts loudest

Understanding what is going on in 'language and media' change is difficult in the case of mobile texting. It may be equally difficult when we move to a different illustration. Consider the styles of language associated with the contemporary promotional culture discussed at various points in this book. A central research question now is not whether technological capability leads to or causes a stylistic shift. It is whether a prevailing set of cultural *values* causes such a shift. We ask: in a competitive information and media marketplace (sometimes called a 'three-minute culture' or an 'attention economy'), does the struggle for viewers' and listeners' attention contribute to a shift of prevailing discourse *style*?

Where can we start with such a question? We might wonder, for example, whether

the intensity of advertising and other kinds of promotional media discourse accentuates discourse choices in each or all of the following more specific areas:

- More frequent or marked use of swearing and other taboo or potentially offensive language in broadcast discourse (see units A8 and C8), in order to create shock value and so stand out from surrounding material. Recent broadcasting controversies suggest that this could be the case.
- Frequency of exaggerated or hyperbolic description (e.g. use of advertising 'trade puff' style (see unit A5) involving expressions such as 'unique', 'excellent', 'outstanding', 'official', 'exclusive', 'film of the year', 'life-changing experience', 'catastrophic', etc.). Such use may over time bleach the meaning of expressions (such as 'excellence' or 'uniqueness') which previously had stronger senses or a lower frequency of occurrence. Such use may appear to be part of a more general phenomenon of 'claim inflation', in which everything must now be the best – or better still, better than the best – if people are to take notice of it. To illustrate this point, Leech (1966) in his study of television advertisements identified the unusual frequency of certain words in advertising, many of which arguably have weaker meanings now than when Leech did his research, in the 1960s (see Table C9.1).

Table C9.1 The twenty most frequently used adjectives (Leech, 1966)

1	new	11	crisp
2	good/better/best	12	fine
3	free	13	big
4	fresh	14	great
5	delicious	15	real
6	full	16	easy
6	sure	16	bright
8	clean	18	extra
9	wonderful	18	safe
10	special	20	rich

- Exaggerated or hyperbolic description may be linked to its opposite: euphemism (or understatement) and circumlocution by politicians and other public figures who are aware of a journalistic desire for controversy that surrounds what they say or write. In a media culture, transmission and recording of what public figures and celebrities say may result in their comments being replayed later to embarrass or incriminate them. Understatement and calculated vagueness, typical of political spin and much issues-management and crisis-management PR, may be used evasively to create what is sometimes called 'wiggle room' or 'plausible deniability'.

Each of these ideas sounds at least plausible. But how can we test whether the general shifts in question are just an impression, or whether they can be precisely demonstrated?

- ❏ What sort of text corpus could you look at, in order to compare promotional or political usage between one period and another? How large a sample would you need and where would you find it? Try drawing up a list of texts or sources that would be useful in pursuing a particular speculation or hypothesis along these lines.
- ❏ What words, expressions or figures of speech would you search for? Would you look for them individually or in clusters or collocations with other terms?
- ❏ What problems would be likely to arise in interpreting the evidence? How much would the significance of particular expressions in your data depend on how you construe the context in which they are used?

Preparing for the future: media literacy

So far in this unit, we have looked at how you might begin to explain (and so explain the merits or dangers of) changes of style in media language. Having a view on such cultural shifts might be thought an important aspect of membership of a media culture.

Such reflection may appear to be a luxury, however, when for many people (especially older people) the more urgent challenges of language and media may include entering text using a keyboard; sending an email successfully; uploading a video to YouTube; or performing a stretch of speech-to-camera without forgetting what to say or becoming embarrassed.

Looking into the future, we should therefore ask what constitutes a suitable level of preparedness for users of communication media of the next generation. We might then ask whether such a level of preparedness is achievable, for what proportion of a population, and by what means. Such a body of skills and awareness is what is usually discussed under the heading of 'media literacy'.

There are many useful discussions of print literacy (e.g. Levine, 1986; Maybin, 2007). In the grid provided in Table C9.2, we ask you to apply your understanding of themes in this book to what constitutes 'media literacy'. Within media literacy, what are the essential language and media skills?

Activity 

For each of the items in a 'basket' of media literacy skills/practices (Table C9.2), assign a number, 5–1, from the scale in the right-hand column.

5 = essential for someone to be thought of as 'media literate';
1 = possibly worthwhile, but superfluous to being 'media literate'.

Make a note where you think an interesting issue or problem arises in relation to the example (e.g. if for some reason it seems impossible to assign a number).

Table C9.2 A 'basket' of media literacy skills/practices

1	Demonstrate proper use and care of media technology (e.g. not scratching DVDs, successfully timer-recording programmes off-air, avoiding crashing PCs, etc.)	5	4	3	2	1
2	Explain what you like and dislike about a TV or radio programme, and why	5	4	3	2	1
3	Differentiate between advertising and editorial content in different media	5	4	3	2	1
4	Produce, save and send (or broadcast) a voice recording	5	4	3	2	1
5	Compare stories represented in media with own experiences	5	4	3	2	1
6	Distinguish fact from opinion across different media	5	4	3	2	1
7	Use a video production studio or set up a desktop video production facility	5	4	3	2	1
8	Discuss how advertising techniques influence consumer decisions	5	4	3	2	1
9	Choose media design elements such as fonts, clipboard images, camera angles and backgrounds, in order to focus attention, suggest a mood, or communicate an idea	5	4	3	2	1
10	Identify news angles in real-world events, and how those news angles would be likely to fit a particular publication's editorial agenda	5	4	3	2	1
11	Write a blog	5	4	3	2	1
12	Evaluate the relative authority of online information sources on the basis of style of presentation, as well as on the strength of external considerations such as reputation	5	4	3	2	1
13	Edit audio/video/web page content	5	4	3	2	1
14	Identify intent, perspective and bias in a news report	5	4	3	2	1
15	Analyse stereotyping in broadcasting and its likely impact on different groups in a diverse audience	5	4	3	2	1
16	Make a storyboard and prop list for a narrative video clip	5	4	3	2	1
17	Put forward explanations of the causes of style shifts in contemporary media discourse	5	4	3	2	1

The list given in Table C9.2 is simply illustrative. Many other skills and kinds of awareness could be added.

- ❏ Pick out elements of reading, writing, speaking and listening in these various 'media literacy' skills. Remember that some language skills will be audible or visible in an utterance or text you produce (e.g. in an email, voicemail or video). Other language skills are needed in order to plan and execute media production techniques in group production (e.g. in making a video). And other language skills again (now metalingual skills, or skills of describing language) are needed to reflect on and discuss media discourse that you produce or which has been produced by others.
- ❏ Throughout the history of literacy debates (and in adopted policies), there has been an imbalance between emphasis on teaching people to read or interpret, and on teaching people to write or produce. This imbalance was notable in controversies during the Christian Reformation, in the century following the invention of printing; emphasis was placed on reading religious works rather than on expressing the learner's own ideas. It was also notable in the period of broadcasting, at least until the arrival of cheap and convenient audio and video recording equipment and uploading to the internet. How important is it now for media literacy programmes to include production skills? And will an imbalance between teaching production and reception skills continue, or has media convergence and new emphasis on interactive communication technologies meant that this division is no longer significant?
- ❏ Until the 20th century, debates about literacy were almost always about 'empowering'. They were concerned with providing skills by which members of a population could gain access to and derive benefit from published texts around them. More recently with print literacy (especially in relation to tabloid newspapers), and most obviously with electronic media, literacy debates have become more concerned with 'protecting'. They are now more about helping the public to escape manipulation or the harm that the media might inflict. Why do you think this shift of emphasis has occurred?

To help find routes through these complex questions, consult the further reading related to this unit, and look at reports of current research on media literacy on sites such as www.ofcom.org or other broadcasting regulation and educational sites.

Section D

Extension
LANGUAGE AND MEDIA READINGS

The following readings have been chosen to provide you with background and familiarise you with the main relevant research directions. The readings are excerpts from books and articles written by leading scholars in the field of language and media and have been selected to present an overview of key issues.

Editorial note

In the extracts which follow, we have omitted bibliographic references wherever it seemed reasonable to do so. This is so that the text does not appear cluttered. The references that are included can be followed up in the list at the end of the book.

Where words or sentences have been omitted from the original text, this is indicated by [. . .]

The typeface of the original works, and features of presentation including some italics and boldface text, have been modified where necessary to achieve consistency and clarity (e.g. in relation to list headings).

How to use the extracts

As you use the readings in this section, consider the following five aspects of *reading* published academic work:

1. Comprehension: grasping what is directly stated, as well as what is implied.
2. Summary or paraphrase: taking 'ownership' of the text, by being able to restate it in your own words and so being able to use or manipulate its ideas for your own purposes (e.g. citing ideas within an argument of your own).
3. Establishing significance: identifying the main claims as well as implications of the claims made in the passage.
4. Evaluating evidence presented: seeing how an argument is put together, and singling out examples or illustrations; then looking for counter-examples or exceptions that may go against what the passage claims.
5. Comparison: placing what is said in a larger context and seeing how it compares with other viewpoints.

These are not separate approaches. They overlap in various ways. But when you set out simply to 'read' something, bear in mind that what is involved will be some combination of these processes – especially if you are going to link your reading of this section to the other sections of the book.

THE MEANINGS OF 'MEDIA'

D1

In this unit, we are concerned with different meanings of the term 'media', and the different, sometimes confusing ways that this term is used in our efforts to understand the forms, channels, and modes of organisation of human communication and interaction. Our first extract is from the anthropologist Ruth Finnegan. In this passage, Finnegan locates our modern idea of 'media' in the larger context of humans' use of a wide range of signs and artefacts as means of communication.

Ruth Finnegan (reprinted from *Communicating: The Multiple Modes of Human Interconnection*, London: Routledge, 2002: 40–3)

Ruth Finnegan

Another way of envisaging human communication and its resources is to consider the technologies and material forms that humans have developed and used in their processes of interconnecting. These are more significant than one might conclude from many accounts of communicating.

'The media' is a much-used phrase nowadays. It proves a somewhat elusive concept however. It often means the 'mass media', usually press, radio and television but also sometimes the cinema, recordings of popular music and some computer-mediated forms. Earlier writers took a less limited conspectus, as in McLuhan's view of the media as all 'the extensions of man' (1964). In wider historical sweeps, broad distinctions have been drawn between writing, print, and electrical media, with the recent addition of electronic computer-based media; sometimes the 'oral medium' of speech starts off the series. Yet other writers use 'media' to refer to concrete forms like coins, maps or graffiti. The magisterial *International Encyclopedia of Communications* lists under 'media' nearly thirty forms of varying levels of generality, including sculpture, photographs, motion pictures, murals, radio, television, books, maps, stamps, portraits, writing and telegraphy, but the list does not seem to be intended as a systematic or comprehensive one (Barnouw et al. 1989). 'Media' and 'medium' are not exact technical terms and will continue to be used, by myself as well as others, in both broad and more specific senses.

The general idea is nevertheless an illuminating one. Humans' interconnectedness is achieved not just through the direct contact of people's bodies but also through external forms – media in the widest sense. People can interact by 'mediational means' (Scollon 1999: 153). This is not just a matter of journalism, television or computer communications, the often assumed meaning of 'the media', for, as Scollon continues, 'virtually everything is a medium or may be a medium for social action' (1999: 153). This 'mediation' may be in the form of other human beings, sometimes a conventional and routinised part of performance. 'Mediators' such as poets and priests or the 'speakers' of West African Akan chiefs communicate in mediational performances on behalf of others (Bauman 2001); so in less formalised settings do many others. But it also often takes place through the use of material objects and technologies, from clothes to seals, tactile maps to scented letters. Even the land around us can be a medium in communicating. [. . .]

This raises two issues that will keep surfacing throughout the later discussion. First,

Ruth Finnegan

these material media of various kinds are often surrounded by clusters of uses and practices which in themselves present accepted options and constraints for communicating. Such conventions form an important dimension of our communicating. At the same time we have to remember that no medium, from stone pebble to written page, ultimately communicates in its own right, but only as it is used and interpreted by human enactors. [. . .] We need to balance the fact that objects do not communicate of themselves with the practices by which human beings on occasion organise them as effective communicative tools, perhaps to do just that.

Second, the apparently straightforward distinction between external media and those more directly located in the body turns out to be far from clear-cut: more a matter of degree than an unproblematic opposition. 'Intrinsic' and 'extrinsic', 'embodied' and 'exosomatic' – such terms are illuminating up to a point but involve continuities and social shaping as well as contrasts. Perhaps the very lack of exactness of the term 'medium' has its uses, reminding us yet again of the multiplicity and relativities of our communicative resources. [. . .]

Issues to consider

- ❑ How should Finnegan's presentation of 'media' as the widest possible range of resources used by human beings in communicating affect our interest in or investigation of contemporary electronic 'media'?
- ❑ You might follow up this reading by finding out more about Marshall McLuhan's notion that modern media communication means that we are accessible all the time. Do you think this is a good thing or would you say it is intrusive?

Our second extract is from Raymond Williams. In his entry for 'media' in his 'vocabulary of culture and society', Williams charts the historical development of the range of contemporary meanings conveyed by the term. He also shows how different uses of the term 'media' affect our appreciation of what contemporary media are – or might be.

Raymond Williams

Raymond Williams (reprinted from *Keywords: A Vocabulary of Culture and Society*, 2nd edition, London: Fontana, 1983: 203–4)

Medium, from *medium*, L – middle, has been in regular use in English from late C16, and from at latest early C17 has had the sense of an intervening or intermediate agency or substance. [. . .] There was then a conventional C18 use in relation to newspapers: 'through the medium of your curious publication' (1795), and this was developed through C19 to such uses as 'considering your Journal one of the best possible mediums for such a scheme' (1880). Within this general use, the description of a newspaper as a **medium** for advertising became common in early C20. The mid-C20 development of media (which had been available as a general plural from mid-C19) was probably mainly in this context. **Media** became widely used, when broadcasting as well as the press had become important in COMMUNICATIONS (q.v.); it was then the necessary

Raymond Williams

general word. MASS (q.v.) **media, media people, media agencies, media studies** followed.

There has probably been a convergence of three senses: (i) the old general sense of an intervening or intermediate agency or substance; (ii) the conscious technical sense, as in the distinction between print and sound and vision as **media**; (iii) the specialized capitalist sense, in which a newspaper or broadcasting service – something that already exists or can be planned – is seen as a **medium** for something else, such as advertising. It is interesting that sense (i) depended on particular physical or philosophical ideas, where there had to be a substance intermediate between a sense or a thought and its operation or expression. In most modern science and philosophy, and especially in thinking about language, this idea of a **medium** has been dispensed with; thus language is not a **medium** but a primary practice, and writing (for print) and speaking or acting (for broadcasting) would also be practices. It is then controversial whether print and broadcasting, as in the technical sense (ii), are **media** or, more strictly, material forms and sign systems. It is probably here that specific social ideas, in which writing and broadcasting are seen as DETERMINED (q.v.) by other ends – from the relatively neutral 'information' to the highly specific 'advertising' and 'propaganda' – confirm the received sense but then confuse any modern sense of COMMUNICATION (q.v.). The technical sense of medium, as something with its own specific and determining properties (in one version taking absolute priority over anything actually said or written or shown), has in practice been compatible with a social sense of **media** in which the practices and institutions are seen as agencies for quite other than their primary purposes.

Issues to consider

- ❑ What do you understand by the term 'media'? Look up the word in several dictionaries (including media subject-specific dictionaries) for different meanings and note down the main meanings that you feel you use the word 'media' to convey.
- ❑ Interview several people from an older generation (e.g. your grandparents' age). How do they understand the term 'media'? What are the main differences between your and their understanding? For example, is the main difference between media and 'new' media, in your terms?

Our third extract is by Katie Wales, who takes up the historical story of the word 'media' and traces the word into its various digital and internet uses.

Katie Wales (reprinted from 'Keywords revisited: media', *Critical Quarterly*, 49 (1) 2007: 6–13)

Katie Wales

In 1976, and indeed seven years later when he revised *Keywords*, Raymond Williams could not have envisaged just how significant the media, one of his lifelong interests, would become to late twentieth-century society. His entry on the term *media* (and also *medium*) comprises just over one page. For linguists or philologists, however, what is of interest is not so much that the last thirty years have brought about a complex technological revolution which has affected every aspect of life at home, school or in the workplace,

Katie Wales

but that the tiny word used to reflect such crucial changes, itself already overloaded in meaning, has had to keep up. [. . .]

There is no doubting the continuing cultural significance of the word *media*, which has hardly yielded to other possible synonyms in the past century. Moreover, it is difficult for lexicographers to keep abreast of the large numbers of new collocations and compounds which in turn reflect the latest technological advances in communications and the *media* or *electronic revolution* which has resulted in what Kristeva sees as our *mediatic* society. Even the OED online entry for the word (last updated in June 2001) has not yet taken *new media* developments into account: *digital* and *computerised media*, *e-media* or *electronic media*, *hypermedia*, *mixed media*, *DIY media* and *multi-media*.[. . .]

In one sense *media* is a classic example of the kind of semantic change that happens when objects change – like *pen*: meanings changing in response to changing social needs. As Williams states: 'words which seem to have been [here] for centuries . . . have come in fact to express radically different or radically variable, yet sometimes hardly noticed, meanings and implications of meaning' . Yet *media* of necessity is more complex than a word like *pen*. There appear to be three main uses of the word, around which different kinds of compounds or collocations tend to cluster. The most up-to-date reference is to the *new media* referred to above, to designate the products of the internet, DVD, mobile phone, satellite and digital TV, et cetera. To the list above can be added *ethernet media*, *Me Media*, *moving image media*, *screen media*, *online news media* and *web-based media*. Lexically we can note how media forms the base of the collocation or compound, reflecting the diversity of types or genres. New media have also, significantly, given the root word *medium* a new lease of life, in that we talk of the medium of Netspeak; or of text-messaging; or of tape or disk for recording and copying; also known as *format*. The second sense, culturally predominant still, is that traced historically by the OED as 'the main means of mass communication', collectively newspapers, radio, television and advertising; and derived from the phrase mass media in the early 1920s, with *mass* very quickly absorbed (referring to the large audience reached). Currently *media* generally refers to news media in popular parlance, despite the influence of advertising revenue for all kinds of news dissemination, including the internet. The *press*, however, is no longer a close synonym, since this tends to be used of traditional printed newspapers (which may themselves be obsolete within a generation). Popular magazines, terrestrial and satellite TV (*broadcast media*) are better served by media. The broadcast media in particular, including the internet, are characterised by *immediacy*: from the same Latin root.

Closely related to this sense is one which has acquired some human connotations: namely that of the reporters or journalists et cetera working for organisations engaged in mass communication: an aspect recognised by the *Encarta World English Dictionary*, for instance. To Williams's own collocations *media people*, *media agencies*, could be added *media consultant*, *media man*, *media pundits* and so forth. This is no metaphorical process, however, [. . .] but the (almost inevitable) less figurative process of metonymy, as in the *Press*, *Board*, *White House* et cetera for people in those institutions as well as the institutions themselves. The human reference is made very obvious in sentences with particular kinds of verbs, e.g. when pop stars and the royal family are either *hounded* or *greeted* by the media; or when the media have *refrained* from comment.

What is needed here, however, is the evaluative dimension to the word: what Bill Louw might call its 'semantic prosody'. This was quite evident when *mass media* was in

Katie Wales

vogue (from the 1920s), since mass could quickly become synonymous not simply with uniform but with *vulgar* or, in contemporary usage, *dumbed down*: cf. *mass-production*, *mass-market*, *mass culture*, *mass leisure*. Even in the late 1950s Hoggart's *Uses of Literacy* uncomfortably implicates the new post-war television culture, a manifestation of the 'mass media of communication', as a kind of opiate of the working classes, alongside the pulp fiction of romance and thriller. Williams's own *Culture and Society*, published around the same time, also criticises the same shallowness of modern mass culture and entertainment. Move on to the last quarter of the twentieth century and the word *media* itself has acquired pejorative connotations, not in consequence of its dissemination across society at large but in consequence of the juxtaposition of certain cultural trends which reflect the media's own agencies: the unquestionable growth in power of the tabloids vis-à-vis the broadsheets; their influence in politics; the rise of *yoof* culture, with its gossip magazines and cult of the pop star and 'celebrity'; and hence the rise of the paparazzi. All these inflationary tendencies can be symbolised in the 1983 ironic respelling meeja, itself self-reflexively coined in the media. The media also gave rise to compounds reflecting this cultural shift (and not all of them noted by the OED), such as *media blitz*, *media circus*, *media coverage*, *media darling*, *media event*, *media exposure*, *media hype*, *media industry*, *media interview*, *media interest*, *media junkie*, *media markets*, *media personality*; *media-friendly*, *media-gate*, *mediagenic*, *media-saturated*, *media-savvy*, *media-shy*, *media-speak*, *media-wise*. [. . .]

Part of the negative prosody or 'vibes' attached to *media* and what it stands for has been displaced onto *media studies*. Although the phrase was first recorded in the OED from 1951, the discipline itself was slow to take root in either the British or American education systems; indeed, Branston and Stafford think it is still a 'young subject', with the syllabuses still being developed at secondary level by the various examining bodies. However, in a form much influenced by cultural studies, communication studies, journalism, film studies, design, semiotics and linguistics, media studies is manifested widely across the Higher Education sector, especially in the arts and humanities. Critics of the discipline, and there have been many, dub it a 'soft' option, a 'Mickey Mouse' degree. [. . .] Nonetheless, many academics themselves recognise that young people have a range of competences to handle the new technology, and a high degree of *media literacy*. Their ranking in status of the mediums (*sic*) of film and printed texts differs from that of older generations.

Issues to consider

- ❏ Each of these three writers highlights the difference between viewing a 'medium' as purely a channel or conduit for carrying information between people and viewing 'medium' as also involving some kind of socially organised practice. By comparing the three passages, summarise the main arguments for and against each view.
- ❏ Research how the term 'media' collocates with other words (e.g. media friendly; media circus, etc.) and contrasts with opposites or other related terms. What if anything do these extra examples suggest about directions in which contemporary media are going?

D2 VARIETIES OF MEDIA LANGUAGE

Our selected extract is by Douglas Biber, who is concerned with the distinctive linguistic features of a given style, in this case of newspaper discourse.

Douglas Biber

Douglas Biber (reprinted from 'Compressed noun-phrase structures in newspaper discourse: the competing demands of popularization vs. economy', in J. Aitchison and D. M. Lewis (eds), *New Media Language*, London: Routledge, 2003: 169–71 and 179–80)

Written registers in English have undergone extensive stylistic change over the past four centuries. Written prose registers in the seventeenth century were already quite different from conversational registers, and those registers evolved to become even more distinct from speech over the course of the eighteenth century (Biber and Finegan, 1989; see also Biber, 1995).

However, over the course of the nineteenth and twentieth centuries, popular written registers like letters, fiction, and essays have reversed their direction of change and evolved to become more similar to spoken registers, often becoming even more oral in the modern period than in the seventeenth century. These shifts result in a dispreference for certain stereotypically literate features, such as passive verbs, relative clause constructions and elaborated noun phrases generally.

Biber and Finegan (1989: 514ff) appeal to both conscious and unconscious motivations to explain these historical patterns for essays, fiction and letters. For example, authors like Samuel Johnson and Benjamin Franklin in the eighteenth century argued that writing should be elaborated and 'ornamental' to effectively persuade readers. At the same time, the eighteenth century witnessed the rise of a popular, middle-class literacy, including writers like Defoe and Richardson, who were from the middle class themselves and addressed themselves primarily to middle-class readers. This popularization of literacy in English gained ground in the nineteenth century, reinforced by mass schooling and the demands of a wider reading public for more accessible written prose; thus the linguistic norms for non-expository registers were reversed during this period, and began to shift towards more accessible, oral styles.

In contrast, informational, expository registers like medical prose, science prose and legal opinions have followed a different course. Rather than evolving towards more oral styles, these expository registers have consistently developed towards more literate styles across all periods. The development of literary linguistic features corresponds to the development of a more specialized readership, more specialized purposes, and a fuller exploitation of the production possibilities of the written mode. That is, in marked contrast to the general societal trends towards a wider lay readership and the corresponding need for popular written registers, readers of medical research prose, science prose and legal prose have become increasingly more specialized in their backgrounds and training, and correspondingly these registers have become more specialized in linguistic form.

The preferred linguistic style of newspaper discourse has also undergone dramatic long-term change, influenced by these same competing forces. Over the course of the eighteenth and nineteenth centuries, newspaper prose was similar to academic prose in developing an increasingly dense use of passive verbs, relative clause constructions and elaborated noun phrases generally. However, the opposing drift towards more oral styles began to influence newspaper prose towards the end of the nineteenth century, followed by more marked change in the twentieth century.

Over the past few decades, these changes towards more oral styles in newspaper language have accelerated. Thus, Hundt and Mair (1999) track several changes in newspaper prose over the thirty-year period from 1960 to 1990, including a greater use of first and second person pronouns, contractions, sentence-initial conjunctions, phrasal verbs, and progressive aspect. Such changes reflect the continuing popularization of newspapers, adopting more oral features in an effort to appeal to a wider reading audience.

Surprisingly, though, newspaper prose has retained some of its nineteenth-century characteristics associated with dense, informational prose. In particular, newspaper prose continues to rely on a dense use of nouns and integrated noun phrase constructions. Thus, modern-day newspaper prose is very similar to academic prose in certain characteristics. These linguistic characteristics seem to be a reflection of two major factors: the informational purpose of newspaper prose, coupled with the influence of economy. That is, the 'informational explosion' has resulted in pressure to communicate information as efficiently and economically as possible, resulting in compressed styles that depend heavily on tightly integrated noun-phrase constructions.

It might be expected that newspaper prose would exhibit an intermediate style generally: relatively oral in some respects, in response to the demands of popularization, but less oral than registers like fiction or letters; and relatively literate in other respects, in response to the demands of economy and informational compression, but much less so than registers like academic or official prose. [. . .]

Several previous studies have documented the ways in which newspaper texts are edited (e.g. van Dijk, 1988; Bell, 1991). Bell (1991: 76–8) identifes 'cutting' as one of the major goals of copy-editing, to reduce the volume of news to a manageable amount. The main editing device for this purpose discussed by Bell is the simple deletion of text.

The present study suggests that newspaper prose has been linguistically innovative in other ways designed to achieve a compressed style. That is, devices like noun–noun sequences, heavy appositive post-modifiers, and *to*-noun complement clauses are especially characteristic of newspaper prose. These features are all literate devices used to pack information into relatively few words. These devices are also commonly used in academic prose, together with functionally-similar devices like attributive adjectives and prepositional phrases as post-modifiers. However, the features discussed above are noteworthy because they are considerably more common in newspaper prose. That is, at the same time that news has been developing more popular oral styles, it has also been innovative in developing literate styles with extreme reliance on compressed noun-phrase structures.

These increasingly compressed styles of expression are at the same time less explicit in meaning. For example, noun–noun sequences can represent a bewildering array of meaning relationships, with no overt signal of the intended meaning. The following list illustrates only a few of these meaning relationships:

Douglas Biber

Noun–noun sequence	**meaning relationship**
air disaster	N1 expresses the location of N2
reprisal raid	N1 expresses the purpose of N2
baggage inspection	N1 expresses the 'patient' of N2
airline officials	N2 is employed by N1
blood pressure	N2 is caused by N1
glass bottle	N2 is composed of N1

It is probably for this reason that news relies primarily on pre-modifying nouns from those semantic domains most commonly associated with current events such as government, business, education, the media and sports. These are areas where news writers can reasonably expect readers to have well-developed pragmatic knowledge, and so be able to decode noun + noun relationships without too much difficulty. However, it seems clear that the concessions to popular literacy associated with a greater use of oral features, like first and second person pronouns, contractions and phrasal verbs, are surprisingly offset by the increasing use of these compressed noun-phrase structures.

From a historical point of view, these developments are relatively recent, accelerating only in the last fifty to one hundred years. Two functional factors have probably been influential in these developments. First, there has been an increasing awareness of the production possibilities of the written mode, offering almost unlimited opportunities for crafting and revising the final text. The availability of typewriters, and more recently word-processors, have been technological developments that facilitate authors' abilities to manipulate the language in written texts. At the same time, we have witnessed an 'informational explosion', resulting in pressure to communicate information as efficiently and economically as possible. Although there may be additional structural and social factors, these two factors can be taken together to explain in part the rapid increase in the use of compressed noun modification devices over the past 100 years.

Issues to consider

- ❑ Collect examples of headlines that exemplify the compressed noun-phrase structures in Biber's list above. Are these front page headlines? How well do they describe the importance of the news item they headline?
- ❑ Biber suggests some reasons why particular registers evolve. How are those reasons related to the wider issues of 'medium' (especially of speech vs. writing) explored in unit D1?
- ❑ Biber links the techniques used in specific styles to the functions that each style serves (such as increased memorability, gaining public attention in a media-saturated environment, condensing information into an especially short stretch of text, etc.). How convincing do you find such linkages between descriptions of selected language forms and their likely social purpose or effect?
- ❑ How far does Biber's extract challenge the widely held view that we can draw a clear distinction between 'information' being transparently communicated and kinds of rhetoric or verbal ornamentation that skew or slant the content being conveyed?

- ❏ Biber notes how discourse styles change over time and alludes to the idea of historical development or 'evolution' of registers. What areas of current media should we look in now for emergent media discourse styles?

MEDIA AND MODERNITY

D3

The extract for this unit is by John B. Thompson, who explores differences between face-to-face verbal interaction and the specialised creation of modern media speech events. In the selected passage, Thompson describes three types of interaction that he suggests are made possible by different forms of communication. He shows how these different forms of interaction contribute to an important historical process of social structuring, and how they have significant consequences in terms of the social relations in which we live.

John B. Thompson (reprinted from *The Media and Modernity*, Cambridge: Polity, 1995: 83–7)

John B. Thompson

In order to explore the kinds of interactional situation created by the use of communication media, it is helpful to distinguish between three forms or types of interaction – what I shall call 'face-to-face interaction', 'mediated interaction' and 'mediated quasi-interaction'. Face-to-face interaction takes place in a *context of co-presence*; the participants in the interaction are immediately present to one another and share a common spatial-temporal reference system. Hence participants can use deictic expressions ('here', 'now', 'this', 'that', etc.) and assume that they will be understood. If the referent of a demonstrative pronoun is unclear, the speaker can remove the ambiguity by pointing to the object in question. Face-to-face interaction is also *dialogical* in character, in the sense that it generally involves a two-way flow of information and communication; recipients can respond (at least in principle) to producers, and producers are also recipients of messages addressed to them by the addressees of their own remarks. A further characteristic of face-to-face interaction is that the participants commonly employ a *multiplicity of symbolic cues* in order to convey messages and to interpret messages conveyed by others. Words can be supplemented by winks and gestures, frowns and smiles, changes in intonation and so on. Participants in face-to-face interaction are constantly and routinely engaged in comparing the various symbolic cues employed by speakers, using them to reduce ambiguity and to refine their understanding of the message. If participants detect inconsistencies, or cues that do not tally with one another, this can become a source of trouble which may threaten the continuation of the interaction and cast doubt on the sincerity of the speaker.

Face-to-face interaction can be contrasted with 'mediated interaction', by which I mean forms of interaction such as letter writing, telephone conversations and so on. Mediated interaction involves the use of a technical medium (paper, electrical wires, electromagnetic waves, etc.) which enables information or symbolic content to be transmitted to individuals who are remote in space, in time, or in both. Mediated interaction is stretched across space and time, and it thereby acquires a number of characteristics which differentiate it from face-to-face interaction. Whereas face-to-face interaction takes place in a context of co-presence, the participants in mediated interaction are located in contexts which are spatially and/or temporally distinct. The participants do not share the same spatial-temporal reference system and cannot assume that others will understand the deictic expressions they use. Hence participants must always consider how much contextual information should be included in the exchange – for example, by putting the place and date at the top of a letter, or by identifying oneself at the beginning of a telephone conversation.

Mediated interaction also involves a certain narrowing of the range of symbolic cues which are available to participants. Communication by means of letters, for instance, deprives the participants of a range of cues associated with physical co-presence (gestures, facial expressions, intonation, etc.), while other symbolic cues (those linked to writing) are accentuated. Similarly, communication by means of telephone deprives the participants of the visual cues associated with face-to-face interaction while preserving and accentuating the oral cues. By narrowing the range of symbolic cues, mediated interaction provides participants with fewer symbolic devices for the reduction of ambiguity. Hence mediated interaction acquires a somewhat more open-ended character than face-to-face interaction. As the range of symbolic cues is narrowed, individuals have to fall back more and more on their own resources in order to interpret the messages conveyed.

Let us now consider the third form of interaction – what I have called 'mediated quasi-interaction'. I use this term to refer to the kinds of social relations established by the media of mass communication (books, newspapers, radio, television, etc.) Like mediated interaction, this third form of interaction involves the extended availability of information and symbolic content in space and/or time – in other words, mediated quasi-interaction is stretched across space and time. In many cases it also involves a certain narrowing of the range of symbolic cues by comparison with face-to-face interaction. However, there are two key respects in which mediated quasi-interaction differs from both face-to-face interaction and mediated interaction. In the first place, the participants in face-to-face interaction and mediated interaction are oriented towards specific others, for whom they produce actions, utterances, etc.; but in the case of mediated quasi-interaction, symbolic forms are produced for an indefinite range of potential recipients. Second, whereas face-to-face interaction and mediated interaction are dialogical, mediated quasi-interaction is monological in character, in the sense that the flow of communication is predominantly one-way. The reader of a book, for instance, is primarily the recipient of a symbolic form whose producer does not require (and generally does not receive) a direct and immediate response.

Since mediated quasi-interaction is monological in character and involves the production of symbolic forms for an indefinite range of potential recipients, it is best regarded as a kind of quasi-interaction. It does not have the degree of reciprocity and interpersonal specificity of other forms of interaction, whether mediated or face-to-face. But mediated quasi-interaction is, none the less, a form of interaction. It creates a certain kind of social situation in which individuals are linked together in a process of communication and symbolic exchange. It is a structured situation in which some individuals

are engaged primarily in producing symbolic forms for others who are not physically present, while others are involved primarily in receiving symbolic forms produced by others to whom they cannot respond, but with whom they can form bonds of friendship, affection or loyalty. [. . .]

In distinguishing between these three types of interaction, I do not wish to suggest that specific interactional situations will always concur neatly with one of the three types. On the contrary, many of the interactions which develop in the flow of day-to-day life may involve a mixture of different forms of interaction – they have, in other words, a hybrid character. For example, individuals may have a discussion with others in the room while they are watching television, thus combining face-to-face interaction and mediated quasi-interaction in the same interactional situation. Similarly, a television programme may involve face-to-face interaction between members of a panel and members of a studio audience, although the relation between these individuals taken together and the diverse recipients of the TV programme remains a form of mediated quasi-interaction. It would be easy to adduce more complex variations (for example, some individuals phone in questions to members of a studio panel, whose responses are heard or seen by listeners or viewers, and so on). One of the merits of the analytical framework outlined above is that it enables us to separate out the different types of interaction involved in complex situations of this kind. It enables us to analyse these situations with some degree of rigour and precision, and thereby to avoid some of the misunderstandings that could arise from a hasty characterization of the interactional situations created by the media. [. . .]

Used historically, this framework can help us to assess the significance of the development of new media of communication from the mid-fifteenth century on. Prior to the early modern period in Europe, and until quite recently in some other parts of the world, the exchange of information and symbolic content was, for most people, a process that took place exclusively within the context of face-to-face situations. Forms of mediated interaction and quasi-interaction did exist, but they were restricted to a relatively small sector of the population. To participate in mediated interaction or quasi-interaction required special skills – such as the capacity to write or read – which were largely the preserve of political, commercial or ecclesiastical elites. However, with the rise of the printing industry in fifteenth- and sixteenth-century Europe and its subsequent development in other parts of the world, and with the emergence of various types of electronic media in the nineteenth and twentieth centuries, face-to-face interaction has been increasingly supplemented by forms of mediated interaction and quasi-interaction. To an ever increasing extent, the exchange of information and symbolic content in the social world takes place in contexts of mediated interaction and quasi-interaction, rather than in contexts of face-to-face interaction between individuals who share a common locale.

The historical rise of interaction and quasi-interaction has not necessarily been at the expense of face-to-face interaction. In some cases, the diffusion of media products has provided a stimulus for interaction in face-to-face situations – in the way [. . .] that books in early modern Europe were commonly read aloud to individuals who had gathered together to hear the written word. Indeed, many books in the sixteenth and seventeenth centuries were composed with a view to being read aloud: they were addressed to the ear as well as the eye, and were thus produced with the aim of being

John B. Thompson

re-embedded in contexts of face-to-face interaction. But the growing importance of mediated interaction and quasi-interaction, and the gradual development of new forms of reception and appropriation (such as the development of reading as a silent, solitary practice), do mean that social life in the modern world is increasingly made up of forms of interaction which are not face-to-face in character. With the rise of mediated interaction and quasi-interaction, the 'interaction mix' of social life has changed. Individuals are increasingly likely to acquire information and symbolic content from sources other than the persons with whom they interact directly in their day-to-day lives.

Issues to consider

- ❑ What are the key differences between the three types of interaction that Thompson describes? List the main differences in three separate columns and find a clear-cut example of each. Then look for some examples where, in your view, the interaction cuts across the categories that Thompson has proposed.
- ❑ The significance of Thompson's arguments, as regards the present, lies mainly in the idea of an 'interaction mix'. By this, he means an overall social make-up, or ecology, of how people interact for different purposes and in different settings, including by using media at a distance. Thompson's historical argument is that the interaction mix has changed between different periods. How should the distinctions that Thompson introduces extend or modify ideas about what media are, as outlined in D1 and D2?
- ❑ Later in the same book, Thompson relates the different kinds of interaction he has described to changing ideas of what he calls public 'visibility'. By 'visibility' he means, for instance, how much we are given to see or know about politicians, celebrities and other public figures. Visibility is an important aspect of social relations, including how power and influence work. Follow up this idea and relate it to established conventions you find in media discourse forms, such as the political media interview genre, which is discussed in unit D4.

D4 BROADCAST TALK

In this unit, we consider the recognised media genres thought to emerge from particular combinations of communicative structure and chosen discourse style. Our first extract is from Martin Montgomery, who locates the genre of the media interview – especially the news interview – by examining different roles performed by the participants and the conventional styles of interaction in which they are engaged.

Martin Montgomery (reprinted from *The Discourse of Broadcast News: A Linguistic Approach*, London: Routledge, 2007: 145–8)

Martin Montgomery

Particularly over the last half of the twentieth century, interviews have become common – not just in news settings – but across the range of media output, frequently being used in entertainment and confessional formats (see Bell and van Leeuwen, 1994). The chat show interview, as one salient type, has been subject to much study and is pervasive enough as a form to be the subject of parody. Perhaps the most important characteristic of the media interviews in general is that they are talk for an overhearing audience. This distinguishes them from everyday talk in canonical speech situations where the prime protagonists are speaker and hearer and where turns at talk alternate between a pair (or members of a group of people) who constitute the immediate participants to the event. Mediated interviews are designed for public consumption, as is evident in many details of their construction – from references to the audience, from the visible and audible reactions of a studio audience, and from particulars of utterance design. Indeed, it is a central and generally understood condition of this talk that a potentially endless number of people may overlook or overhear it – not as active interlocutors but as an indefinitely large audience. Interviewers and interviewees know, therefore, that what they say will be appraised not just by their immediate interlocutor but by who-knows-how-many beyond. This is not merely a matter of pressure towards increased circumspection in one's choice of words, though that must undoubtedly exist. It is also a matter of the public performance of talk – of talking adequately for the public purposes of the encounter and of acquitting oneself well in public.

In addition, they are characterised by the previously mentioned differentiation or pre-allocation of roles: one speaker asks questions and the other answers them. The speaker who asks questions does so from an institutionally defined position – one in which they hold some responsibility for setting the agenda, the terms or the topic of the discourse. Nor is it a case of simply asking questions; the media interviewer also controls the length, shape and even the style of the encounter. Conversely, of course, the interviewee has not achieved that role by accident. In some way or other they have earned, by virtue of a distinctive attribute, their 'communicative entitlement' as material for a documentary case study, as witness, as celebrity. And always the nature of the entitlement is 'evidenced' or constituted in practice within the interview: in other words, witnessing, 'celebrity-ness', or 'documentary-ness' (Corner, 1995) is an outcome of the kinds of interrogation pursued within the interview. The interviewee 'does witnessing' in the interview in response to questions designed to display it.

The news interview itself, therefore, is simply one manifestation of a widely available mediated public genre, but one that offers journalists a crucial device for supplying quotable material to underpin the news. In practice, of course, broadcast news interviews are themselves not all of a single type. We may distinguish four principal sub-genres: (1) interviews with correspondents (reporting and commenting); (2) interviews with ordinary people affected by, or caught up in, the news (witnessing, reacting and expressing opinion); (3) interviews with experts (informing and explaining); and (4) interviews with 'principals' – public figures with some kind of responsible role in relation to the news event (accounting). These four sub-genres may be defined – as here – by characterising the social identity and role of the person being interviewed and their

characteristic contribution to the interview; but they could equally have been described in terms of the kinds of lead-in that set the agenda of the interview or the kinds of question that form its spine. For instance, a prototypical question to a correspondent is "Can you tell us more about what is going on?" (see Haarman, 2004). A prototypical question to an ordinary witness or bystander is "What could you see . . .?", or "What did/does it feel like . . .?". And the question to an expert explores the implications of a situation: "Given X, can you explain its implications?".

This repertoire of different types of news interview provides multiple threads out of which the web or tapestry of the news programme is woven. In bulletin news programmes, for instance, they are routinely used in edited fragments rather than in their entirety, providing perspectival sound-bites for an item (see Ekstrom, 2001). And so, by the use of interviews, the news becomes a thing of many voices – even if they are ultimately orchestrated in performance by the voice of the presenter. One highly significant aspect, which is mostly overlooked in studies of broadcast news interview, is their quite specifically occasioned character. They arise out of the need to cover journalistically an event or issue and they are inserted into an item or programme to cast light on or fill out an item or report. For this reason their relevance is routinely provided for at or near the beginning of the interview or extract.

Among the main sub-genres of news interview, the broadcast encounter with a public, often political, figure has received by far the greatest attention – in part because they are seen as instances of the classic public sphere in action. The focus of discussion in treatments of interviews of this type is on topics such as bias/neutrality, adversarialness, 'holding to account' and evasion. Indeed, the amount of attention devoted to political interviews might be seen as disproportionate, especially since it leads to this one sub-type coming to define the genre and practice of the news interview as a whole even though they are in practice extremely rare within the context of the standard bulletin news programme. On the contrary, they are the rather exclusive preserve of those extended news programmes that aim to offer in-depth coverage of current affairs [. . .]. Accordingly, to focus on the political interview as if it were typical of news interviewing in general is neither supported by the history of the journalistic interview nor justified by a survey of current broadcasting practice.

In what follows, therefore, we set out to characterise the news interview in general, situating the political interview as merely one type among the major kinds of interview that make up the news and offering a typology that distinguishes between them. The four main types of interview are termed the accountability interview, the experiential interview, the expert interview and the news interview with a correspondent, reporter, editor which we term the affiliated interview. [. . .]To help define the position of an interview within a typology of news interview types it is useful to distinguish between four broad parameters or axes. The first parameter defines the interviewee as affiliated with the news institution or not. The second parameter defines the interviewee as involved with the news event as an actor or responsible agent. The third parameter defines the interviewee as having first-hand knowledge of the event or holding knowledge about it. And the fourth stipulates the nature of their presumed alignment with the audience set up by the interview – whether with the interviewee or not.

On this basis, the following matrix can be constructed.

	Affiliation	Knowledge	Agency	Audience alignment	
				with inter'er	with inter'ee
Accountability interview	–	(of)	+	+	–
Experiential interview	–	(of)	+	+	–
Expert interview	–	(about)	–	+	–
Affiliated interview	+	(of/about)	–	–	–

Although this matrix generates a set of ideal-typical classifications to which many actual broadcast news interviews unproblematically correspond, there are in practice some instances of mixed or undecidable cases, or instances where an interview starts out as one type and shifts into another. Nonetheless, such typifications are associated with recognisable differences in interview in terms of both broad purpose (within the overall discursive economy of the news) and particular discursive practice (for instance, type of lead-in or question), even though it must be accepted that part of the difficulty in defining the sub-generic types is that the roles of participants may on occasion be re-defined through shifts of discursive practice.

Issues to consider

- ❑ Like linguistic registers, genres change. Do the question/dialogue types that Montgomery outlines as being the main resources of media news fit current forms of news delivery on the internet as well as those of radio or television?
- ❑ Montgomery states that 'Perhaps the most important characteristic of the media interviews in general is that they are talk for an overhearing audience'. What are the strategies employed in these interviews to make audiences feel they are part of a wider group of 'participants' in this interaction?
- ❑ Montgomery's matrix of features offers a way of classifying an 'ideal type' of news interview genre. Create a corresponding matrix for features of a related media genre (e.g. for interviews incorporated into a celebrity or music programme format, or for the contributing voices that make up a political documentary on radio or television).
- ❑ Find an example of an interview which seems to cut across Montgomery's categories. Do modifications to his matrix suggest themselves on the basis of such examples?

Our second extract is from Steven Clayman and John Heritage. In this piece, Clayman and Heritage stress the importance of close analysis of the actual conversational interaction that takes place in an interview. They also offer guidelines as regards how the structure of genres enacted by the form of conversational interaction can be researched.

Steven Clayman and John Heritage

Steven Clayman and John Heritage (reprinted from *The News Interview: Journalists and Public Figures on the Air*, Cambridge: Cambridge University Press, 2002: 6–25)

If the news interview is not scripted in any strong sense of the word, neither is it a disorganized free-for-all in which "anything goes." Indeed, as we will be arguing throughout the book, the parties to a news interview observe an elaborate set of social conventions associated with the roles of interviewer and interviewee. These conventions are largely tacit and taken for granted – they are rarely commented upon within interviews themselves, and they receive only cursory and superficial attention in journalism textbooks and manuals of interviewing technique. And yet, these conventions of interaction are very real and very powerful. Adherence to the conventions is what distinguishes the news interview from other genres of broadcast talk and other forms of interaction more generally. These conventions are robust and remarkably similar in both Britain and the United States, although they are subject to cross-cultural variation and historical change. In all of these ways, the news interview can be understood as an organized social institution in its own right.

At the same time, the news interview is deeply intertwined with other societal institutions, most notably journalism and politics. It is a public arena in which representatives of these institutions encounter one another and strive to pursue their respective goals and agendas. Accordingly, what transpires within a news interview both reflects and contributes to the current state of journalism, politics, and their co-evolution over time. [. . .]

The news interview as a genre

The news interview is a familiar and readily recognizable genre of broadcast talk. But what makes it so? What sets news interviews apart from talk shows, panel discussions, debates, audience participation programs, and other interaction-based genres of broadcast programming? Like most ordinary language categories, the "news interview" has fuzzy boundaries – its members share a loose family resemblance rather than a rigid set of defining attributes. [. . .]

Studying the news interview requires a distinctive mode of analysis appropriate to its distinctive character. To clarify this point, it is useful to begin by considering, by way of contrast, how news is typically analyzed when it appears in story form. Traditional content analyses tend to focus on matters such as the themes that predominate within a given range of stories, and the balance and diversity of viewpoints represented therein. For example, studies of election news are concerned with the proportion of coverage devoted to each candidate, and the tendency for stories to concentrate on the theme of the horse race (e.g., who's ahead, campaign strategy, publicity efforts, etc.) to the exclusion of more substantive matters (e.g., the candidates' qualifications, issue positions, policy proposals, etc.). Studies of political news beyond the confines of the campaign have revealed a similar emphasis on political strategy over policy substance.

When we turn from the story form of news to consider the news interview, a different mode of analysis is in order. While overarching themes – such as political strategy – are highly significant to the organization of news narratives, they are rather less central within a mode of discourse that is organized interactionally rather than thematically. The

news interview is, first and foremost, a course of interaction to which the participants contribute on a turn-by-turn basis, for the most part by asking and answering questions. Of course, particular themes are expressed within each successive contribution, but these contributions are not merely understood in terms of their thematic content. They are also understood in terms of how they bear on the unfolding interactional "game" being played by interviewer and interviewee.

To illustrate this point, consider the questions that interviewers ask. The sense and import of any given question depends in part on how it functions as a "move" within the interview game at a particular point in its state of play. Each question has a retrospective import – some questions accept and build upon the interviewee's previous remarks in a way that moves the discussion along, while other questions subject prior remarks to challenge. Each question also has a prospective import – some questions are relatively open-ended and allow the interviewee maximum leeway to respond, whereas others narrow the parameters of an acceptable response and exert pressure on the interviewee to answer in a particular way. Correspondingly, the sense and import of an interviewee's response depends in part on how it deals with the agenda established by the question – whether it is dutifully answering, or resistant in some way, or downright evasive . . .

[. . .] Given its manifold significance, how does one go about analyzing the interactional game of the news interview? In light of the preceding, it may be tempting to begin by examining how the game is played differently by different participants and in different social environments. For instance, focusing on the interviewer's role in the game, one could chart the relative prevalence of polite or deferential styles of questioning versus more aggressive or adversarial styles of questioning across particular interviewers, interviewees, news programs, broadcasting media, national boundaries, or historical eras.

However, a comparative analysis of this sort cannot proceed without a thorough understanding of the various practices that constitute deference or adversarialness in this context. Such practices are numerous, complex, and by no means transparent. To take just one example [. . .], one way of expressing adversarialness is via questions that are opinionated or assertive – such questions display an expectation about the type of answer that would be correct or preferable, and thus exert pressure on the interviewee to answer in a particular way. Pressure of this sort can be encoded in a variety of ways, some of which may be available to a priori intuition while others most certainly are not. For example, it turns out that when yes/no questions are negatively formulated (e.g., "Didn't you," "Aren't you," "Isn't it true that") they embody so strong a preference for an affirmative answer that they are often treated by interviewees as if they were expressing an opinion rather than merely asking a question. [. . .]

More generally, any attempt to document systematic variations in interview conduct presupposes that one already has a grasp of the broad array of practices that comprise such conduct, and the sense and import that such practices have for the participants themselves (Schegloff, 1993). [. . .] What are these practices? How do they affect the conduct of interviewers and interviewees? What are the institutional norms to which they are responsive, and what happens when these norms are transgressed? Once these practices have been described, what can they tell us about how the news relates to its social context and how it has evolved over time? Clearly no analysis of the news interview can come to terms with its journalistic, political, and cultural power without attending seriously to such questions.

Issues to consider

- ❑ How do Clayman and Heritage suggest it may be possible to move from recordable data of interaction that actually takes place to the less evident intentions and strategies of the participants in this kind of media genre?
- ❑ Use Hymes's SPEAKING grid presented in unit B4 to analyse a news interview at the level of speaker, norms of interaction, goal, etc.
- ❑ What are the main linguistic strategies associated with the news interview as a speech event? Are these universal (i.e. common to all cultures) or culture-specific? If you are able to, investigate this question by examining a news interview from a different culture.
- ❑ How well does Montgomery's development of an interview matrix in the previous extract reflect the research approach advocated by Clayman and Heritage?

D5 NEWS AND ADVERTISING ANGLES

In this unit, we continue with news as our example of genre. We are interested in how a process of selection and arrangement transforms raw events or information into the expected conventional form of the news genre. We present three readings which highlight how the process of discourse construction can slant or skew information for the purpose of persuasion (or even, in worst cases, for deliberate manipulation or deception).

Our first extract is from Allan Bell. Bell describes and comments on an influential list of qualities that make a story not simply *informative* but typically *newsworthy* (i.e. eligible for coverage as material suited to the news genre). The original list was devised by two news researchers, Johan Galtung and Mari Ruge, in their 1973 paper, 'Structuring and selecting news'. While other expositions of the same list can be found, Bell offers a particularly insightful explanation and illustration of the implicit news agenda that Galtung and Ruge revealed.

Allan Bell

Allan Bell (reprinted from *The Language of News Media,* Oxford: Blackwell, 1991: 156–8)

NEGATIVITY is what comes to people's minds as the basic news value. Negative events make the basic stuff of 'spot' news. It is a true platitude that news is bad, although it is a difficult question *why* the negative makes news. Involved in negativity are a number of concepts such as damage, injury or death, which make disasters and accidents newsworthy (and unchallengeable subjects for narratives). Conflict between people, political parties or nations is a staple of news. Indeed the ultimate in conflict news, war reporting, is one of the earliest historical forms of news and a stimulus for the growth of news media. Deviance is another negative characteristic with proven news interest.

RECENCY (Bell 1983) means that the best news is something which has only just happened. Time is a basic dimension of news stories. Recency is related to Galtung and Ruge's

concept of FREQUENCY – how well a story conforms with news work cycles. The day is the basic news cycle for the press and principal television and radio news programmes, while staple radio news works on an hourly cycle. This means that events whose duration or occurrence fits into a 24-hour span are more likely to be reported. So the murder is more newsworthy than the police investigation, the verdict more than the trial.

PROXIMITY means quite simply that geographical closeness can enhance news value. The minor accident is reportable only in the settlement where it happens, not a hundred miles away. The carnival coming to town is news only in the town it comes to. Related is Galtung and Ruge's factor of MEANINGFULNESS – the cultural familiarity and similarity of one country with another, not just the physical distance between them.

The CONSONANCE of a story is its compatibility with preconceptions about the social group or nation from which the news actors come. Thus editors have stereotypes about the manner in which Latin American governments or the British royal family behave. Schank and Abelson (1977) developed the concept of *script* to explain this. People have a mental script for how certain kinds of events proceed. [. . .]

UNAMBIGUITY indicates that the more clearcut a story is, the more it is favoured. Ifs, buts and maybes are minimal. The 'facts' are clear, the sources impeccable.

UNEXPECTEDNESS means the unpredictable or the rare is more newsworthy than the routine. Closely related is NOVELTY. 'New' is the key word of advertising, and one of the main factors in news selection. Science is a low-priority news area, but gains coverage when there is a 'breakthrough' to report.

SUPERLATIVENESS says that the biggest building, the most violent crime, the most destructive fire gets covered (Galtung and Ruge's term is THRESHOLD).

RELEVANCE is the effect on the audience's own lives or closeness to their experience. Achieving relevance for a story causes much head-scratching and labour in newsrooms. A common angle on economic announcements, political decisions or scientific breakthroughs is to lead with what they supposedly mean for the ordinary reader: more money in the pocket or a better paint for houses. Relevance need not be the same as proximity. Many decisions relevant to New Zealand are made 15,000 km away in Washington, DC.

PERSONALIZATION indicates that something which can be pictured in personal terms is more newsworthy than a concept, a process, the generalized or the mass. Striving for personalization has brought journalists to grief – for instance in the *Washington Post*'s Janet Cooke affair. Cooke's feature writing about an eight-year-old drug addict won a 1981 Pulitzer Prize which was withdrawn when it was found the boy did not exist.

ELITENESS of the news actors plays an important role in news decisions. Reference to elite persons such as politicians or film stars can make news out of something which would be ignored about ordinary people. Similarly, the elite nations of the First World are judged more newsworthy than the non-elite nations of the South.

The quality of ATTRIBUTION – the eliteness of a story's sources – can be crucial in its news chances. Highly valued news sources need to be elite on some dimension, particularly socially validated authority. The unaffiliated individual is not well regarded as a source. In a study of climate change news (Bell 1989) I found that only two out of the 150 sources cited were not backed by affiliation with some organization or institution.

Finally FACTICITY (Tuchman 1978) is the degree to which a story contains the kinds of facts and figures on which hard news thrives: locations, names, sums of money, numbers of all kinds.

Issues to consider

- Think of some recent news stories that have stood out and try and say what it is about these stories that makes them newsworthy. Use Bell's list to identify the qualities in each of the stories.
- Do you agree with the qualities listed by Bell? Are some of these qualities more or less important than others? Discuss the list in pairs and arrange the various qualities in order of most important to least important explaining why.
- The original research on which the list presented here was based is now 40 years old. How much – and in what ways – have the properties of newsworthiness changed in the intervening period?
- How well does the list outlined by Bell here fit different kinds of media news delivery (e.g. contemporary online news sources)?
- A news agenda involves a public, editorial decision. There are also personalised lists, feeds and alerts that reshape the relation between you and the news. The search agenda is now yours, and so the news values are yours – rather than shared public property. What are the advantages of pursuing your own news agenda by means of such personalised search and RSS feed possibilities? And what are the advantages of subscribing to, or continually witnessing, a public news agenda and set of values that have been subjected to editorial judgements directed towards wider public reception?

Our second extract, from Greg Myers, looks at how the language of advertising is designed to maximise its persuasive potential. The extract describes various linguistic resources that characterise what is often considered a distinctive style of persuasive advertising language.

Greg Myers

Greg Myers (reprinted from '"Beanz Meanz Heinz": what makes slogans stick?', in *Words in Ads*, London: Arnold, 1994: 30–44)

Let's compare two slogans, both of which try to get us to think of chocolate products as healthy foods rather than as indulgences. The first is for Van Houten's Cocoa, and appeared in an ad in 1904.

> A COCOA YOU CAN ENJOY. SUPPLIES THE ENERGY FOR WORK AND STUDY.

Even with some very nice allegorical figures of work and study accompanying it, this is an unmemorable slogan. The second example is a slogan recognisable to most British people:

> A MARS A DAY HELPS YOU WORK, REST AND PLAY

Why is this more memorable? To begin with, it rhymes, and runs in a fairly regular rhythm (though the regularity follows some rather complex metrical rules). The sentence structure places work, rest, and play as parallel activities [. . .] and the rhyme comes on play. And of course it echoes an even older saying, 'An apple a day keeps the doctor away', which gives it a sound of familiarity and perhaps inevitability.

The Mars slogan sticks with us because it draws attention to its form. Most of our daily uses of language do not draw attention to the form of the language itself this way. If I tell my daughter, 'Have a Mars bar', she is interested in what is said (and eaten) and not how it is said. We usually assume that language is transparent, that we can express ourselves through it without the exact words and sounds mattering. Poetry often tries to break down this transparency, with rhythm and rhyme and other patterns that make us respond to the form, even if we do not analyse it. Jokes, too, often play on the forms of language; most jokes fall flat when the punch line is changed even slightly. It is part of the fascination of ads that they play with language in similar ways. And in ads, as in poems and jokes, the patterning of the form of the ad – the product name or the jingle or the headline – may lead us to important meaning relations – as in the way play is stressed in the Mars slogan by being last.

Theorists of literature writing in Russia in the 1920s, who have been very influential on later writers, suggested that literature is distinguished, not by its subject matter (heroes, heroines, romantic or tragic events) but by a use of language in a way that would stand out against ordinary uses. Literature would make the language strange to us and thus renew our perception of it. Their term for this standing out is translated as *foregrounding*, drawing on a metaphor from painting, the way some things in the composition draw our attention while others fade into the background. Foregrounding in language can be achieved either by unexpected regularity or unexpected irregularity. An unexpected regularity is called *parallelism*, and an unexpected irregularity is called *deviation*. (The terms here are not important in themselves, but the patterns they describe are important in most theories of poetry.) The rhyme in the Mars slogan is an example of parallelism, because we don't expect the first part of a sentence to rhyme with the second part. An example of deviation would be the name for what was once the Standard Oil Company of New Jersey, or Esso; *Exxon* is deviant in that we do not expect double Xs in English words or names.

Most critics would now question the idea that literature can be defined as a special type of language; they would see it as a special way of using language. After all, we have just seen two of the best known literary devices, rhyme and rhythm, in a decidedly non-literary text, the Mars slogan. Instead of trying to fence off kinds of language, we can look at how any text builds up and defies expectations. In this chapter, I will point out some of the most common kinds of patterning in ads at the most basic level of sounds and letters. Most readers can agree that these patterns are there, so they are a good place to start any analysis. But the meanings with which they are associated can be highly complex and variable, as you will see if you groan at some of my examples.

Catchy sounds

Alliteration

The basic move in many advertising slogans is to build up a pattern of similarity, so that they can break it for effect. [. . .] In many cases the pattern of similarity in sound in a

slogan will play against a dissimilarity in meaning, making us more aware of the contrast. For instance, this is the headline on an ad for olive oil, above a picture of a pot of paella:

> For a moment, Morecambe became Madrid

This is not just playing on the opening letters – if it was, they could have used 'Manchester became Madrid'. Morecambe shares the /m/ with moment, and /m/ and /k/ with became, as well as the /m/ with Madrid. The joke for the British audience is that *Madrid* is the capital of the exciting country in which the British like to take their holidays, and *Morecambe* (pronounced morkum) is seen (unfairly I am sure) as a gloomy, rundown, and terribly ordinary working-class seaside resort, popular in the 1950s. The parallelism links two places with completely different associations, two places that can only be linked by using olive oil; there is a kind of wit in being reminded that they share some accidental similarities in sound. [. . .]

Assonance

So far I have been talking about the repetition of consonant sounds, *alliteration*. Linguists and literary critics usually distinguish this from the repetition of vowel sounds, *assonance*, and it is worth maintaining this distinction when talking about advertising because the effect of assonance is usually more subtle. There are many vowel sounds (how many depends on which variety of English you speak), all made by changing the shape of the lips or the mouth cavity; they are represented by the letters *a*, *e*, *i*, *o*, *u*, and various combinations. Because the effect is subtle, I had a hard time finding examples at first. Here is the current Gillette slogan:

> Gillette – the best a man can get. [. . .]

Rhyme

[. . .] Even three-year-olds recognise rhyme when they hear it, but it is a bit more complicated to define it. Rhyme is the repetition of ending sounds; technically it is the similarity of all the last sounds of two words, from the ending of the last stressed syllable on. (This is a complicated way of saying that *motion* is a full rhyme with *lotion* but only a half rhyme with *caution*.) Rhyme was used in ads from the beginning, so that it was taken as part of the genre. [. . .] Rhymes are used today more cautiously, perhaps because they carry associations with the mindless hard sell. In some cases, they are presumably meant to sound over insistent, as in this ad that appeared around Christmas.

> If men are wise they socialize with Appletise

Part of this oddity comes from the fact that the last two rhymes (*ize* and *ise*) are on less stressed syllables, so to make the rhyme come out you have to stress them more in your reading. [. . .] One important point to remember with rhyme, as with the other patterns of repeated sounds, is that it refers to *sounds*, not spellings. By the time we get through school, we sometimes get so used to spelling that we forget that most letters have several sounds, and most sounds can be spelt with several letters. For instance, in –

> Pilkington Glass. Amazingly Pays in Your Glazing.

– a company that makes double glazing gets in three rhyming words, with two different spellings. [. . .]

Tunes and Intonation

Of course words don't always stand by themselves on the page; the most insistent slogans are in broadcast ads, where words often work with and against music. [. . .] Where the music is written for the ad (instead of borrowed from an already popular song, a currently popular form of intertextuality), it often sets up patterns of similarity and difference in the same way as the words. [. . .] The loudness, pitch, and grouping of the spoken voice can also interact with what might be the expected patterning of a slogan; these aspects of pronunciation are called *intonation*. In the intonation of radio advertising, some words that would not be stressed in normal reading (such as *so* and *the* and *and*) are stressed to shift emphasis:

> I exercise, AND I eat the right sort of breakfast.
>
> SO, if ordinary shampoos don't fix your problem, try this.
>
> You have the Bible, but do you have the OTHer Testament of Jesus Christ [it's the Book of Mormon]
>
> Intermountain Design Inc., 521 South 8th Street, IN Boise

In each of these cases, the emphasis on a usually unstressed word shifts attention to some relevant relation: the need to link exercise to diet, the link between dandruff and trying a new shampoo, the existence of another religious book, the nearness of the location. [. . .]

Catchy print

Some advertisers try to get attention for print ads by making the ad as much as possible like face to face interaction. [. . .] But another approach is to call attention to the printedness of it, to the artificiality of the symbols. This section is about how the letters (not the sounds) are presented, what is called in linguistics *graphology*. Just as repeated sounds attract attention, so do repeated letters. In print, they can be emphasised by enlarging them, or using one letter to fill several slots. So if a firm has a name like Kopy Kwik, it may appear on the logo with a huge K in front of *opy* and *wik*. Where alliteration arises by chance, as with Minnesota Mining and Manufacturing, it can be brought out in the print version, so the company name becomes 3M. [. . .]

Frequency of letters

When advertisers make up names (instead of keeping the name of, say, the founder) they very often use less common letters to make the name stand out. X is particularly popular. I tried the experiment of going down the aisles at our local supermarket, and found *Radox*, *Dettox*, and *Biotex*. And of course there's the beef stock cube OXO, which has the advantage of reading the same, not only backwards and forwards, but upside down and

right way up. Other names used in marketing include *Dulux*, *Halifax*, *Kleenex*, and *Exxon*. [. . .]

Unpredictable spelling

Even when the advertiser is stuck with an existing product name, it may attract attention by deviating from expected spelling. I think the most famous British example is:

> Beanz Meanz Heinz

This is a good example of deviation in graphology, that is, attracting attention by spelling, because read aloud it doesn't sound odd. This spelling emphasises the fact that the three final consonant clusters sound the same, even if they are spelt differently. (To get this parallelism, one has to read it as referring to the word *beans*, as singular.) The deviation brings out what is unusual, and therefore memorable, about the brand name. [. . .]

Between languages

We may read English words without thinking of the spelling. Foreign words attract attention in ads when they provide unfamiliar spellings. The advertisers can either try to conceal the non-Englishness of the sequences, or emphasise them by juxtaposing them with English words. [. . .] Perhaps the best known example of this kind of spelling play between languages is the Perrier campaign that replaced the sound *o* with the French word, pronounced more or less the same in a bad French accent, *eau*. So the heading *H2Eau* went with a bottle of water, *Picasseau* went with a cubist representation of the bottle, *Incogniteau* went with the bottle without a label (still recognisable by its shape), and *The Sole eau* with the bottle on stage in front of a curtain. They even managed to get the British version of *Cosmopolitan* to print its name on its spine as *Cosmeau*. As the series ran on and on, it became another test of the copywriters' ingenuity. Note that this deviation in spelling serves two functions, both of reminding us of the water and reminding us that it is French.

Names and shapes

One further kind of deviation with graphology occurs when the advertisers ask us to take an image on the page as both a letter in a word and a picture or name in itself. So in the UK public-information campaign to get parents to lay children on their backs rather than their fronts, to reduce the risk of cot deaths, the headings was

> BACK TO SLEEP

with the B on its side, in the shape of a sleeping baby. [. . .] Another way to draw attention to print is to the names of individual letters, as we call them when we recite the alphabet. Of course, this particular kind of play will be untranslatable. I was at first baffled by the name of a French pop radio station NRJ because I failed to give the letters their French names – it comes out sounding like the French word *energie*. A similar play in English, in an ad for Lucozade, says *NRG*.

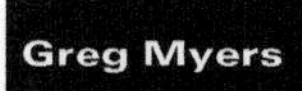

Homophones

In English, there are many words that sound the same (or can be made to sound similar) but are spelled differently – what linguists call *homophones*. This kind of play works especially well in print because of the tension between the spelling and the apparent meaning; we have to work harder so the joke comes as more of a surprise. For instance when we read this –

> Sainsbury's have discovered that the finest whisky is kept under loch and quay.

– the spelling and pictures make us think of the relevant Scottish meanings first, but we must also recall the idiomatic phrase that fits in this sentence, *lock and key*. [. . .]

Conclusion

I have been pointing out some of the ways that slogans can be catchy rely on their sound and print forms, and some of the uses of this catchiness. [. . .] These patterns are not automatic in their effect. They require activity on the part of the hearer or reader, and the advertisers use this investment of effort to make their messages stick. [. . .] We can say that this sort of play attracts attention to the physical form of the ad, spoken or written, while most daily language use leads us to ignore this physical form. Sometimes, as with the sillier jingles and altered spellings, that is all it does. But with most of these ads, the play led to some aspect of meaning to be associated with the product.

Issues to consider

- ❑ Recall the advertising slogans or jingles that you know. Can you say why they have remained memorable? Are these features in Myers's list? Are there any features that Myers does not describe?
- ❑ Look at some adverts (in magazines, newspapers, posters, etc.) and see how many of the linguistic devices that Myers describes in this reading you can identify. Which of these devices seem to you to be the more characteristic of 'advertising language'?
- ❑ In this passage, Myers suggests that linguistic resources used in creating 'advertising language' are also found in other kinds of discourse style, including literary writing and slogans in other fields (e.g. newspaper headlines, political slogans). Find examples of advertising language in other fields and evaluate how successful they are.
- ❑ Is it possible to refine the linguistic approach Myers outlines in order to distinguish advertising language from those other uses? Or, are the further distinctions needed likely to be ones of social function and use, rather than of linguistic form?

Our third extract is by Norman Fairclough. Fairclough works carefully through the sorts of questions that it is helpful to ask in order to unpick the persuasive design of texts of all kinds. He focuses on the sorts of questions readers and viewers need to ask if they are to engage critically with texts that present a particular viewpoint or ideological position. In this closing section of his book, Fairclough is especially concerned with what specific questions we should ask about the process of discourse construction in order to throw light on priorities, strategies and values circulating in media communication. Such questions form the core of any idea of contemporary critical media literacy.

Norman Fairclough

Norman Fairclough (reprinted from *Media Discourse*, London: Arnold, 1995b: 201–5)

I suggest that it ought to be an objective of media and language education to ensure that students can answer four questions about any media text:

1 How is the text designed, why is it designed in this way, and how else could it have been designed?
2 How are texts of this sort produced, and in what ways are they likely to be interpreted and used?
3 What does the text indicate about the media order of discourse?
4 What wider sociocultural processes is this text a part of, what are its wider social conditions, and what are its likely effects?

These are of course very general questions, which can be developed into more specific ones. [. . .] I shall discuss them in turn.
1 How is the text designed, why is it designed in this way, and how else could it have been designed?

This question highlights the idea that texts are based upon choices, and that alternative choices might always have been made. Sometimes the question will direct attention to the variation that currently exists in media practices – for instance, the sort of variation in radio science that was brought out in Chapter 7 in the comparison between *Medicine Now* and *High Resolution*. Sometimes the question will suggest that current practices are shaped by (and help shape) current social and cultural circumstances – and that things might be (and perhaps once were, and will be) different.

The question of how texts are designed has received more attention in the book than any other. I have provided a 'metalanguage' for talking about the language and intertextuality of texts. Such a metalanguage is essential for a critical literacy of media language, but developing a metalanguage which can be made generally accessible through the educational system is a formidably difficult problem which I have not addressed in this book. Let me summarize as a further and more specific series of questions the main forms of analysis introduced in the book. I also include some of the types of linguistic and textual analysis used in connection with each group of questions.

(a) Intertextuality

- What genres, voices and discourses are drawn upon, and how are they articulated together?

– direct and indirect speech, generic structure or 'staging', narrative analysis (story, presentation), conjunctions, collocations

(b) Language
i Representations
- What presences and absences, foregrounding and backgrounding, characterize the text?
- What process and participant types are there? How are processes and participants categorized and metaphorized?
- What relationships are set up between propositions (clauses) in texts?
  – presupposition, process and participant types, nominalization, agency and voice (active and passive), categorization and wording, metaphor, main and subordinate clauses, theme, local and global coherence relations

ii Relations and identities
- What are the participants (voices) in the text, and how are they constructed?
- What relationships are set up between participants – specifically between:
  – media personnel (journalists, presenters) and audiences/readerships
  – 'others' (e.g. experts, politicians) and audiences/readerships
  – media personnel and 'others'
- Are constructions of participants and relationships simple, or complex/ambivalent?
- What relative salience do institutional and personal identities have in the construction of participants?
  – oral delivery, body movement, key (serious or humorous), conversationalization, vocabulary, mood, modality, interactional control features, lists

iii Image and text
- In the case of television, how are visual images constructed, and what relationships (e.g. of tension) are set up between language and image?

2 How are texts of this sort produced, and in what ways are they likely to be interpreted and used?

[. . .] With respect to production, it is important to be aware that what we read in a newspaper or see on the television screen is not a simple and transparent representation of the world, but the outcome of specific professional practices and techniques, which could be and can be quite different with quite different results. It is also important to be aware that the practices which underlie texts are based in particular social relations, and particular relations of power. With respect to consumption, important issues are the diversity of practices of reading, listening and viewing (and their social conditions), and the potential for divergent interpretations and uses of any given text by different sections of a readership or audience.

3 What does the text indicate about the media order of discourse?

Part of critical media literacy is an overall sense of the practices of media and of the media order of discourse, and a sensitivity to significant tendencies of change. This question assumes that any given media text will shed some light upon these issues, in that it will be a product of a particular state and evolution of the order of discourse. Particular questions here include:

- Is the text indicative of stable or unstable relationships, fixed or shifting boundaries, between discursive practices within the order of discourse, and between the media order of discourse and socially adjacent orders of discourse?
- What particular choices (inclusions/exclusions, of genres or discourses) is this text associated with?
- What chain relationships across the media order of discourse and/or socially adjacent' orders of discourse is this text situated within?
- What particular tendencies of change (e.g. commodification or conversationalization of media discourse) does this text exemplify?

4 What wider sociocultural processes is this text a part of, what are its wider social conditions, and what are its likely effects?

This question brings into the picture wider social conditions (including economic and political ones) which constrain media discourse and media texts, and their social effects – in terms of systems of knowledge and beliefs (and ideologies), social relations of power, and the positioning of people as social subjects. It also draws attention to changes in society and culture which frame the sort of changes in the media order of discourse alluded to in question 3 above. [. . .] The analysis of any media event links together statements about:

– the text and its linguistic properties
– the discourse practice – processes of text production and consumption (recall that intertextual analysis links text to discourse practice)
– the sociocultural practice which the discourse practice and the text are embedded within.

We might add to the four questions so far a fifth question [. . .]:

5 What can be done about this text?

The point of this question is to highlight the status of media texts as a form of social action which can be responded to with other forms of social action. These may be other texts – letters of congratulation or complaint, reviews, discussions – or nontextual forms of action. Some media texts, for instance, can stimulate public campaigns, meetings and demonstrations. [. . .] One effect of this question, within a programme of critical literacy awareness, may be to encourage people to move beyond reception of media texts to action in response to those communicative events.

Issues to consider

- ❑ Fairclough provides a 'metalanguage' for talking about the language and intertextuality of texts, something which is 'essential for a critical literacy of media language'. How much is critical media literacy a matter of learning ways of expressing intuitions we already have about texts? How much is the approach a way of learning to see new qualities, detail or problems in any text we choose to investigate?
- ❑ Fairclough points out that what we see on the television screen or read in a newspaper is 'not a simple and transparent representation of the world, but the outcome of specific professional practices and techniques'. Think of examples where the ideology implicit in a particular newspaper or television channel 'imposed' its 'representation of the world' on the viewer. What were the main linguistic strategies used to achieve this?
- ❑ Fairclough's final suggestion is that it should be possible to move from detailed analysis of the language of media discourse to kinds of public engagement (e.g. complaining, contesting, rebutting). How far do you think such social action can take place in the language of linguistic analysis? Will an alternative metalanguage need to be developed for a day-to-day discourse of public contestation and debate?

NARRATIVE STRATEGIES

D6

In this unit we are concerned with the transformation that takes place in media discourse – by means of particular discourse choices and organisation – from information, ideas, events or situations into public textual presentation. Our extract is by Michael Toolan, who in this passage investigates what he calls the 'political orientation of a narrative'. Processes of discourse transformation are to be found, he suggests, in media forms that either overtly or indirectly tell stories, or convert story material into other kinds of general statement. Toolan argues that in doing so media narrative often presents ideological viewpoints, or what he calls 'slant'.

Michael Toolan (reprinted from *Narrative: A Critical Linguistic Introduction*, 2nd edition, London: Routledge, 2001: 221–8)

Michael Toolan

The linguistic apparatus of political construal: notes on key resources

Here is a brief review of some of the key linguistic phenomena it seems sensible to examine when analyzing the political orientation of a narrative. Most are lexicogrammatical systems where choice of formulation, or 'slant', is possible; they can all contribute to the discoursal variations, transformations, or alternations to be found where different treatments of a news item are compared.

Michael Toolan

1 *Transitivity*. Following Halliday's account of clause transitivity as the representation of reality, it is reasonable to look at just which entities are presented as participants in a text's representation of events. Which individuals or groups tend to be cast as agent (sayer, thinker), and which tend to be cast as affected medium, in the text (see also Passivization, below)? What *kinds* of process are particular protagonists reported as initiating? And which relevant parties are scarcely mentioned at all?

Consider the protest against the Seattle WTO talks: was this chiefly a physical battle (as the abundant television coverage of police–protestor confrontations and the now-standard designation as *The Battle of Seattle* would suggest) or a conflict of wills, or more one than the other? Similarly, are protests against foxhunting, or against genetically-modified experimental crops, as essentially physical (as distinct from mental and ethical) as they are often represented? The media, in their pursuit of exciting copy and a more dramatic portrait of the day's happenings, are surely likely to represent matters in a more material and less mental way than might be the case. The success or failure of various campaigns (political, military, commercial) may have even more to do with winning hearts and minds than we tend to think. And it may be that the dominant party seeks to reinforce whatever physical/material advantage they have, by their emphasis on that advantage in their statements (= stories) to the press, so that mental (and verbal) opposition is worn down. These are highly speculative comments, but they seem to be important issues to do with textual presentation – and they are issues that a Hallidayan anatomy of transitivity enables us to explore.

Besides the processes and participants of transitivity analysis, it is often crucial to examine that content that a text casts as the third and back-grounded component, circumstantial elements. [. . .] Deciding whether surrounding circumstances are ever indirect causes is often difficult, and a circumstance that is actually foregrounded in a headline is definitionally no longer neutral background: at the very least, to highlight a circumstance is to suggest that it is rather less tenuously involved in whatever incident has occurred. All of these implications are strengthened by the use in headlines of such conjunctions as *as*. Recall *The Times* headline discussed by Trew:

> Rioting blacks shot dead by police as ANC leaders meet

'As' rarely explicitly expresses a causal connection in headlines, usually serving as the most succinct means of reporting temporal connection or simultaneity; but since it does elsewhere express causal relation, readers may attribute a residually causal emphasis even while assuming that the 'declared' interpretation is temporal.

2 *Passivization*, especially with agent-deletion. Passive voice sentences are a significant representational variant, which need to be seen alongside their closest counterpart, the active mood sentence. For example, an initial representation of a key event may use a transitive material process clause, that is to say, a clause containing a physical process done by one participant to another. Active voice, the normal and simpler ordering, places the agent as subject, followed by the process undergone, followed by the affected entity as object, e.g.

Police shoot Africans
Youths stab boy

A common variant of this is the complex transitive clause where an attribute or condition of the affected, perhaps arising as a result of the process stated, is also mentioned:

Police shoot Africans dead
Youths stab boy to death

But a further alternative, often with a distinctly different effect, is the passive construction. By passivization the affected participant is brought to the focal subject position in the sequence, and the semantic agent can optionally be deleted:

Africans (are) shot dead (by police)
Boy stabbed to death (by youths)

With reference to informativeness, the reformulation says less: we no longer have an indication of the cause or agent of the process of shooting. But it does thematize (bring to the front) the most affected or changed participants.

3 *Suppletion of agentless passives by intransitive clauses.* An (agentless) passivized or complex-transitive clause can be supplanted by an intransitive clause relatively smoothly. Typically, both clauses will have the structure S-P-(A), and while there may have to be a change of lexical verb, the new verb choice can be close in meaning to the original:

Africans shot dead (in Salisbury riot)
Africans die (in Salisbury riot)
Boy stabbed to death on crime-ridden estate
Boy dies on crime-ridden estate

The affected participant formerly in object position is now the sole stated participant, occupying subject position, and the former description of a causal relation, what x did to y, is now simply a report of what happened to y, or even, of what y 'does'.

4 *Nominalization.* A nominalization is a conversion and encapsulation of what is intrinsically a clausal process in the syntactic form of a noun phrase, hence treating the entire process as an established 'thing' – which can then serve as a participant in some other more directly reported and inspectable process. Nominalization 'de-narrativizes' a process, making the process mere background to a product or thing. This formulation:

Damilola Taylor died of stab wounds

is a process and a narrative. But the following equivalent

The death of Damilola Taylor from stab wounds

is a nominalization, assuming a narrative but not telling it. Similarly, in the Salisbury riot story –

> The deaths of 13 Africans

– nominalization can attenuate the sense of 'shooting dead' or 'dying' as experienced processes. The reformulations deflect the reader's attention further from questioning whether these deaths were killings or not, and if so who the killers were. Nominalization transformations such as this recast an implicit process into the form of a static condition or thing. This nominal condition or thing can then be used as the agent or affected participant or carrier of some other process, now become the focus of our attention:

> The Taylors had accused Mr Hague of using **their son's death** as a 'political football'.
> **The deaths of 13 Africans** triggered a further wave of violence in Salisbury townships today.

Nominalization is one of the crucial linguistic resources deployed in news reports. But as the examples above suggest, it can also be exploited and abused: it enables the user to refer without narrating, without clear and explicit report. The teller can be economical with the facts (as they see them). Nominalizations are exploited, used as sword and as shield, by every political and ideological faction or persuasion. In the explicitly political arena, they often serve to contrive implicit or explicit transfers of responsibility – unsurprisingly, in view of the fact that varying answers to the question, 'Who is to blame?' lie at the heart of much political discourse. It is not that nominalization is inevitably 'wrong' or undesirable – it is an invaluable means of textual condensation, e.g. in academic and scientific writing. But it clearly can be used, in barely perceptible ways, to background what arguably should be in the foreground. [. . .]

5 *Modality and evaluation* [. . .]. Within systemic linguistics more recently, the systems of lexical resource available for conveying evaluation have been brought together under the cover-term of Appraisal. Appraisal theory postulates that, by means of complex networks of vocabulary expressing various kinds of appreciation, judgement, and affect, speakers can 'encode' their interpersonal evaluations of the subject-matter. [. . .]

6 *Namings and descriptions* [. . .]. Consider again Trew's news stories about riots and killings (we can note, relevantly, that the *Salisbury, Rhodesia* of the 1970s has become *Harare, Zimbabwe*). Were those who acted *rioters*, *demonstrators*, or *troublemakers*; were they a unified group or was there a ruthless, violent minority among the majority; were those actually shot representative of the entire group, or innocent bystanders, or ringleaders, or what? Notice, in passing, the contrasting evaluations carried by the words *leader* and *ringleader*. Were the police ordinary police or special police, black or white or mixed or both-but-stratified. If trained to deal with riots, trained by whom, with what objectives? How many police actually opened fire, were they young, nervous recruits, or hardened old stagers? All the foregoing questions are probing both the facts and, by implication, their proper reported description; and all descriptions carry some interpretative and

political charge. [. . .] Some sets of variant description are particularly familiar, and often contain noticeably positive or negative evaluation: cf. *terrorist* versus *freedom fighter* versus *gunman* versus *men* [sic] *of violence*; *question* versus *allegation*; *reply* versus *rebuttal*; *answer* versus *refute*; *opinion* versus *allegation*; *opinion* versus *fact*; *answer* versus *justification*; *national security* versus *government cover-up*; *policy* versus *expediency*. [. . .]

7 *Collocational incongruity*. Under this label may be gathered all the demonstrably atypical or infelicitous constructions – clearly having most impact in headlines and leads – of the kind discussed [above] and thus not elaborated here. By contrast with some of the other discourse-transformative resources discussed in this list, these clashes of idiom or usage may well not be deliberate, even though, ironically, they seem to arise after much careful deliberation over individual word selection. Mr Hague is defiant so that the verb *defies* is selected; the Taylors' request for their tragedy not to be used in a policy debate is nominalized as a *plea*. But the chaining of these in text gives rise to the incongruity of a powerful person *defying a plea*, possibly reflective of ideological and narrative turbulence, amenable to Bakhtinian explanation as a clash of voices.

8 *Presupposition*. This is the term used to describe a speaker's backgrounding, in their utterance, of various kinds of assumptions that are nevertheless retrievable from that utterance. Thus if I say the car battery is flat again I presuppose that the battery has been flat before. Even if the sentence is cast in the negative – *Thankfully the battery isn't flat again* – the presupposition remains true (the battery was flat before). [. . .] The most strategic use of presupposition in public or political discourse is so as to 'insert' into the record (but in the background, as if they were uncontroversial facts, common ground) propositions that are contestable or slanted. To take two examples from *The Daily Telegraph* story discussed above, when this reports

> [Mr Hague] said he would not be bullied into silence on inner city crime, falling police numbers and morale.

it relays without objection Mr Hague's presupposition that somebody has been intent on bullying him into silence on inner city crime, etc. Notice by contrast that *The Independent* questions Mr Hague's presupposition by using scare quotes:

> [Mr Hague] warned that he would not be 'bullied' into dropping the issue.

[. . .] Often as interesting to reflect upon are the cultural or societal presuppositions that can be inferred from what members of a community talk or write about, and from how they do so. The community or culture involved need not be coterminous with nationality, but could be based on a sport, music, a religion, a hobby – every imaginable grouping that might sustain a monthly magazine or an internet discussion group. Clearly, very different kinds of things will be narratively 'tellable' (being significant, or calamitous, or amusing, or a triumph, etc.) for each of these communities, and strikingly different cultural presuppositions will form a backcloth to the foregrounded tellable material.

Issues to consider

- Take a news story either from a newspaper or an online news report. Try to find, within the single story, an example of each of the features that Toolan points to. Use Toolan's description as a model of how to describe and explain the significance of each feature.
- The process of 'nominalisation' that Toolan describes intersects with the style of news discourse analysed by Douglas Biber in the second extract in unit D2. But there are differences of approach. What are the main differences between these two treatments of this feature of verbal discourse in the media?
- Toolan describes as features of narrative form some aspects of news discourse that many readers would not readily see as being involved in telling stories (e.g. presupposition and naming, which pervade all discourse). Is his wide concept of narrative an important broadening of what we understand by storytelling, or is the concept of narrative made weaker by subsuming so many different aspects of how discourse works?
- Lambrou (2007) argues that the element of 'Trouble' is an important condition for making personal narratives reportable, as 'Trouble' guarantees a crisis that needs to be resolved. Moreover, it justifies their telling in the first place. How far do you think that 'Trouble' is a necessary condition of news stories? Is it true to say that the greater the crisis the more memorable the news stories? How does this relate to Bell's notion of 'NEGATIVITY' as a condition of 'newsworthiness', in D5?

D7 WINDOWS ON THE WORLD

Our two extracts in this unit look at aspects of how different sign systems – visual, audio, and verbal – combine to create meanings that are presented as to different degrees true or convincing depictions of reality.

Our first extract is by David Graddol, who questions the idea of media discourse as a transparent 'window on the world'. Graddol emphasises the role played in creating a sense of truth or reality by the organisation of visual material as a kind of rhetoric. He also shows how linguistic categories can be applied, with suitable modification, to visual discourse. Graddol compares the different resources of verbal and visual styles of discourse when it comes specifically to creating a sense of reality.

David Graddol

David Graddol (reprinted from 'The visual accomplishment of factuality', in D. Graddol and O. Boyd-Barrett (eds), *Media Texts: Authors and Readers*, Clevedon: Multilingual Matters/Open University, 1994: 136–42)

The idea that television offers a 'window on the world' in which events and places 'out there' are unproblematically made available to viewers in the home has often been remarked upon. Yet everything which is seen on the TV screen arrives there only after a complex process of mediation involving many people and institutions and a great deal of

technology and artifice. TV news is expected to provide a window which is more transparent than most, but it is no different from other TV genres in these respects. Its transparency and perceived factuality is a testament to the extent to which its conventions of representation have become naturalized. Understanding the semiotics of factuality is perhaps one of the most important literacy skills required by readers and viewers in the modern industrial world. But the ways in which information and entertainment have become inextricably linked in most TV genres means that the task of identifying and evaluating claims to factuality has become more complex than ever before.

The visual element in news reports has often been discounted as being less important than the words of a newsreader. Ellis (1982), for example, suggests that, in TV generally, sound is a far more important channel than vision; that pictures are illustrations to the sound, and that, in comparison to the cinema, they lack detail. 'Sound tends to anchor meaning on TV, where the image tends to anchor it with the cinema' (Ellis, 1982: 129).

On the other hand, some researchers have pointed to the cultural importance of the visual image in establishing truth. 'Seeing is believing':

> Seeing has, in our culture, become synonymous with understanding. We 'look' at a problem. We 'see' the point. We adopt a 'viewpoint'. We 'focus' on an issue. We 'see things in perspective'. The world 'as we see it' (rather than 'as we know it', and certainly not 'as we hear it', or 'as we feel it') has become the measure for what is 'real' and 'true'. (Kress and van Leeuwen, 1990: 52)

The visual element of news is perhaps the most under-theorised element of an otherwise well researched genre. Of all semiotic codes, it has been regarded as the most straightforward and transparent. The relationship between words and pictures in news reports has been regarded as a relatively simple one: the pictures may be selective in what they show but without words they cannot tell the truth, nor for that matter can they lie. Factuality is thus assumed to be accomplished by the words rather than the pictures. [. . .]

Modality systems

Factuality is not merely a question of truth or lies, but a more complex semiotic system which provides for varying authority, certainty and appropriateness to be allocated to particular representations of the world. This semiotic system is called the modality system. That which has definiteness, certainty, lack of ambiguity is said to have high modality. That which is less definite, possible rather than certain, is said to have low modality. Factuality is not quite the same as modality (you can have high modality in fiction, for example), but it is a key part of the semiotic mechanism by which factuality is accomplished.

Verbal modality

Verbal language uses a number of devices to express modality. Modality is so central to communication that in the English language it is an integral part of the verb. Things can happen, could happen, will happen, have happened, or happened. It is not possible to speak of a process or action without encoding modality. But modality is also signalled in ways other than through modal auxiliaries: through 'projecting' verbs like 'think' ('I thought it happened'), or through the use of hedges like 'possibly', 'perhaps'. The evaluations of factuality are usually those of the speaker or narrator, but they can be easily attributed to others. Indeed, attribution is a key part of news reporting – the status of a fact depends largely on the authority of the source and how distant a reporter was from sources and events. In the following fragment of a news report:

> The British maintain they cleaned the site up in 1957

the verb 'cleaned' is high modality (the implicit claim is that there is no argument over this point), but the evaluation of its factuality is not that of the speaker. Responsibility for the claim of factuality has been shifted to the 'British' through the verb 'maintain'. The narrator thus expresses high modality for 'maintain' (the British definitely made this claim), but distances herself and us as viewers from the factual status of the cleaning up.

Factuality depends on high modality but also on the genre of the text in which a claim was made. For example, the truth value of the news fragment cited above would be quite different if it were embedded in a novel rather than a news report:

> Effects of factuality or non-factualness are produced by the formal structures of genres: so, for example, the genre of the scientific paper or of a newspaper editorial produces the former, while the genre of the novel or of casual gossip produces the latter. (Kress, 1985: 143)

[. . .]

TV news is both a knowledge system and a genre. That is, the news system represents a particular way of collecting and establishing 'facts' which are different from, say, the institutions of science or the courts, and there are conventional ways of organising and presenting these facts on television. In western society the status of TV news as a knowledge system is regularly called into question. As a genre, it is also very vulnerable, and has difficulty in maintaining its generic distinctiveness from other TV genres such as faction, docu-drama, documentary, current affairs, chat shows. [. . .] The authority, quality of sources and interpretations which TV news offers are thus always potentially contestable. Its audience is heterogeneous and the social relations and values which are in play are various. In order to accomplish factuality, TV news must work hard to maintain the security of its knowledge-system, must establish the distinctiveness of the genre, and must use all the resources at its disposal for achieving high modality in its presentation. The visual component of TV news provides crucial resources in all three areas.

Visual modality

Modality operates in visual representation as well as verbal, though the devices which express it are less systematic. Hodge and Kress (1988) prefer to use the term 'modality cues' in relation to visual texts. For example, in cartoons, some figures may be drawn more realistically and in greater detail than others:

> a 'dense', detailed image can stand for realism or proximity, which can stand for present time, which can stand for factuality. An image lacking in detail and denseness

> can stand for unreality or distance, which can stand for past time, which can stand for fictionality (Hodge and Kress, 1988: 134).

In TV advertising, such devices as soft focus and colour saturation are routinely used to indicate forms of visual idealisation and fantasy, but in such landscapes the image of the advertised product will be shown as detailed and well focused. [. . .]

The modality conventions which operate in TV news are not those of science, though news reports may draw on the resources of science genres occasionally. High modality in TV news is more typically achieved by showing the context in which events occur – indeed, that is sometimes all that news images do show. TV news needs also to report a variety of perspectives and points of view and to evaluate these. The world which it describes is the transient world of today and what is news tonight is not news tomorrow. Above all, TV news needs to communicate immediacy, geographical and temporal location. It regularly succeeds in evoking emotional responses from its audience. Despite these subjective aspects of its reporting, it must simultaneously persuade viewers of the authority and credibility of the world which it portrays. It must present the world in a way which does not jeopardise the idea that it objectively exists, independently of partial accounts of it.

The key to understanding how TV news accomplishes factuality lies in recognising this tension between objectivity and subjectivity. It goes some way to explaining the complex and eclectic nature of the visual modality system which TV news employs.

The realist tradition

TV news tells stories about the world and the dominant narrative technique for such storytelling is what is called realism. Realism of the kind I am referring to here first arose as a literary convention. Realist novels typically employ an omniscient narrative voice, one who can see things which individual characters cannot see and who is in all places at once. [. . .]

The cinema adopted and adapted the realist narrative techniques of the novel. In a realist film, we see the same action from different angles and points of view as the camera moves position; we move instantly from location to location. The camera in this way provides the all-seeing narrative voice. Within this narrative structure, the camera can take up the perspective of various characters. [. . .] The reliability of different protagonists' accounts is cued by a number of different devices in realist film. Less reliable characters might be left partly in shadow; the shots in which they appear may be shorter or less frequent; they may be shown in extreme close up, so they appear threatening; the camera may look down upon them in a way which positions them as less powerful; it may look up to them in a way which makes them appear menacing; it may show them from an oblique angle which situates them as 'other', not one of us. In addition, a character's social role in the narrative may indicate whether they are 'hero', 'helper', 'victim', 'villain'. None of these devices by themselves will establish the modality of a character's world-view, but together they can encourage the viewer to accept that the perspective of certain characters is more authoritative than others.

As in the narration of novels, the film-goer is thus exposed to the world-views of

David Graddol

many characters, and the reliability of each is established through visual techniques. In addition, the viewer is given the privileged knowledge provided by the omniscient camera. Any event shown by this camera is given the highest modality: it is the objective realist narrative voice. It shows the world as it appears without characters and their individual perspectives. Realism thus provides a powerful visual technology for cueing narrative modalities. The regime of camera work and editing is so naturalized that we rarely stop to think about its artifice.

Realism in news

Indeed, the realist technique is so naturalized that TV news cannot avoid drawing on its resources when telling its own narratives. Failure to use it would run the risk that its representation of the world would appear unrealistic. Realism also provides what at first glance seems a perfect resolution to the tension between objective and subjective. It allows news to encompass a variety of voices and accounts, yet maintain through the device of the omniscient camera/narrator the belief in an objective world. It provides the viewer with a privileged account of this objective world, and gives the news producer a means of steering the viewer authoritatively through the maze of partial accounts.

Issues to consider

- ❑ Do you agree that the visual elements in news reports are less important than the words of a newsreader or do you agree more with the notion that 'seeing is believing'?
- ❑ Find a newspaper or magazine article that contains modal expressions (e.g. can, might, would, will, could, etc.). Could you argue that the lack of certainty or authority suggested by the use of these types of words is a reflection of 'bad' or imprecise reporting? When is it acceptable to make hypothetical claims about what might or could happen in the media news beyond the gossip pages?
- ❑ Find an example of an audio-visual text in which the truth-claims apparently made by the visual resources that Graddol outlines clash with a more hedged or modulated view being expressed verbally, for instance in an accompanying voice-over? What effect is created by such dissonance between the two different discourse modes?
- ❑ Some contemporary, 'postmodern' accounts of media suggest that media discourse conventions have been so routinely questioned, treated with irony, and turned into pastiche that the power of any dominant truth-telling voice has been seriously weakened. Are you convinced by Graddol's claim that there is usually a dominant, omniscient voice in place to anchor all other voices or points-of-view in an overall sense of realism created by a piece of media discourse?

Our second extract is by Gunther Kress and Theo van Leeuwen and explores wider issues raised by the way that contemporary media texts combine different modes. Kress and van Leeuwen draw out general issues for discussion of language and media presented by increasingly common forms of 'multimodality' and identify challenges in investigating these new forms of 'meaning making'.

Gunther Kress and Theo van Leeuwen (reprinted from *Multimodal Discourse: The Modes and Media of Contemporary Communication*, London: Arnold, 2001: 1–9)

Gunther Kress and Theo van Leeuwen

For some time now, there has been, in Western culture, a distinct preference for monomodality. The most highly valued genres of writing (literary novels, academic treatises, official documents and reports, etc.) came entirely without illustration, and had graphically uniform, dense pages of print. Paintings nearly all used the same support (canvas) and the same medium (oils), whatever their style or subject. In concert performances all musicians dressed identically and only conductor and soloists were allowed a modicum of bodily expression. The specialised theoretical and critical disciplines which developed to speak of these arts became equally monomodal: one language to speak about language (linguistics), another to speak about art (art history), yet another to speak about music (musicology), and so on, each with its own methods, its own assumptions, its own technical vocabulary, its own strengths and its own blind spots.

More recently this dominance of monomodality has begun to reverse. Not only the mass media, the pages of magazines and comic strips for example, but also the documents produced by corporations, universities, government departments etc., have acquired colour illustrations and sophisticated layout and typography. And not only the cinema and the semiotically exuberant performances and videos of popular music, but also the avant-gardes of the 'high culture' arts have begun to use an increasing variety of materials and to cross the boundaries between the various art, design and performance disciplines, towards multimodal Gesamtkunstwerke, multi-media events, and so on. [. . .]

In this book we make this move our primary aim; and so we explore the common principles behind multimodal communication. We move away from the idea that the different modes in multimodal texts have strictly bounded and framed specialist tasks, as in a film where images may provide the action, sync sounds a sense of realism, music a layer of emotion, and so on, with the editing process supplying the 'integration code', the means for synchronising the elements through a common rhythm. Instead we move towards a view of multimodality in which common semiotic principles operate in and across different modes, and in which it is therefore quite possible for music to encode action, or images to encode emotion. This move comes, on our part, not because we think we had it all wrong before and have now suddenly seen the light. It is because we want to create a theory of semiotics appropriate to contemporary semiotic practice. In the past, and in many contexts still today, multimodal texts (such as films or newspapers) were organised as hierarchies of specialist modes integrated by an editing process. Moreover, they were produced in this way, with different, hierarchically organised specialists in charge of the different modes, and an editing process bringing their work together.

Today, however, in the age of digitisation, the different modes have technically become the same at some level of representation, and they can be operated by one multi-skilled person, using one interface, one mode of physical manipulation, so that he or she can ask, at every point: 'Shall I express this with sound or music?', 'Shall I say this visually or verbally?', and so on. Our approach takes its point of departure from this new development, and seeks to provide the element that has so far been missing from the equation: the semiotic rather than the technical element, the question of how this technical possibility can be made to work semiotically, of how we might have, not only a unified and unifying technology, but also a unified and unifying semiotics. [. . .] In this book we want to pause, as it were, to take stock of what general picture is emerging. We want to sketch a multimodal theory of communication based, not on ideas which naturalise the characteristics of semiotic modes by equating sensory channels and semiotic modes, but on an analysis of the specificities and common traits of semiotic modes which takes account of their social, cultural and historical production, of when and how the modes of production are specialised or multi-skilled, hierarchical or team-based, of when and how technologies are specialised or multi-purpose, and soon. [. . .]

The issue of meaning in a multimodal theory of communication

We indicated [in the Preface] that it was our focus on *practices* and our use of the notion of *resources*, rather than a focus on fixed, stable entities, which allowed us to make progress with a multimodal approach to representation and communication. In relation to one specific question this has been particularly crucial, namely the question of meaning. The traditional linguistic account is one in which meaning is made once, so to speak. By contrast, we see the multimodal resources which are available in a culture used to make meanings in any and every sign, at every level, and in any mode. Where traditional linguistics had defined language as a system that worked through double articulation, where a message was an articulation as a form and as a meaning, we see multimodal texts as making meaning in multiple articulations. Here we sketch the four domains of practice in which meanings are dominantly made. We call these strata to show a relation to Hallidayan functional linguistics, for reasons of the potential compatibility of description of different modes. We do not however see strata as being hierarchically ordered, as one above the other for instance, or some such interpretation. Our four strata are discourse, design, production and distribution. [. . .]

Stratal configurations

At the level of the social organisation of semiotic production different configurations of discourse, design, production and distribution may occur. Three of these may be merged for instance, as in everyday conversational speech, where any speaker or listener incorporates discourse, design and production skills and probably experiences them subjectively as one and the same. Nevertheless, even here they do remain distinct strata. Speakers need access to discourses, knowledges which are socially structured for the purpose at hand; they need to know how to formulate these knowledges in the

appropriate register and how to embed them in an (inter)active event; and they need to be able to speak. Much as we might take these skills for granted and see them as a unified whole, they are distinct, as would quickly become apparent if any one of them became impaired.

At the other end of the scale from everyday conversation we might have the speech, say, of professional voice-over specialists. Here the division of labour is maximised. Each stratum involves different people and different skills. Expert sources provide the discourse, scriptwriters the design, voice specialists the voices, recording engineers the recordings, and so on. Yet the division of labour is not total. The experts will be hand-picked for their understanding of what the media need and their ability to provide the kinds of discourse appropriate to television documentaries. The scriptwriters will have to know something about television production so as not to write things which cannot be filmed or are too expensive to film, and so as to make good use of the medium's specific 'production values'. The voice-over specialists must understand what they are reading and take account of the requirements of the recording engineers, by keeping their voice at an even level, not rustling the paper, and so on. In other words, what we shall call 'stratal uncoupling' is never absolute.

Moreover, the two types of semiotic production exist in the same society.

Issues to consider

- ❑ How convincing, historically, is Kress and van Leeuwen's claim of a major step-change in terms of media discourse modality? Trace different forms of combination of modes in the history of communication, using a history of media (see Further reading for suggestions).
- ❑ How would you explain Kress and van Leeuwen's important distinction between meaning being made just once (in verbal discourse) and meaning being re-made, continuously, in multimodal discourse? Can you work through an example of multimodal discourse to show how this happens?
- ❑ Kress and van Leeuwen investigate the semiotic organisation of multimodal discourse more than they do the complex forms of interaction that such discourse seems to make possible (see units A3, B3, C3 and D3). How can we begin to describe the overall effect of some channels in a multimodal mix being interactive, while other channels or modes are not? To help you think about this, consider for example, a website. Some material may be fixed but other material may be selectable. Or, some material is linked by hypertext to other content, and some material can be resized but other material not. What about those materials that invite reply while others do not?

D8

MEDIA TROUBLE

Our extract in this unit, by Alan Durant, addresses the social problem of friction at the edges or boundaries of what is accepted as public media discourse. Durant outlines the challenge of resolving disputes over media discourse, and contrasts efforts to resolve what discourse means in face-to-face interaction with more elaborate forms of dispute that he claims are prompted by disagreement over media texts. The mediated characteristics of such texts act as an important constraint on the kinds of reply that are possible, he argues, and shape the sorts of social action that can be mounted in response to media texts (social actions of the kind Fairclough advocates in the final extract in D5).

Alan Durant

Alan Durant (reprinted from *Meaning in the Media: Discourse, Controversy and Debate*, Cambridge: Cambridge University Press, 2009: 9–12)

If you watch a film or television programme and wish to query its terms or point of view, or if you see yourself referred to in a public notice or publication, you cannot negotiate meaning in the 'dialogic' way outlined. This is not just because the social relationships involved are different, and more remote. Media communication events are structured differently from person-to-person conversation. As a result they present greater difficulty when misunderstanding, disagreement over meaning, or a sense of being offended arises. And where divergent interpretations go beyond resolution in the flow of communication, an escalation of the scale and ramifications of conflict follows. Grievance, in this area, incubates at a distance. [. . .] The varying degree of publicness of media texts increases their potential for offence, but also complicates how to establish the competing interpretations from which arbitration must start. In these different and more formal scenarios, relations between participants are those of a more complex kind of speech event than face-to-face conversation.

In this context, it is ironic that part of the celebrated power of modern media discourse is its apparent closeness to 'ordinary, everyday language': how it transmits and reproduces textures and patterns of personal speech and dialogue. While media discourse may appear in this way to *be the same as* everyday discourse, however, that sameness is 'mediated' (or as some writers prefer, 'mediatized') in ways that significantly affect how much and also in what manner discourse meaning can be queried or challenged.

The history of communication media is not only a history of successive technologies and institutions. It is also one of changing social relations governing interaction between people. If we are to get a precise sense of the *object* of media disputes over meaning – the contested media discourse – then we need to disentangle often hybrid forms and genres in our contemporary mix of technical resources and media institutions. A great deal of simplification enters into discussion if we model interpretive dispute on a default setting of two people talking to each other face-to-face [. . .]. Yet it is equally simplistic to see dispute as a matter of an isolated textual object [. . .] simply exhibited, published or posted in the public domain in such a way as to make available around it a cluster of positions from which reactions are stated, without acknowledging either intention, different anticipated interpretations, or complicating social facts about reception. To make progress in understanding contested media meanings, attention must be given to *processes* involved in media communication as well as to assumed properties of the *object* of contestation. [. . .]

The distinctions I have made so far may seem commonsense. We communicate all the time and mostly have firm intuitions about communicative intent. We easily understand, for instance, how and when we can answer back and when we can't; and we have rich intuitions as regards who is getting at what when they say something, what tone they are adopting, in what adopted role or persona, and for roughly what purpose. It is true that we can spell these things out more carefully. But intuitively we are mostly quite good at Harold Lasswell's 'who, what, when, where, why' questions about communication. As regards media discourse in particular, skills of instant recognition seem to be especially pronounced among young people, who grow up surrounded by the latest mix of media technologies, forms and styles.

Recognising what is going on is one thing, but things become less straightforward where interpretations have to be verbalised and defended against disagreement, particularly in formal contexts such as tribunals or legal proceedings. Developing an ability to talk about meaning is an important aspect of engaging actively with a changing media environment. Such skill is part of 'media literacy'.

Difficulties in formulating and explaining competing interpretations of a discourse that is contested are significant enough to make it useful to group disputes together for closer consideration: a class of what I will call 'meaning troublespots'. 'Meaning troublespot' is an informal rather than technical notion. It is based on an analogy between the personal, social and financial cost to protagonists involved in disputes over meaning and the serious damage and injury associated with physical accidents and political conflicts.

Disputes over meaning take many forms. But only some of the features that characterise those disputes make them 'meaning troublespots' in my sense. [. . .]. Disputes occur, for instance, in different media (newspaper, TV, radio, internet page or blog); they also occur in different genres (in news, documentary, fiction, magazine features). The controversies they precipitate are handled by different regulatory procedures (in the courtroom, by extrajudicial media regulators, in discussion by TV commentators and in newspaper columns). Yet none of these classes of difference will be relevant to whether a situation constitutes a meaning troublespot in my sense: the category I am proposing includes examples of each. Disputes also differ as regards the scale or amount of discourse involved. They vary from controversies focused in a precise crux (say a single word or phrase), through contested episodes within longer stories, or about a single fictional character (e.g. where a description is alleged to be defamatory of a living person), to problems surrounding a whole text (e.g. where adverts or whole campaigns of related adverts are considered deceptive, or novels or films are claimed to be obscene or blasphemous). Again, all of these I include in my meaning troublespot category.

What makes a meaning troublespot distinctive and worth investigating, for me, is *how* the meanings to be contested are put forward and argued over, as well as how some outcome to contestation – some kind of effective calming or closure – is achieved. In each instance of what I will call a meaning troublespot, what is involved is a pattern of events that is not necessarily fixed but (as the sociologist John Thompson has shown for

political scandal) which unfolds unevenly over time, with distinct contours and dynamics. Here is a rough outline of typical processes involved at a 'meaning troublespot':

- An utterance (or representation) is made public by being published, broadcast or exhibited, involving (a) words (or images, or both), in (b) some specific social setting and (c) against a backdrop of expectations, attitudes and beliefs that shape how the communicator anticipates the message will be understood.
- Various readers, hearers or members of an audience who encounter the utterance or text attribute a meaning to it; on the basis of that meaning, they derive some particular significance or effect that they associate with what has been said, written or shown.
- One or more people claim, given their particular way of interpreting the piece of discourse, to have experienced an effect which they believe to be harmful (they may feel they were lied to, misled or misrepresented, or they may feel in some way let down or offended).
- To seek some relief from or remedy against the perceived harmful effect, the party who feels injured sets in motion some form of public complaint, protest or litigation.
- The producer of the utterance or text denies that it means what the injured party *says* it means, and puts forward an alternative, competing account.
- A relevant adjudicating body (or the wider 'court of public opinion') scrutinises the discourse in question. Because discussion of the discourse is not, in its reproduced media form, dialogic or immediately interactive, commentary and analysis interrupt the flow of social action and present the question of 'meaning' as a kind of 'freeze frame' or reconstruction, an exercise temporarily offline from the continuing interests and agendas of the participants.

Put like this, the step-by-step unfolding of the essential stages of a meaning troublespot may appear mechanical. In any given instance, those stages are unlikely to be experienced as if they permit logical dissection. Precise boundaries will not line up neatly and stages will be experienced as overlapping and having blurred edges.

Even this simple outline of a meaning troublespot, however, can help to highlight important differences between the sorts of cases I want to discuss and either the simple model of face-to-face communication or of textual 'objects' placed in the public domain and contemplated from different perspectives. 'Meaning', in my 'meaning troublespots' framework, is constructed in interaction between the different parties, who act strategically in relation to one another against the changing backdrop of a developing interpretive situation. This timeline and apparent fluidity stand in contrast to analysis of a publication, recorded broadcast, single printed-off email, or website visited on a given day, each of which cuts a slice through temporal flow and fixes a snapshot of a particular state of play between the parties at a given moment. On the other hand, at the core of a meaning troublespot there is very often media speech, as much as writing, fixed in a recorded form. Negotiation of verbal or textual meaning places this frozen object derived from speech under intense interpretive scrutiny, in ways that differ fundamentally from the dialogic conditions I outlined.

Issues to consider

- ❏ Does Durant's description of the differences between face-to-face dispute and media complaint apply equally to all forms of media? If not, why not?
- ❏ The kinds of dispute referred to in this passage arise mainly where people disagree over what a text means. In other units, we see that many media controversies are not about meaning but about fundamental differences of taste, belief, standard of civility, or willingness to tolerate. Do all such disputes about media discourse run along similar lines to those indicated in this extract, or do some need a different model or approach to explanation?
- ❏ Durant's notion of 'meaning troublespot' covers a wide range of different sources of (or triggers to) public dispute and controversy, from adverts that are considered deceptive to comments that are alleged to be defamatory and news that is felt to be untrue or biased. Think of some recent instances of meaning troublespots in the media. How were those instances reported and resolved, if at all? Try to map each dispute or controversy onto Durant's list of staged processes above.

MEDIA LANGUAGE AND SOCIAL CHANGE

D9

Each of our two extracts in this unit considers major historical change in language use in communication media.

Our first extract, by Walter Ong, looks at the major transformation brought about by the capability of 20th-century media to broadcast and reproduce speech. In this passage, Ong describes a major social contrast he sees between 'non-media' or 'primary oral' speech (face-to-face interaction, or spoken rhetoric directly addressed to a crowd) and 'secondary oral' media that permit recorded and broadcast sound.

Walter Ong (reprinted from *Orality and Literacy: The Technologizing of the Word*, London: Routledge, 1982 [2002]: 133–4)

Walter Ong

[. . .] With telephone, radio, television and various kinds of sound tape, electronic technology has brought us into the age of 'secondary orality'. This new orality has striking resemblances to the old in its participatory mystique, its fostering of a communal sense, its concentration on the present moment, and even its use of formulas. But it is essentially a more deliberate and self-conscious orality, based permanently on the use of writing and print, which are essential for the manufacture and operation of the equipment and for its use as well.

Secondary orality is both remarkably like and remarkably unlike primary orality. Like primary orality, secondary orality has generated a strong group sense, for listening to spoken words forms hearers into a group, a true audience, just as reading written or printed texts turns individuals in on themselves. But secondary orality generates a sense for groups immeasurably larger than those of primary oral culture – McLuhan's 'global

village'. Moreover, before writing, oral folk were group-minded because no feasible alternative had presented itself. In our age of secondary orality, we are group-minded self-consciously and programmatically. The individual feels that he or she, as an individual, must be socially sensitive. Unlike members of a primary oral culture, who are turned outward because they have had little occasion to turn inward, we are turned outward because we have turned inward. In a like vein, where primary orality promotes spontaneity because the analytic reflectiveness implemented by writing is unavailable, secondary orality promotes spontaneity because through analytic reflection we have decided that spontaneity is a good thing. We plan our happenings carefully to be sure that they are thoroughly spontaneous.

The contrast between oratory in the past and in today's world well highlights the contrast between primary and secondary orality. Radio and television have brought major political figures as public speakers to a larger public than was ever possible before modern electronic developments. Thus in a sense orality has come into its own more than ever before. But it is not the old orality. The old-style oratory coming from primary orality is gone forever. In the Lincoln–Douglas debates of 1858, the combatants – for that is what they clearly and truly were – faced one another often in the scorching Illinois summer sun outdoors, before wildly responsive audiences of as many as 12,000 or 15,000 persons [. . .], speaking for an hour and a half each. The first speaker had one hour, the second an hour and a half, and the first another half hour of rebuttal – all this with no amplifying equipment. Primary orality made itself felt in the additive, redundant, carefully balanced, highly agonistic style, and the intense interplay between speaker and audience. The debaters were hoarse and physically exhausted at the end of each bout. Presidential debates on television today are completely out of this older oral world. The audience is absent, invisible, inaudible. The candidates are ensconced in tight little booths, make short presentations, and engage in crisp little conversations with each other in which any agonistic edge is deliberately kept dull. Electronic media do not tolerate a show of open antagonism. Despite their cultivated air of spontaneity, these media are totally dominated by a sense of closure which is the heritage of print: a show of hostility might break open the closure, the tight control. Candidates accommodate themselves to the psychology of the media. Genteel, literate domesticity is rampant. Only quite elderly persons today can remember what oratory was like when it was still in living contact with its primary oral roots. Others perhaps hear more oratory, or at least more talk, from major public figures than people commonly heard a century ago. But what they hear will give them very little idea of the old oratory reaching back from pre-electronic times through two millennia and far beyond, or of the oral life-style and oral thought structures out of which such oratory grew.

Issues to consider

- ❑ Ong suggests that one of the major differences between primary and secondary orality is that the latter 'has generated a strong group sense'. Can this be likened to the notion of a discourse community (see unit C2, where individuals share communicative practices to achieve common goals)? Think of some other examples of practices associated with secondary orality.

- ❑ Ong argues that modern-day political oratory differs greatly from old-style political oratory, which was embedded in primary orality. Is this a fair comment, especially in light of Barack Obama's presidential acceptance speech (see C5), which has been widely praised for its eloquence and evocation of Lincoln?

Our second extract, from David Crystal, outlines contemporary challenges facing language as a result of rapid expansion of the internet. In this passage, Crystal brings together his findings from a detailed description of internet language, and speculates about the present and future impact of new uses of language that we are yet to fully understand.

David Crystal (reprinted from *Language and the Internet*, 2nd edition, Cambridge: Cambridge University Press, 2006: 258–61 and 271–2)

David Crystal

The Internet has been the focus of this book, within which I have looked at seven situations – email, synchronous and asynchronous chatgroups, virtual worlds, the World Wide Web, blogging, and instant messaging. In each case, I have found clear signs of the emergence of a distinctive variety of language, with characteristics closely related to the properties of its technological context as well as to the intentions, activities, and (to some extent) personalities of the users. But the Net is only a part of the world of computer-mediated language. Many new technologies are anticipated, which will integrate the Internet with other communication situations, and these will provide the matrix within which further language varieties will develop. We have already seen this happen with broadcasting technology: radio brought a new kind of language, which quickly yielded several sub-varieties (commentary, news, weather . . .); then television added a further dimension, which similarly evolved sub-varieties. How many computer-mediated varieties of language will eventually emerge, it is difficult to say; but we can be sure of one thing – it will be far greater than the seven identified in this book. As Bob Cotton and Malcolm Garrett say, in the title of their review [1999] of the future of media and global expert systems, 'You ain't seen nothing yet'.

Immediate innovation is anticipated in each of the three traditional domains of communication: production, transmission, and reception. Cotton and Garrett, somewhat analogously, describe the future in terms of major developments in delivery systems, processing power, and access devices. All of these will have an impact on the kind of language we use. The heart of the matter seems to be the immense increase in bandwidth, already seen in ISDN, cable, and optical fibre technologies, which will permit many channels to be simultaneously available within a single signal, and thus allow hitherto separate communication modalities to be integrated. The two main modes, sound and vision, have already begun to be linked in this way; and there is in principle no reason why other modes (tactile, olfactory, gustatory) should not also be incorporated. The various established media elements are already becoming increasingly integrated, in a frame of reference neatly captured by the phrase 'streaming media'. It would appear that the aim is to make anything speedily available with anything – Web with sound and video, personal digital assistants with Web access, television with Internet access, Internet with television access, radio programmes with pictures, and so on. [. . .]

David Crystal

From a linguistic point of view, the developments are of two broad kinds: those which will affect the nature of language use within an individual speech community; and those which bring different languages together. Under the former heading, there will be linguistic implications when speech is added to already existing visual modalities, as in Internet telephony [. . .]with the microphone and loudspeakers giving the Net the functionality of a phone. In due course, we will be able to interact with systems through speech – already possible in a limited way – with speech recognition (at the sender's end) making it unnecessary to type messages into a system, and speech synthesis (at the receiver's end) providing an alternative to graphic communication. Then there is the complementary effect, with vision being added to already existing speech modalities (both synchronous and asynchronous), as in the case of the personal videophone, video-conferencing using mobile phones, and video extensions to email and chat situations. Here we shall experience real-time smooth visibility of the person(s) we are talking to – and also, in some applications, the option of seeing ourselves as well [. . .]. Of course, whether these technologies will be welcomed or implemented by, for example, the members of those synchronous chatgroups, where anonymity and fantasy are the essence of the interaction, remains to be seen.

The developments which will bring languages together take me away from the theme of this book, but they should at least be mentioned for the sake of completeness. Here we are talking about the provision of automatic translation of increasing quality via multilingual browsers. It will still take some decades for translation devices to leave behind their errorful and pidgin-like character, and routinely achieve a language level with high-quality grammatical, semantic, and discourse content; but once available, it will be routinely accessible through the Internet. We can also envisage the translating telephone, where we speak into a phone, and the software carries out the required speech recognition, translation, and speech synthesis, enabling the listeners to hear our speech in their own language. It is only a short step from here to Douglas Adams' 'Babel fish', inserted into the ear to enable the same thing to happen in face-to-face communication. The implications of such technologies on languages have yet to be fully appreciated. Plainly, the arrival of automatic translation will act as a natural force counteracting the currently accelerating trend towards the use of English (or any other language) as a global lingua franca. But there are more fundamental implications, for, in a world where it is possible to translate automatically from any one language into any other, we have to face up to the issue of whether people will be bothered to learn foreign languages at all. Such a world is, of course, a very long way off. Only a tiny number of languages are seen to be commercially viable prospects for automatic translation research, and few of the world's languages have attracted linguistic research of the magnitude required to make machine translation viable. The issue is, accordingly, only of theoretical interest – for now. [. . .]

What kind of impact might we expect a 'force of unimaginable power' [i.e. the internet] to make on language? We have seen [. . .] a range of intriguingly new and still evolving linguistic varieties, characterized by sets of specific adaptations, in graphology, grammar, semantics, and discourse, to the properties of the technology and the needs of the user. They suggest an answer to the second of the two questions I raised in Chapter 1: is the Internet emerging as a homogenous linguistic medium or is it a collection of distinct dialects? The latter, surely, is the case. Although there are a few properties

David Crystal

which different Internet situations seem to share, these do not in aggregate make a very strong case for a view of Netspeak as a variety. But if Netspeak is not a variety, what is it? Is there anything at all to be said, if we step back from the detail of these situations, and 'take a view' about Internet language as a whole? The first question I asked [. . .] was whether the 'electronic revolution' was bringing about a linguistic revolution. The evidence suggests that it is. The phenomenon of Netspeak is going to 'change the way we think' about language in a fundamental way, because it is a linguistic singularity – a genuine new medium.

[. . .] Linguists, stylists, editors, and other observers have groped for analogies to express what they find in Internet language, and have failed. The kind of language which is on the Internet in its different situations, though displaying some similarities with other forms of communication, is fundamentally different from them. Comparisons with note-taking, letter-writing, amateur radio, citizens'-band radio, and all the other communicative acts mentioned in earlier chapters prove to be singularly unilluminating. For Netspeak is something completely new. It is neither 'spoken writing' nor 'written speech'. [. . .] It is something fundamentally different from both writing and speech, as traditionally understood. It is, in short, a fourth medium. In language studies, we are used to discussing issues in terms of 'speech vs. writing vs. signing'. From now on we must add a further dimension to comparative enquiry: 'spoken language vs. written language vs. sign language vs. computer-mediated language'. Netspeak is a development of millennial significance. A new medium of linguistic communication does not arrive very often, in the history of the race.

Issues to consider

- ❑ Crystal is wary of making predictions, but he does nevertheless make some. How reliable do you think those predictions are (especially given the lapse of time since even the latest edition of this book was published)? What kinds of evidence could you look for in order to confirm Crystal's account – or alternatively to provide counter-examples?
- ❑ Is it possible to make worthwhile connections between the detailed description Crystal offers of internet language and the large-scale social transformations suggested by Ong (and other writers referred to above such as Fang)?
- ❑ Can you make any predictions about mediated language and innovations in how we will communicate in the future? Do you think the most significant changes will be at the level of the 'linguistic' or at the level of mode of communication?

KEY DATES IN THE HISTORY OF MEDIA

Below we present a basic chronology of inventions and related developments in media history. This list should help you form a large-scale view of media development. It should also dispel any sense that most relevant media history has happened in the present generation. More comprehensive lists can be found in specialised works such as Briggs and Burke (2005: 269–80), which links its list of dates to detailed commentary elsewhere in that book on the relevant social history. Other sources of useful information on media history can be found in our guide to Further Reading. A usefully detailed timeline can be found online at http://www.mediahistory.umn.edu/timeline.

We hope even our highly selective list will be useful, if read in conjunction with general reference works or a historical timeline of the kind you can find in most print or online encyclopaedias. As you use our list, remember that the history will make more sense if you relate media developments to other aspects of social history: what was going on economically and politically, what international relations may have been like at the time, what sort of lives people of different classes and social groups were actually living, etc.

The picture we present of media history can be misread and create quite distorting impressions. Note, for instance, that our timeline is skewed in favour of Western, especially British, developments. The history of writing and printing looks very different, if viewed from a Chinese perspective. It is a good follow-up activity, therefore, to try to adapt a thread or period in our list for a cultural focus on another part of the world. You can do this by consulting even quite a small number of reference works. Also, we haven't given much prominence to the names of individual inventors, or to exactly what roles inventors, entrepreneurs, public institutions and other social agents played in the evolution of particular technologies, or to the gradual development of media developments signalled here by a single-date entry. Nor have we distinguished between technical inventions, media institutions and social (e.g. regulatory) policies. Each of these aspects of media history is important in any given case. Such details are a lower priority here, however, than outlining the longer historical processes.

Finally, we haven't tried to fix a boundary between 'communication' technologies and other kinds of invention. Few people will dispute that printing and television should be included in a media timeline. Some may question whether carrier pigeons, canals, motorways and space rockets should be included in the same list. Others may argue that a history of mediated communication should go wider. If we tried to reflect the widest version of media history here, however, our list would quickly become a general social history.

Date	*Invention/innovation*
45,000–5000 BCE	Cave paintings and carvings, at different locations and in different periods
c. 5000 BCE	Invention of writing
c. 2200 BCE	Oldest surviving papyrus document
c. 2000 BCE	Earliest alphabetic writing
1200s BCE	Egyptians use carrier pigeons for military communication
295 BCE	Founding of library at Alexandria
c. 195 BCE	Carving of the Rosetta Stone, in three simultaneous language forms: hieroglyphics, hieratic script and Greek
c. 350	Development of xylography, or printing of books from wooden blocks (in China)
c. 400	Books cut into pages, and bound in a codex manner, begin to replace scrolls
c. 615	First records of the teaching of Mohammed
868	First printed book (in China – sometimes dated considerably earlier)
983	An encyclopedia, the *Taiping Yulan*, produced in China.
1038	Arab scholar Alhazen describes a room-size camera obscura
c. 1120	Chinese craftsmen sew pages together to make stitched books
c. 1300	Kublai Khan establishes a 'pony express' message delivery service in China
c. 1400	Earliest surviving woodcuts (of images) in Europe
c. 1400	Movable type used to print books (Korea)
1448	Gutenberg sets up his printing shop in Mainz.
1452	Gutenberg begins printing the 42-line Bible in two volumes
1465	First printing of musical notation
1460s and 1470s	First presses established in various parts of Europe
1476	William Caxton brings Gutenberg's invention of printing to England
1500	First recorded etchings
1500	Lead pencils first used in England

Date	*Invention/innovation*
1517	Martin Luther nails his 'Ninety-five Theses' to a church door in Wittenberg. His Theses are printed in vernacular German, ushering in the Christian Reformation.
1536	A proto-newspaper is printed: the 'Gazetta' in Venice.
1544	First Index of prohibited books (published in Paris)
1557	Stationers' Company, London, is given printing monopoly for the whole of England, and becomes in effect a licensing and regulatory body
1563	First printed timetable of postal services
1576	First London theatre
1600s	Early development of sign language (initially in Italy)
c. 1610	First news sheets (in Germany)
1611	King James version of the Bible (the 'Authorised Version') is published
1620	News sheets called 'corantos' are sold in Europe, especially in Italy
1630s	First coffeehouses in London, which become centres for communication and the formation of opinion (mainly influential 50–100 years later)
1631	Early French newspaper carries classified advertisements
1642	Puritans close all theatres in England
1644	John Milton's *Areopagitica* defends freedom to publish (and outlines main arguments for freedom of expression)
1702	First daily newspaper in English, the *Daily Courant*
1709	England's Copyright Act offers basis for protecting intellectual property
1712	Stamp duty imposed on publications
1725	First circulating library in London
1755	Publication of Dr Johnson's Dictionary
1750s	Regular mail ship runs between England and its colonies
1765	Repeal of the Stamp Act
1771	First edition of *Encyclopædia Britannica*
1775	Watt and Bolton's steam engine sets off the Industrial Revolution

Date	*Invention/innovation*
1780s	Use of coaches, and in USA stagecoaches, to deliver mail between towns
1788	Founding of *The Times* newspaper
1790	Hydraulic press invented, based on earlier steam inventions
1790	British adopt secret ship-to-ship code, using ten coloured flags (four years later, in France, Claude Chappe creates semaphore signalling system)
1790	First US patent law (conferring property rights on registered inventions)
1791	Congress passes First Amendment to the US Constitution (of 1787), protecting freedom of expression
1796	Invention of lithography
1798	Development of mechanised papermaking
1798	Stamp tax imposed on newspapers published in Britain, and imports of foreign newspapers prohibited
1803	First steam-powered ship, heralding replacement of sail-powered sea travel
1805	Completion of the Grand Union Canal as means of north–south communication and transport in England
1806	Carbon paper invented
1807	Camera lucida invented, improving image tracing
1811	Koenig's steam printing press first used
1821	Invention by Louis Braille of Braille, a system of writing for blind people based on rectangles representing characters by means of six raised-point positions
1822	Jean Champollion deciphers hieroglyphics by translating the Rosetta Stone
1822	Diorama paintings, lit in a dark room, are notable forerunner of cinema projection
1823	Charles Babbage builds a calculating machine called a 'difference engine' (a sort of mechanical computer)
1827	First comic strip, drawn by Swiss teacher Rodolphe Topffer
1830s	First typewriters

Date	*Invention/innovation*
1834	Zoetrope, or toy using a rotating drum, creates illusion of movement
1837	Isaac Pitman's *Stenographic Soundhand* introduces shorthand
1837	Commercial telegraph line sends messages (London)
1840	Penny post (postal system) adopted in England
1844	First telegraph message sent using Morse code (between two US cities)
1846	Rotating cylinder press used in printing
1849	The term 'advertising agency' used to describe a specialised professional service
1850	First typewriter with continuous paper feed (ribbons for typewriters invented five years previously)
1850	First cable laid under the sea between Britain and France
1851	Photography (by means of wet plates)
1851	Reuters news agency founded
1853	Envelopes made mechanically by a paper-folding machine
1850s	Photojournalism begins with pictures from the Crimean War
1858	Phonautograph (early sound recording machine)
1860	First aerial photographs taken from balloon over Paris
1865	First transatlantic cable
1868	Invention of the stapler
1869	First postcards (from Austria)
1869	Opening of Suez Canal (joining Mediterranean Sea and the Gulf of Suez)
1872	Eadweard Muybridge photographs a horse in motion, and links his photographs together, in a forerunner of film (sometimes dated five years later)
1873	Western typewriters adopt QWERTY keyboard
1876	Alexander Graham Bell's telephone invented
1876	Melvil Dewey develops library classification system for books on different subjects ('the Dewey decimal system')
1877	Introduction of photography (by means of dry plates)

Date	*Invention/innovation*
1877	Thomas Edison's phonograph; also Charles Cros's phonograph; also, Emile Berliner's microphone and David Hughes's microphone
1879	First American telephone exchange, as well as formation in USA of the National Bell Telephone Company
1879	Introduction of electric light bulbs
1880	Discovery of radio waves (by Heinrich Hertz)
1880s	Trains deliver newspapers on a daily basis
1883	Invention of a newspaper folding machine
1886	Motion picture camera developed
1886	Berne Convention finalises international copyright agreement
1886	Eastman's hand-held camera leads to highly influential Kodak box camera and Brownie camera
1880s	First four-wheeled cars (*not* SUVs)
1890	First electric underground trains in London
1892	First portable typewriters
1895	Discovery of X-rays
1895	Lumière brothers' portable movie camera (France) also projects films; films exhibited in Berlin (and following year in London)
1896	First flying machine
1897	In England, Marconi sets up wireless telegraphy business
1898	First airship flight (Zeppelin)
1900–5	Magnetic recorded and broadcast voice messages (first achieved technically by the Dane, Valdemar Poulsen, five years earlier)
1901	Hearing aid patented
1901	First electric typewriter
1905	Neon signs first used (sometimes dated twenty years later)
1906	Lee De Forest's three-element vacuum tube, the audion, invented
1907	Photograph transmitted by wire across France
1907	Dialogue titles added to silent films
1911	First Hollywood studio
1912	Motorised film cameras replace hand cranks

Date	*Invention/innovation*
1920s	Early radio stations go on air
1920s	Experimentation starts with colour film
1921	Public address (PA) system of amplifier and loudspeakers first used, in a military ceremony
1922	BBC goes on air (granted Royal Charter in 1927)
1925	Goodyear blimp displays advertisements while floating across the sky
1925–6	Warner Bros. start experiments to make films with synchronised sound, followed a year later by *Don Juan*, the first publicly shown 'talkie' (synchronisation of sound and film achieved technically in the early 1900s by machines such as the Vivaphone, Chronophone and Kinetophone)
1927	Movietone newsreels start to exhibit with sound
1928	John Logie Baird demonstrates the possibility of television using mechanical scanning
1930	Flashbulbs invented for use in conjunction with cameras
1930	Hays Office creates Production Code in Hollywood (restricting certain kinds of on-screen action)
1934	Nuremberg rally (Germany)
1935	Invention of radar
1936	Live broadcast from a Spanish Civil War battle
1936	BBC starts first regular television service, three hours a day
1936	Alan Turing describes a general purpose computer
1938	Orson Welles' radio drama, *The War of the Worlds*, starts panic when interpreted by many as real 'Martian invasion'
1939	Air mail service first offered across the Atlantic
1941	First touch-tone dialling and push-button telephones
1943	'Walkie-talkie' FM radio, carried as backpack
1947	Transistor shows potential to replace vacuum tubes
1948	LP records
1949	Network TV established (USA)
1950	Xerox photocopiers (the xerography process used in photocopying invented by Chester Carlson in the 1930s)

Date	*Invention/innovation*
1951	Colour television sets
1952	IBM computers
1954	Independent, commercial television in UK; regular colour broadcasts in USA
1956	Transatlantic telephone cable
1956	Cordless remote for TV
1957	Sputnik (first space satellite)
1958	LP records produced in stereo
1959	First stretch of motorway in Britain
1959	Xerox manufactures plain paper copier
1959	Development of microchip (integrated electronic circuitry)
1960	Voice communication for people who can't talk: an electronic larynx
1961	Carousel projector introduced as aid to lecturers showing slides
1962	First satellite TV broadcast (Telstar satellite sends television signal across the Atlantic)
1962	Audio cassettes (from Dutch company, Philips)
1963	Patent taken out on computer mouse
1964	Pirate radio stations off English coast challenge BBC monopoly
1964	Olympic Games telecast by satellite live, globally, from Tokyo
1965	Ban on tobacco advertising on television in Britain
1965	Video recorders on sale for home use
1965	Development of hypertext, prefiguring internet links
1966	Development of optical fibre
1967	BBC local radio
1967	Cordless telephones for the home (not cell phones/mobile phones)
1968	Magnetic-stripe credit cards
1969	Neil Armstrong becomes first man to broadcast from the moon: 'The Eagle has landed . . . That's one small step for man, one giant leap for mankind.'
1969	Regular colour TV broadcasting in UK

Date	*Invention/innovation*
1971	Commercial availability of microprocessors
1971	First word-processor (Wang 1200)
1971	Independent local radio in Britain
1972	Capability to send emails (only widely in use two decades later)
1972	Home video cassette recorders (VCRs) commercially available, with cassettes available for rent and purchase
1972	First cable pay-TV services
1972	Satellites first used in incorporating location material into television news reports
1975	Bill Gates and Paul Allen start 'Micro-Soft' (later becomes Microsoft)
1975	British teletext systems (Ceefax by cable from 1972; Teletext to TV sets from 1974)
1976–7	Portable Apple computers (Apple I in 1976, Apple II from 1977)
1977	Fibre-optic cable (in California)
1978	Availability of first cellular phones (mobile phones)
1979	Speech recognition device achieves vocabulary of 1,000 words
1979	Atari game computers (also, text-only Multi-User Dungeon (MUD) game appears)
1979	Sony Walkman tape player
1981	IBM PC (fully compatible IBM clones appear two years later); also, first laptops
1983	Sony and Philips bring out compact discs (CDs)
1983	Internet domains given names instead of numerical addresses
1984	Machine translation from basic Japanese into English (with many mistakes)
1984	Commercial availability of video camcorders
1984	Portable CD players
1984	High-quality fax machines demonstrated
1985	Voice synthesiser text-to-speech computer function pronounces 20,000 words
1989	Transatlantic optical fibre cable

Date	*Invention/innovation*
1989	Digital editing of photographs on home computers
1990	World Wide Web originates at CERN in Switzerland. Tim Berners-Lee writes the main program
1991	ISDN in Britain
1991	Sony PlayStation game console
1991	Hypertext Markup Language (HTML) accelerates development of the World Wide Web
1991	X-ray photograph taken of someone's brain recalling a word
1993	Nokia experiments with text messages sent between mobile phones
1993	First Hollywood film edited on non-linear editing computer system
1993	Pentium chip (Intel)
1995	Internet opens to commercial interests (process begun on small scale around 1980)
1995	First internet phone calls: VoIP
1995	Direct Broadcast Satellites (DBS) beam TV programmes to home dishes
1996	Commercial availability of digital video discs (DVDs)
1997	Streaming of audio and video on the internet
2000	Camera phones
2001	Wireless laptops
2001	iPod music player
2003	Social networking sites: MySpace.com, then Facebook in 2004
2003	Cell phones/mobile phones incorporate computer and internet capabilities
2004	'Podcasting' coined as term for internet delivery of radio-style content
2004	Sudden expansion in popularity of blogging
2005	YouTube first video
2006	First reports of internet 'telemedicine', in which doctors can 'see' patients at a distance
2009	Inventions and developments continue across digital media, including especially internet delivery systems and increased wi-fi communication

To appreciate the interest and value of this kind of historical grid, try asking yourself questions that oblige you to link the availability, or state of development, of a particular media technology to surrounding social conditions. Questions to get you started might include:

- Could a literate person have read about what was going on in the French Revolution in a daily newspaper – either in France or in Britain?
- Should you expect to be able to look at photographs of the American Civil War?
- If someone travelled from China to London in 1850, what means were available to that person to send messages back to their family: phone?/telegraph?/postal service?

Such questions quickly lead into others. We ask many such questions throughout the book. Read this list in conjunction with topics explored in various threads above (especially threads 1, 3, 7 and 9).

FURTHER READING

1 Media as language use

Ong (1982) is a classic text for reading about the impact of speech, writing and print on our thought processes, personality and social structures. For a contemporary approach to media language, see Fairclough (1995b). Scollon (1999) provides discussion on mediated language, while Boyd-Barrett in Graddol and Boyd-Barrett (1994) provides a historical overview of approaches to language and media study. For an overview of literacy studies, see Levine (1986), Street (1984, 1995) and Maybin (2007).

2 Varieties of media language: register and style

See Graddol, Cheshire and Swann (1994) for a clear introduction to differences between speech and writing and dimensions underlying the two channels of communication. Register and style are discussed in Stockwell (2007), and style is discussed in Swales (1990). Van Dijk provides a useful analysis of the language of news (1988). For an insight into the 'hysterical' style in newspapers, see Fowler (1994). Jenkins (2003) is a useful text for a discussion on standard language ideology. For an introduction to the language used in newspapers, see Reah (2002), and for an equivalent introduction to television language, see Marshall and Werndley (2002).

3 Mediated communicative events

For classic texts on how modern linguistics can analyse language as a functioning system, see de Saussure (1983) and Lyons (1977). For a discussion of communication models, see McQuail (1969) and McQuail and Windahl (1993). Thompson (2000) is a useful text that provides a systematic analysis of the phenomenon of political scandal and the implications on media self-presentation.

4 Media discourse genres

For a conceptual discussion of genre in language use, see Swales (1990). For discussion of the genre of the TV commercial, see Chandler (2008). Lorenzo-Dus (2008) focuses exclusively and explicitly on the discourse of television and four main features: storytelling, closeness, conflict and persuasion. See Hymes (1972, 1977) for an in-depth discussion of speech events and how these are determined by a number of factors such as participants, goals and norms of interaction. For a generic analysis of media discourse types, see Fairclough (1995b).

5 Media information and persuasion

See also Palmer (1998) for a broad discussion of news values and approaches to the criteria of newsworthiness in additon to Bell's (1991) list. For a clear and practical introduction to rhetoric in both spoken and written mediums, see Cockcroft and Cockcroft (2005); also see Gill and Whedbee (1997). Gibbs (1994) provides a useful discussion of metaphor and the human mind, while Lakoff and Johnson (1980) *Metaphors We Live By* is a classic text for understanding metaphors or metaphorical mappings that occur throughout everyday non-literary discourse.

6 Media storytelling

Labov (1972) is a classic text for the narrative schema model and Simpson (2004) provides a clear introduction to developments in structural narratology. Toolan (2001) provides both. Fulton, Huisman, Murphet and Dunn (2005) provide a collection of texts that apply contemporary narrative theory to media texts, and Cobley (2001) provides a comprehensive historical overview of narratives, from those in oral cultures to modernism, and cinema to cyberspace. For an understanding of what defines a narrative from a non-narrative, such as a recount, see Lambrou (2007).

7 Captions, soundtracks and multimodality

The essays in Barthes (1977) remain a classic source for this topic. For a contemporary discussion of multimodal discourse, see Kress and van Leeuwen (1990, 2001), as well as Scollon and Levine (2004). MacDonald (2003) offers an approach to analysing discourse simultaneously involving visual and verbal modes, while Montgomery (2007) studies broadcast discourse in particular. Further discussion of how words and images are combined in new media can be found in Hocks and Kendrick (2005).

8 Boundaries of media discourse

For a survey of the authoritarian 'scissors' over the past 400 years, read Thomas (2007). For a comprehensive reference guide to American media censorship and in-depth coverage of each media format – newspapers, magazines, motion pictures, radio, television, and the internet – see Foerstel (1998). For a social history of swearing, see Hughes (1998 [1991]). Also see Greenawalt (1996), Neu (2008) and Durant (2009) on meanings and interpretations of offensive language in the media. For a lively discussion of contemporary uses of swearing and offensive language in the media, see Pinker's (2007) chapter 'Seven words you can't say on television'.

9 The future of media language

For an overview of the social history of developments in the media, including developments of the early 21st century, see Briggs and Burke (2005). Snoddy, in Aitchison and Lewis (2003) makes predictions on the future of communications and media in his chapter 'Modern media myths'.

REFERENCES

Abercrombie, N. (1996) *Television and Society*, Cambridge: Polity Press.

Andersson, L.-G. and Trudgill, P. (1992) *Bad Language*, London: Penguin.

Barnouw, E. (editor-in-chief) (1989) *International Encyclopedia of Communications*, Oxford: Oxford University Press.

Baron, N. (2000) *Alphabet to Email*, London: Routledge.

Barthes, R. (1975) *S/Z*, London: Cape.

Barthes, R. (1977a [1966]) 'Introduction to the structural analysis in narratives', in *Image-Music-Text*, London: Fontana.

Barthes, R. (1977b [1961]) 'The photographic message', in *Image-Music-Text*, London: Fontana.

Barthes, R. (1977c [1964]) 'Rhetoric of the image', in *Image-Music-Text*, London: Fontana.

Bartlett, F. C. (1932) *Remembering*, Cambridge: Cambridge University Press.

Barton, D. (1994) *Literacy: An Introduction to the Ecology of the Written Language*, Oxford: Blackwell.

Bauman, R. (2001) 'Verbal art as performance', in A. Durant (ed.), *Linguistic Anthropology: A Reader*, Oxford: Blackwell.

Beard, A. (2000) *The Language of Politics*, London: Routledge.

Bell, A. (1983) 'Broadcast news as a language standard', in Gerhard Leitner (ed.), *Language and Mass Media* (*International Journal of the Sociology of Language* 40), Amsterdam: Mouton, pp. 29–42.

Bell, A. (1989) 'Hot news – media reporting and public understanding of the climate change issue in New Zealand: a study in the (mis)communication of science' (Project report to DSIR and Ministry for the Environment), Wellington: Victoria University, Department of Linguistics.

Bell, A. (1991) *The Language of News Media*, Oxford: Blackwell.

Bell, A., and van Leeuwen, T. (1994) *The Media Interview: Confession, Contest, Conversation*, New South Wales: New South Wales University Press.

Bhopal Medical Appeal advert, *The Guardian*, 19 May 2007.

Biber, D. (1988) *Variation across Speech and Writing*, Cambridge: Cambridge University Press.

Biber, D. (1995) *Dimensions of Register Variation: A Cross-linguistic Comparison*, Cambridge: Cambridge University Press.

Biber, D. (2003) 'Compressed noun-phrase structures in newspaper discourse: the competing demands of popularization vs. economy', in J. Aitchison and D. M. Lewis (eds), *New Media Language*, London: Routledge, pp. 169–71, 179–80.

Biber, D. and Finegan, E. (1989) *Sociolinguistic Perspectives on Register*, Oxford: Oxford University Press.

Big Brother transcript (http://www.telegraph.co.uk/news/uknews/1553807/Channel-4-hit-by-new-racism-controversy.html), 8 June 2007.

Big Words . . . Small Worlds (Broken English Productions for Channel 4 television, UK, 1987), written and narrated by the novelist David Lodge. Producer: Alan Durant. Executive producer: Colin MacCabe.

Blake, N. (1981) *Non-standard Language in English Literature*, London: Deutsch.

Blunt, J. (2005) 'You're Beautiful': *Back to Bedlam*.

Bourdieu, P. (1991) *Language and Symbolic Power*, translated by Gino Raymond and Matthew Adamson, Cambridge: Polity Press.

Boyd-Barrett, O. (1994) 'Language and media: a question of convergence', in D. Graddol and O. Boyd-Barrett (eds), *Media Texts: Authors and Readers*, Clevedon: Multilingual Matters/Open University, pp. 22–39.

Bradbury, R. (1953) *Fahrenheit 451*, New York: Ballantyne Books.

Briggs, A. and Burke, P. (2005) *A Social History of the Media: From Gutenberg to the Internet*, Oxford: Polity.

Bruner, J. (1990) *Acts of Meaning*, Cambridge, MA, and London: Harvard University Press.

Cameron, D. (1995) *Verbal Hygiene*, London: Routledge.

Castells, M. (2000) *The Rise of the Network Society*, Oxford: Blackwell.

Caughie, J. (ed.) (1990) *Screen*, 31: 1.

Chandler, D. (1997) *An Introduction to Genre Theory* [www document] (http://www.aber.ac.uk/media/Documents/intgenre/chandler_genre_theory.pdf), 29 August 2008.

Chandler, D. (2008) 'The genre of the TV commercial', in G. Creeber (ed.), *The Television Genre Book*, 2nd edition, London: BFI.

'Character matters' (http://www.onthemedia.org/transcripts/2008/02/22/05), 22 February 2008.

Clayman, S., and Heritage, J. (2002) *The News Interview: Journalists and Public Figures on the Air*, Cambridge: Cambridge University Press.

Cobley, P. (2001) *Narrative*, London: Routledge.

Cockcroft, R. and Cockcroft, S. (2005) *Persuading People*, London: Macmillan.

Cook, G. (1992) *The Discourse of Advertising*, London: Routledge.

Corner, J. (1995) *Television Form and Public Address*, London: Edward Arnold.

Cotton, B. and Garrett, M. (1999), *'You Ain't Seen Nothing Yet': The Future of Media and the Global Expert System*, London: Institute of Contemporary Arts.

Crystal, D. (2000) *Language Death*, Cambridge: Cambridge University Press.

Crystal, D. (2006) *Language and the Internet*, 2nd edition, Cambridge: Cambridge University Press.

Davies, N. (2008) *Flat Earth News*, London: Chatto and Windus.

Derrida, J. (1981) 'The law of genre', in W. J. T. Mitchell (ed.), *On Narrative*, Chicago: University of Chicago Press.

Dictionary of Media Studies (2006) London: A. & C. Black.

Durant, A. (2009) *Meaning in the Media: Discourse, Controversy and Debate*, Cambridge: Cambridge University Press.

Eco, U. (1990) *The Limits of Interpretation*, Bloomington: Indiana University Press.

Eisenstein, E. (1979) *The Printing Press as an Agent of Social Change: Communications and Cultural Transformations in Early Modern Europe*, 2 vols, Cambridge: Cambridge University Press.

Ekstrom, M. (2001) 'Politicians interviewed on television news', *Discourse and Society*, 12 (5): 563–84.

Ellis, J. (1982) *Visible Fictions: Cinema, Television, Video*, London: Routledge.

Fairclough, N. (1989) *Language and Power*, London: Longman.

Fairclough, N. (1994) 'Conversationalization of public discourse and the authority of the consumer', in R. Keat, N. Whiteley and N. Abercrombie (eds), *The Authority of the Consumer*, London: Routledge.

Fairclough, N. (1995a) *Critical Discourse Analysis: The Critical Study of Language*, London: Longman.

Fairclough, N. (1995b) *Media Discourse*, London: Arnold.

Fang, I. (1997) *A History of Mass Communication: Six Information Revolutions*, Burlington, MA: Elsevier Science.

Feuer, J. (1992) 'Genre study and television', in R. C. Allen (ed.), *Channels of Discourse, Reassembled: Television and Contemporary Criticism*, London: Routledge, pp. 138–59.

Finnegan, R. (2002) *Communicating: The Multiple Modes of Human Interconnection*, London: Routledge.

Fiske, J. (1987) *Television Culture*, London: Routledge.

Foerstel, H. N. (1998) *Banned in the Media: Reference Guide to Censorship in the Press, Motion Pictures, Broadcasting and the Internet (New Directions in Information Management)*, Westport, CT: Greenwood Press.

Forster, E. M. (1927) *Aspects of the Novel*, Orlando, FL: Harcourt.

Fowler, R. (1994) 'Hysterical style in the press', in D. Graddol and O. Boyd-Barrett (eds), *Media Texts: Authors and Readers*, Clevedon: Multilingual Matters/Open University, pp. 90–9.

Freire, P. and Macedo, D. (1987) *Literacy: Reading the Word and World*, London: Routledge.

Fulton, H., Huisman, R., Murphet, J. and Dunn, A. (2005) *Narrative and Media*, Cambridge: Cambridge University Press.

Galtung, J. and Ruge, M. (1973) 'Structuring and selecting news', in S. Cohn and J. Young (eds), *The Manufacture of News: Social Problems, Deviance, and the Class Media*, London: Constable, pp. 62–72.

Geis, M. (1982) *The Language of Television Advertising*, New York: Academic Press.

Gelb, I. (1952) *A Study of Writing*, Chicago: University of Chicago Press.

Genette, G. (1997) *Paratexts: Thresholds of Interpretation*, Cambridge: Cambridge University Press.

Gibbs, R. (1994) *The Poetics of Mind*, Cambridge: Cambridge University Press.

Gill, A. M. and Whedbee, K. (1997) 'Rhetoric', in A. van Dijk (ed.), *Discourse as Structure and Process*, London: Sage, pp. 157–84.

Gimson, A. C. (1962) *Introduction to the Pronunciation of English*, London: Edward Arnold.

Goddard, A. (2002) *The Language of Advertising*, London: Routledge.

Goffman, E. (1981) *Forms of Talk*, Oxford: Blackwell.

Goody, J. (1977) *The Domestication of the Savage Mind*, Cambridge: Cambridge University Press.

Goody, J. (1987) *The Interface between the Written and the Oral*, Cambridge: Cambridge University Press.

Goody, J. and Watt, I. (1963) 'The consequences of literacy', *Comparative Studies in Society and History*, 5 (3): 304–45.

Graddol, D. (1994) 'The visual accomplishment of factuality', in D. Graddol and O. Boyd-Barrett (eds), *Media Texts: Authors and Readers*, Clevedon: Multilingual Matters/Open University, pp. 136–57.

Graddol, D., Cheshire, J. and Swann, J. (1994) *Describing Language*, Oxford: Oxford University Press.

Greenawalt, K. (1989) *Speech, Crime and the Uses of Language*, Oxford: Oxford University Press.

Greenawalt, K. (1996) *Fighting Words*, Princeton, NJ: Princeton University Press.

Gunter, B. (1997) *Measuring Bias on Television*, Luton: University of Luton Press.

Haarman, L. (2004) '"John, what's going on?": some features of live exchanges on television news', in A. Partington, J. Morley and L. Haarman (eds), *Corpus and Discourse*, Bern: Peter Lang.

Hall, S. (ed.) (1997) *Representation: Cultural Representations and Signifying Practices*, London: Sage.

Halliday, M. A. K. (1978) *Language as Social Semiotic*, London: Edward Arnold.

Harris, R. (1995) *Signs of Writing*, London: Routledge.

Hartley, J. (1982) *Understanding News*, London: Routledge.

Hocks, M. and Kendrick, M. (2005) *Eloquent Images: Word and Image in the Age of New Media*, Cambridge, MA: MIT Press.

Hodge, R. and Kress, G. (1988) *Social Semiotics*, Cambridge: Polity Press.

Hoggart, R. (1957) *The Uses of Literacy*, London: Penguin.

Hughes (1998) *Swearing: A Social History of Foul Language, Oaths, and Profanity in English*, London: Penguin.

Hundt, M. and Mair, C. (1999) '"Agile" and "uptight" genres: the corpus-based approach to language change in progress', *International Journal of Corpus Linguistics*, 4 (2): 221–42.

Hymes, D. (1972) 'Toward ethnographies of communication: the analysis of communicative events', in P. Giglioli (ed.), *Language and Social Context*, Harmondsworth: Penguin, pp. 21–43.

Hymes, D. (1977) *Foundations in Sociolinguistics: An Ethnographic Approach*, Philadelphia: University of Pennsylvania Press.

Jakobson, R. (1960) 'Concluding statement: linguistics and poetics', in T. Sebeok (ed.), *Style in Language*, Cambridge, MA: MIT Press, pp. 350–77.

Jenkins, J. (2003) *World Englishes*, London: Routledge.

Jones, D. (1924 [1917]) *English Pronouncing Dictionary*, 2nd edition, London: J. M. Dent & Sons.

Kent, R. (ed.) (1994) *Measuring Media Audiences*, London: Routledge.

Knight, D. (1994) 'Making sense of genre', *Film and Philosophy 2* [www document], http://www.hanover.edu/philos/film/vol_02/knight.htm.

Kress, G. (1985) *Linguistic Processes in Sociocultural Practice*, Geelong, Victoria: Deakin University Press.

Kress, G. (1988) *Communication and Culture: An Introduction*, Kensington, New South Wales: New South Wales University Press.

Kress, G. and van Leeuwen, T. (1990) *Reading Images*, Geelong, Victoria: Deakin University Press.

Kress, G. and van Leeuwen, T. (2001) *Multimodal Discourse: The Modes and Media of Contemporary Communication*, London: Arnold.

Labov, W. (1966) *The Social Stratification of English in New York City*, Washington, DC: Center for Applied Linguistics.

Labov, W. (1972) *Language in the Inner City*, Philadelphia: University of Pennsylvania Press.

Labov, W. and Waletzky, J. (1967) 'Narrative analysis: oral versions of personal experience', in J. Holm (ed.), *Essays on the Verbal and Visual Arts*, Seattle: University of Washington Press, pp. 12–44.

Lakoff, G. (2004) *Don't Think of an Elephant! Know Your Values and Frame the Debate*, White River Junction, VT: Chelsea Green.

Lakoff, G. and Johnson, M. (1980) *Metaphors We Live By*, Chicago: University of Chicago Press.

Lakoff, R. (2003) 'The new incivility: threat or promise', in J. Aitchison and D. M. Lewis (eds), *New Media Language*, London: Routledge, pp. 36–44.

Lambrou, M. (2007) 'Oral accounts of personal experiences: when is a narrative a recount?', in M. Lambrou and P. Stockwell (eds), *Contemporary Stylistics*, London: Continuum.

Lasswell, H. D. (1948) 'The structure and function of communication in society', in L. Bryson (ed.), *The Communication of Ideas*, Urbana: University of Illinois Press, pp. 117–30.

Leech, G. (1966) *English in Advertising: A Linguistic Study of Advertising in Great Britain*, London: Longman.

Levine, K. (1986) *The Social Context of Literacy*, London: Routledge.

Lorenzo-Dus, N. (2008) *Television Discourse: Analysing Language in the Media*, Basingstoke, Hants: Palgrave Macmillan.

Luke, A., O'Brien, J. and Comber, B. (1994) 'Making community text objects of study', *The Australian Journal of Language and Literacy*, 17 (2): 139–49.

Lyons, J. (1977) *Semantics*, 2 vols, Cambridge: Cambridge University Press.

MacDonald, M. (2003) *Exploring Media Discourse*, London: Arnold.

MacQueen, H., Waelde, C. and Laurie, G. (2008) *Contemporary Intellectual Property: Law and Policy*, Oxford: Oxford University Press.

Marshall, J. and Werndley, A. (2002) *The Language of Television*, London: Routledge.

Maybin, J. (2007) 'Literacy under and over the desk: oppositions and heterogeneity', *Language and Education*, 21 (6): 515–30.

McCrum, R., Cran, W. and MacNeil, R. (1986) *The Story of English*, New York: Viking.

McLuhan, M. (1964) *Understanding Media: The Extensions of Man*, London: Ark.

McQuail, D. (1969) *Towards a Sociology of Mass Communications*, 5th edition, London: Sage.

McQuail, D. and Windahl, S. (1993) *Communication Models for the Study of Mass Communication*, London: Pearson.

Millwood-Hargrave, A. (2000) 'Delete expletives? Research undertaken jointly by the Advertising Standards Authority, British Broadcasting Corporation, Broadcasting Standards Commission and the Independent Television Commission' (http://www.asa.org.uk/asa/research/archive/), 9 March 2009.

Montgomery, M. (2007) *The Discourse of Broadcast News: A Linguistic Approach*, London: Routledge.

Montgomery, M., Durant, A., Fabb, N., Furniss, T. and Mills, S. (2006) *Ways of Reading*, London: Routledge.

Morley, D. (1992) *Television, Audience and Cultural Studies*, London: Routledge.

'Mother in photos survived tsunami' (http://news.bbc.co.uk/1/hi/world/europe/4141733.stm), Sunday, 2 January 2005, 18:21 GMT.

Mott, F. L. (1950) *American Journalism*, London and New York: Macmillan.

Myers, G. (1994) *Words in Ads*, London: Arnold.

Myers, G. (1999) *Ad Worlds: Brands, Media, Audiences*, London: Arnold.

Neale, S. (1995) 'Questions of genre', in O. Boyd-Barrett and C. Newbold (eds). *Approaches to Media: A Reader*, London: Edward Arnold, pp. 460–72.

Neu, J. (2008) *Sticks and Stones: The Philosophy of Insults*, Oxford: Oxford University Press.

O'Donnell, W. R. and Todd, L. (1980) *Variety in Contemporary English*, London: Allen and Unwin.

O'Keeffe, A. (2006) *Investigating Media Discourse*, London: Routledge.

O'Reilly, T. (2007) 'The language of blogs', *The Guardian*, 14 April 2007.

Ong, W. (1982) *Orality and Literacy: The Technologizing of the Word*, London: Routledge.

Orwell, G. (1949) *1984*, London: Penguin.

Palmer, J. (1998) 'News production', in A. Briggs and P. Cobley (eds), *The Media: An Introduction*, pp. 376–91.

PermaBlog, *The Guardian*, 25 April 2007 (http://www.guardian.co.uk/), Wednesday, 5 November 2008, 05:24 GMT.

Pinker, Steven (2008 [2007]) *The Stuff of Thought*, London: Penguin.

Polanyi, L. (1981) 'Telling the same story twice', *Text*, 1(4): 315–36.

Polanyi, L. (1982) 'Linguistic and social constraints on storytelling', *Journal of Pragmatics*, 6: 509–24.

Police top misheard lyrics chart (http://news.bbc.co.uk/1/hi/entertainment/7574541.stm).

Preston, I. L. (1994) *The Tangled Web They Weave: Truth, Falsity, and Advertisers*. Madison: The University of Wisconsin Press.

Propp, V. (1968 [1928]) *Morphology of the Folktale*, Austin: University of Texas Press.

Quinn, F. (2007) *Law for Journalists*, Harlow: Pearson Education.

Reah, D. (2002) *The Language of Newspapers*, London: Routledge.

Root, G. (2008) 'Writing exhibition captions', unpublished student guide. Church Farmhouse Museum, Hendon.

Rotten tomatoes (http://uk.rottentomatoes.com/movie-1069340/), 30 August 2008.

Saussure, F. de (1983 [1915]) *Course in General Linguistics*, edited by Roy Harris, London: Duckworth.

Scannell, P. (ed.) (1991) *Broadcast Talk*, London: Sage.

Scannell, P. and Cardiff, D. (1991) *A Social History of British Broadcasting: 1922–39 – Serving the Nation*, Oxford: Blackwell.

Schank, R. C. and Abelson, R. P. (1977) *Scripts, Plans, Goals and Understanding*, London: Lawrence Erlbaum.

Schegloff, E. A. (1993) 'Reflections on quantification in the study of conversation', *Research on Language and Interaction*, 26: 99–128.

Scholes, R. and Kellogg, R. (1966) *The Nature of Narrative*, New York: Oxford University Press.

Scollon, R. (1999) *Mediated Discourse and Social Interaction*, London: Routledge.

Scollon, R. and Levine, P. (2004) *Discourse and Technology: Multimodal Discourse Analysis*, Washington, DC: Georgetown University Press.

Simpson, P. (1993) *Language, Ideology and Point of View*, London: Routledge.

Simpson, P. (2004) *Stylistics*, London: Routledge.

Snoddy, R. (2003) 'Modern media myths', in J. Aitchison and D. M. Lewis (eds), *New Media Language*, London: Routledge, pp. 18–26.

Stockwell, P. (2002) *Cognitive Poetics: An Introduction*, London: Routledge.

Stockwell, P. (2007) *Sociolinguistics*, London: Routledge.

Street, B. (1984) *Literacy in Theory and Practice*, Cambridge: Cambridge University Press.

Street, B. (1995) *Social Literacies: Critical Approaches to Literacy in Development, Ethnography and Education*, London: Longman.

Swales, J. (1990) *Genre Analysis*, Cambridge: Cambridge University Press.

Talbot, M. (2007) *Media Discourse: Representation and Interaction*, Edinburgh: Edinburgh University Press.

Tannen, D. (1982) 'The oral/literate continuum in discourse', in D. Tannen (ed.), *Spoken and Written Language: Exploring Orality and Literacy*, Norwood, NJ: Ablex, pp. 1–16.

Tannen, D. (1998) *The Argument Culture: Changing the Way We Argue*, London: Virago.

Thomas, D. (2007) *Freedom's Frontier: Censorship in Modern Britain*, London: John Murray.

Thomas, J. (1983) 'Cross-cultural pragmatic failure', *Applied Linguistics*, 4: 91–112.

Thompson, J. B. (1995) *The Media and Modernity: A Social Theory of the Media*, Cambridge: Polity Press.

Thompson, J. B. (2000) *Political Scandal: Power and Visibility in the Media Age*, Cambridge: Polity Press.

Thwaites, T., Lloyd, D. and Warwick, M. (1994) *Tools for Cultural Studies: An Introduction*, South Melbourne: Macmillan.

Titunik, I. R. (1973) 'The formal method and the sociological method (M. M. Baxtin, P. N. Medvedev, V. N. Volosinov) in Russian theory and study of literature', in V. N. Volosinov (ed.), *Marxism and the Philosophy of Language*, London: Academic Press.

Todorov, T. (1981) *Introduction to Poetics*, Brighton: The Harvester Press.

Todorov, T. (1990) *Genres of Discourse*, Cambridge: Cambridge University Press.

Toolan, M. (2001 [1988]) *Narrative: A Critical Linguistic Introduction*, 2nd edition, London: Routledge.

'Tsunami tragedy: your e-mails', Monday, 24 January 2005 (http://www.cnn.com/2004/WORLD/asiapcf/12/28/more.emails/), posted: 11:01 AM EST (16:01 GMT).

Tuchman, G. (1978) *Making News*, New York: The Free Press.

van Dijk, T. (1988) *News as Discourse*, London: Lawrence Erlbaum Associates.

Wales, K. (2007) 'Keywords revisited: media', *Critical Quarterly*, 49 (1): 6–13.

Wellek, R. and Warren, A. (1963) *Theory of Literature*, Harmondsworth: Penguin.

Wernick, A. (1991) *Promotional Culture: Advertising, Ideology and Symbolic Expression*, London: Sage.

Whorf, B. L. (1956) *Language, Thought and Reality: Selected Writings of Benjamin Lee Whorf*, edited by J. B. Carroll, Cambridge, MA: MIT Press.

Williams, R. (1974) *Television: Technology and Cultural Form*, London: Fontana.

Williams, R. (1983 [1976]) *Keywords: A Vocabulary of Culture and Society*, London: Fontana.

Winston, B. (1998) *Media Technology and Society: A History*, London: Routledge.

Wray, A. and Bloomer, A. (2006) *Projects in Linguistics: A Practical Guide to Researching Language*, 2nd edition, London: Hodder Arnold.

INDEX

http://www.routledge.com/textbooks/reli

Visit the *Routledge English Language Introductions* series website portal and discover a range of online resources designed to test and support your understanding of books from the RELI series.

For *Language and Media,* you'll find extra exercises to take your reading further and related weblinks to apply your understanding to fresh material from the media.

Our online portal for the series features a host of materials including:

- additional activities
- more passages for analysis and discussion
- links to relevant websites
- information about the series and how to use the books
- suggestions of related Routledge titles for further study.